Bill, I hope you find these room
of general interest.

For your birthday 12/04/2014

Best wishes Peter

THE MEN WHO FLEW THE
MOSQUITO

Other books by the same author:

B-24 Liberator, 1939–45
Castles in the Air
Classic Fighter Aircraft
Eighth Air Force at War
Famous Bombers
Fields of Little America
Flying to Glory
Four Miles High
Great American Air Battles of World War Two
Home By Christmas?
Modern Military Aircraft
Spirits in the Sky (with Patrick Bunce)
The Bedford Triangle
The Encyclopedia of American Military Aircraft
The World's Fastest Aircraft
Thunder in the Heavens (with Patrick Bunce)
Wellington: The Geodetic Giant

Patrick Stephens Limited, an imprint of Haynes Publishing, has published authoritative, quality books for enthusiasts for over a quarter of a century. During that time the company has established a reputation as one of the world's leading publishers of books on aviation, maritime, military, model-making, motor cycling, motoring, motor racing, railway and railway modelling subjects. Readers or authors with suggestions for books they would like to see published are invited to write to: The Editorial Director, Patrick Stephens Limited, Sparkford, Nr Yeovil, Somerset BA22 7JJ.

THE MEN WHO FLEW THE
MOSQUITO

Compelling accounts of the Wooden Wonder's triumphant WW2 career

Martin W Bowman

Patrick Stephens Limited

First published in 1995

British Cataloguing-in-Publication Data:
A catalogue record for this book is available
from the British Library

ISBN 1 85260 488 3

Library of Congress catalog card no. 94 79673

Patrick Stephens Limited is an imprint of
Haynes Publishing, Sparkford,
Nr Yeovil, Somerset, BA22 7JJ

Typeset by J. H. Haynes & Co. Ltd.
Printed and bound in Great Britain by
Butler & Tanner Ltd., London and Frome

Contents

Introduction

It has been particularly difficult to embrace all the activities of the Mosquito in this one volume, and since I began researching and interviewing for *THE MEN WHO FLEW THE MOSQUITO* it has become obvious that an entire book on 100 Group, RAF, should be written. This is now in progress. That said, I think everyone will be more than happy at the selection herein of new, and in many cases, freshly researched material, on this superb aircraft and its wonderful crews. Alongside the Lancaster, Spitfire and Hurricane, the Mosquito is, as schoolboys of all ages know, an endearing, perennial favourite whose famous and oft-quoted nickname, 'Wooden Wonder', is part of aviation folklore; especially today, when the skies are filled with the sights and sounds of aviation 'heavy metal' more often than wood and fabric. Surprisingly, it is never difficult when exploring aviation, to uncover caches of hidden gems, even when the aircraft concerned is as famous as the Mosquito; so I know that there is much here to interest past, present and future generations of devotees. To the Mosquito's already thrilling history I have added much rare and lesser known, but equally spectacular and compelling accounts, including ferrying adventures over the Arctic and USAAF spy-dropping and OSS *Redstocking* communications flights, together with many rare and exciting photographs.

Enough of the nuts and bolts – or rather wood and glue – for *THE MEN WHO FLEW THE MOSQUITO* is, as the title suggests, a book about the actual 'men', in every sense of the word. Quite simply, I have not found a more interesting, dedicated and harmonious band of British, Commonwealth and American pilots and navigators as these men. Having interviewed most of the 'cast' in this book, I doubt whether there was ever a greater team effort than that made by those Mosquito crews. 'Mossie' pilots and navigators generally stress that they were an 'entity'. This human quality was certainly evident in 8 Group, whose use of the Mosquito is graphically recounted in the late John Clark's vivid account, included by kind permission of his wife, Ann Solberg Clark. At the time of writing, Ed Boulter and Philip Back, two more from 8 Group, still fly regularly; Philip even flew me from Norfolk to Oxfordshire to see his wartime navigator, Derek Smith so that we could all meet and talk. It is one of a number of Mosquito memories I shall cherish forever.

Memories are precious, but we can all admit to having embellished them, or failed to point out that we might have got them slightly out of kilter as the years have passed. No man is an island. Fortunately, people like Geoff Thomas, Tommy Cushing, and Bob Collis and his allies, have made every effort to keep me, and contributors with hazy memories, on track with input from original research material.

All of us know that the Mosquito was built of wood and glue, as most books on this fine aircraft have pointed out. But while there is no room, or need, for repetition here, ponder for a moment the ramifications of events recorded in Chapter 15, for which I am most grateful to Geoff Thomas who introduced much of the research. Bob Collis, more than most, has made strenuous efforts on my behalf to ensure accuracy, although this has meant that, on occasion, we have had to disregard some reputations, assertions, and myths perpetrated and perpetuated in some quarters. All of this should ensure that this book is an accurate tribute to THE MEN WHO FLEW THE MOSQUITO.

Martin W. Bowman

"Come out of the road—you'll get run over."

Sunday Express, Mar. 5th, 1944

Acknowledgements

I am enormously grateful to the following people for making it possible to include as much diverse information and anecdotes on Mosquito operations as was possible in the space allowed. Bob Collis provided his customary expertise in matters concerning crashes and crews, and he furnished much missing information on German crews in the form of police reports, combat encounter details and detailed correspondence. If there is a finer researcher in the UK at this time, I have yet to meet him.

I am indebted also to Tom Cushing for his gracious help in locating Mosquito crewmen and for furnishing No 23 Squadron historical details and rare photos. Jerry Scutts and Philip J. Birtles also added many missing pieces to the jigsaw with some superb photos. I am, as always, most grateful to Mike Bailey for his guidance, checking and supply of much needed books for research purposes. I would also like to pay tribute to my friends and fellow researchers in France, Belgium and Norway, who came to my aid when I most needed it. The peoples of these countries of course hold great admiration for the Mosquito, and some of them actually saw the aircraft bomb targets in their country during the Second World War. Let me not forget too the welcome correspondence and photos from former 'Mossie' men in Australia, Canada and the United States of America.

My heartfelt thanks to all those named below who furnished such marvellous help and support throughout: Steve Adams; Michael Allen DFC; Sidney Allinson; Don F. Aris; Jim Avis; Philip Back DFC; David Backhouse; Norman Bacon; H. Barker; Tim Bates; AVM H. Bird-Wilson CBE DSO AFC Retd; Philip J. Birtles, Chairman, Mosquito Air Museum; Barry Blunt BA Hons, Archivist to the Mosquito Aircrew Association; Warren Borges; Terrence Boughton; Ed Boulter DFC; Michael J. F. Bowyer; Tommy Broom; S/L Ed Bulpett RAF Retd; Jeff Carless; John Carnegie; Mrs S. A. Chadderton; Dorothy Chaloner; Des Curtis; S/L Mike Daniels RAF Retd; *Eastern Daily Press*; *Eastern Evening News*; Grenville Eaton; Roy Ellis-Brown DFC; Reg Everson; Mrs P. Jane Fox, *Legion* Magazine; J. D. S. Garratt DFC & Bar; Rev Nigel Gilson; AVM Bill Gill DSO; Val Grimble; Ken Godfrey; Richard T. Goucher RAF Retd; Cato Guhnfeldt; Leo Hall; Capt Pete Hardiman; Lewis Heath; Raymond Hicks; W/C Gerry Honey OBE MRAeS MIMgt RAF Retd; G. Horsfield; Richard Howard; S/L Stephen J. Howard RAF; M. Howland; Dennis Hudson; Harry Jeffries; Bernard M. Job; *Lancashire Evening News*; E. W. Lawson; W/C R. W. Leggett RAF Retd; Frank Leyland, Andrew Long; S/L George Lord RAF Retd; Ron Mackay; G. F. Mahony; Norman Malayney; Capt Bill McCash AFM; Noelle Meredith, PRM, The Royal Aeronautical Society; Eric Mombeek; W/C A. P. Morgan;

F. G. Morris; Jean Nater; W/C George Newby RAF Retd; Wiley Noble; Merle Olmsted; J. A. Padilla; Charles Parker DFM; Simon Parry, Air Research Publications; W/C George Parry DFC DSO RAF Retd; Andre E. Pecquet; Allan Pudsey; Ralph Ramm; John Rayner; Barbara Rayson; John Rayson G.Av.A; W. F. Rhodes; The late Peter Richard; S/L Derek Rothery RAF Retd; S/L Philip Russell DFC RAF Retd; B. W. Salmon; Alan Sanderson; S/L E. J. Saunderson RAF Retd; George Sesler; W/C Joe Singleton RAF Retd; Jerry Scutts; Richard T. Sizemore; Colin R. Smith; Derek Smith; Mrs Ann Solberg Clark; Dr Robin Steel; Robert 'Bob' Stembrowicz; Gerald Stevens DFC; C. Tarkowski; Geoff Thomas; S/L A. M. Tomalin RAF; Henk Van Baaren; John Vasco; Paddy Walker; Peter Waxham; Alan B. Webb; Harry Welham; Brian Williams; W. C. Woodruff CBE FRAeS; *Worcester Evening News*. My thanks also to the dedicated PSL editorial team for their forbearance, and their skill in ensuring that accuracy prevails.

Glossary

AA	Anti-Aircraft
AAA	Anti-Aircraft Artillery
ADLS	Air Delivery Letter Service
AF	Air Force
AFC	Air Force Cross
AI	Airborne Interception (radar)
AM	Air Marshal
Anvil	Use of aged PB4Y-1s as radio-controlled bombs
AOC	Air Officer Commanding
Aphrodite	Use of aged B-17s as radio-controlled bombs
ASH	AI.XV narrow-beam radar used for low-level operations
ASR	Air-Sea Rescue
ATS	Air Training Squadron
AVM	Air Vice Marshal
BBC	British Broadcasting Corporation
BEA	British European Airways
BG	Bomb Group (USAAF)
Blip	Radar echo or response
Bogey	Unidentified aircraft
BS	Bomb Squadron (USAAF)
BSDU	Bomber Support Development Unit (RAF)
C-scope	CRT showing frontal elevation of target
Capt	Captain
CCU	Combat Crew Unit
CH	Chain Home (early warning radar station)
Chaff	American *Window*
CHEL	Chain Home Extra Low
CHL	Chain Home Low

CO	Commanding Officer
CoG	Centre of Gravity
Col	Colonel
CRT	Cathode Ray Tube
Day Ranger	Operation to engage air and ground targets within a wide but specified area, by day
DCM	Distinguished Conduct Medal
DFC	Distinguished Flying Cross
DFM	Distinguished Flying Medal
Diver	V1 flying bomb operation
Drem lighting	System of outer markers and runway approach lights
DSC	Distinguished Service Cross
DSO	Distinguished Service Order
Düppel	German code name for *Window*. Named after a town near the Danish border where RAF metal foil strips were first found.
e/a	Enemy Aircraft
ETA	Estimated Time of Arrival
F/L	Flight Lieutenant
F/O	Flight Officer
F/Sgt	Flight Sergeant
FIDO	Fog Investigation and Dispersal Operation
Firebash	100 Group Mosquito sorties using incendiaries/napalm against German airfields
Flensburg	German device to enable their night fighters to home in on *Monica* radar
Flg	Flieger: Airman (German)

FNSF	Fast Night Striking Force	Maj	Major
Freelance	Patrol with the object of picking up a chance contact or visual of the enemy	Maj	Major: Squadron Leader (German)
		Maj Gen	Major General
Fw	Feldwebel: Sergeant (German)	*Mandrel*	100 Group airborne radar jamming device
G/C	Group Captain	MC	Medium Capacity bomb
GCI	Ground Control Interception (radar)	MCU	Mosquito Conversion Unit
Gee	British medium-range navigational aid using ground transmitters and an airborne receiver	Met.	Meteorological
		MG	Maschinengewehr: Machine gun (German)
Gen	General	*Monica*	British tail warning radar device
GP	General Purpose bomb	MTU	Mosquito Training Unit
Gruppe	German equivalent of RAF Wing	NCO	Non-Commissioned Officer
Gruppenkommandeur		NFS	Night Fighter Squadron
	Officer commanding a Gruppe (German)	*Night Ranger*	
			Operation to engage air and ground targets within a wide but specified area, by night
H2S	British 10-cm experimental airborne radar navigational and target location aid		
		NJG	Nachtjagdgeschwader: Night Fighter Group (German)
HE	High Explosive (bomb)	*Noball*	Flying bomb (V1) or rocket (V2) site
'Heavies'	RAF/USAAF four-engined bombers		
		OBE	Order of the British Empire
HEI	High Explosive Incendiary	Obgefr	Obergefreiter: Corporal (German)
HMS	His Majesty's Ship	Oblt	Oberleutnant: Flying Officer (German)
Hptm	Hauptmann: Flight Lieutenant (German)		
		Oboe	Ground-controlled radar system of blind bombing in which one station indicated track to be followed and another the bomb release point
HRH	His Royal Highness		
IAS	Indicated Air Speed		
IFF	Identification Friend or Foe		
Intruder	Offensive night operation to fixed point or specified target	Obst	Oberst: Group Captain (German)
		Ofw	Oberfeldwebel: Flight Sergeant (German)
IO	Intelligence Officer		
JG	Jagdgeschwader: Fighter Group (German)	op	Operation
		OSS	Office of Strategic Services. The US intelligence service activated during the Second World War, and disbanded on 1 October 1945
KG	Kampfgeschwader: Bomber Group (German)		
KüFlGr	Küstenfliegergruppe: Coastal Flying Wing (German)		
		OT	Operational Training
LAC	Leading Aircraftsman	OTU	Operational Training Unit
Lichtenstein	First form of German AI radar	P/O	Pilot Officer
LMF	Lack of Moral Fibre	PFF	PathFinder Force
LNSF	Light Night Striking Force	PoW	Prisoner of War
LORAN	Long-Range Navigation	PR	Photographic Reconnaissance
Lt	Leutnant: Pilot Officer (German)	PRU	Photographic Reconnaissance Unit
Lt	Lieutenant	R/T	Radio Telephony
Lt Cmdr	Lieutenant Commander	RAAF	Royal Australian Air Force
Lt Col	Lieutenant Colonel	RAE	Royal Aircraft Establishment
Luftflotte	Air Fleet (German)	RAFVR	Royal Air Force Volunteer Reserve
M/T	Motor Transport		

RCAF	Royal Canadian Air Force	Sub/Lt	Sub-Lieutenant
RCM	Radio CounterMeasures	TI	Target Indicator
RNorAF	Royal Norwegian Air Force	TNT	TriNitroToluene
RN	Royal Navy	'Torbeau'	Torpedo-carrying Beaufighter
RNVR	Royal Naval Volunteer Reserve	U/S	Unserviceable
RP	Rocket Projectile	Uffz	Unteroffizier: Sergeant (German)
S/L	Squadron Leader	UHF	Ultra-High Frequency
S/Sgt	Staff Sergeant	USAAF	United Sates Army Air Force
SASO	Senior Air Staff Officer	VC	Victoria Cross
SD	Special Duties	VHF	Very High Frequency
SEAC	South-East Asia Command	WAAF	Women's Auxiliary Air Force
Serrate	British equipment designed to home in on *Lichtenstein* AI radar	W/C	Wing Commander
Sgt	Sergeant	*Window*	Metal foil strips dropped by bombers to confuse enemy radar systems
SKG	Schnelles Kampfgeschwader: Fast Bomber Group (German)	W/O	Warrant Officer
SOE	Special Operations Executive	W/T	Wireless Telephony
Staffel	German equivalent of RAF squadron	Y-Service	British organization monitoring German radio transmissions to and from aircraft
Staffelkapitan			
	Squadron Commander (German)	*	(medal) and Bar

Chapter One

Wing-tips Over the Wave Tops

'Last night, aircraft of Bomber Command made a heavy attack on objectives in the Ruhr. Large fires were seen on both banks of the Rhine,' says an Air Ministry communique. 'Aircraft of Fighter Command attacked enemy airfields and railways in France and the Low Countries. Six enemy aircraft were destroyed.'

'One of our aircraft is missing.'

Each night, from 1939 until 1945, avid listeners huddled around their wireless sets and paused to hear the clipped tones of the British announcer on the BBC Home Service deliver his chilling rejoinder. Night after night, RAF bomber crews flew deep into Germany and the occupied territories of Europe. Each time their wives, girlfriends and families prayed it was not them that had 'Bought it' or 'Gone for a Burton', as it was termed in the idiom of the day.

Bomber crews had been flying night ops for as long as 'Peggy' could remember. She had met Roy Dow, her Canadian pilot husband, on Saturday, 2 September 1939, at the Maison de Dance in Stockton-on-Tees when Roy, from Fort William, Ontario, was on a navigation course nearby. The date had been prophetic. Next morning, at 11:00 a.m., British Prime Minister Neville Chamberlain sombrely announced that 'Britain is now at war with Germany'. In the heady war-charged atmosphere of the time, Thomas Roy Asquith Dow and Virginia 'Peggy' Scott had enjoyed a whirlwind courtship, and despite little money (Roy was paid just £21 a month) and with death around every corner, they

got married on 9 November. Roy whisked 'Peggy' off in his Morgan Four-Four, painted British Racing Green, for a lightning 56-hour honeymoon in her home town of Newcastle, before rejoining his squadron at Thorney Island, Hampshire. He would fly 49 ops on Beauforts of Coastal Command and turn down a G/C post in Canada before finally being granted his greatest wish: he wanted to fly the Mosquito.

Most RAF pilots wanted to do the same, ever since that raw 15 November day in 1941, at the 2 (Light Bomber) Group airfield at Swanton Morley, Norfolk. For some time now, 105 Squadron observers at the large grass airfield had attended conversion training on a new W/T and the gunners had started navigation courses, all amid rumours of receiving a revolutionary type of aircraft built largely of wood, to replace the squadron's outdated Blenheim IVs. 105 Squadron had flown its first operation on 7/8 November with a raid on Essen. After a short day-and-night bombing campaign the squadron had switched to suicidal anti-shipping strikes in the North Sea. W/C H. I. 'Hughie' Edwards, the then CO, was awarded the Victoria Cross for his bravery and leadership on an operation at roof-top height over Bremen on 4 July 1941. Operation *Wreckage*, as it was code-named, cost four crews, and Edwards landed back at Swanton Morley minus most of his port wing-tip and with telephone wire wrapped around the tailwheel. During September and October, 105 Squadron flew anti-shipping operations from Malta. Losses were high. Returning to Swanton Morley, the surviving crews were due for a rest

W4050, the prototype Mosquito B.IV bomber, fitted with two Rolls-Royce Merlin 21s and built in just 11 months, and which astounded officials when it flew for the first time at Hatfield on 25 November 1940. (ARP)

and in bad need of a morale boost. The arrival of the Mosquito provided it.

The grey and green shape approached the aerodrome from the north-west. First it flew over at about 500 ft, at a speed of some 300 mph; then it approached the Watch Office and hangar from the west and went into a vertical bank at a height of 2–3,000 ft before turning a circle so tight and at such a speed that vapour trails streamed from his wing-tips. This was followed by a normal circuit and landing. Compared to the Blenheim IV 105 Squadron was used to, this performance was quite breathtaking.

The tall frame of Company Chief Test Pilot Geoffrey de Havilland Jr. emerged from the tiny cockpit of the 'Wooden Wonder' and he climbed down the ladder to be received like a conquering hero by G/C Battle OBE DFC, the station commander and W/C Peter H. A. Simmons DFC, CO 105 Squadron, with his air and ground crews.

Among the gathered throng of seasoned pilots and their navigators at Swanton Morley on 15 November to admire 'the Mosquito's beautiful shape' was F/L D. A. G. Parry, who, like his CO,

was a veteran of two tours on Blenheims. He was always known as 'George' because, like the autopilot of the same name, he always came home! Parry had recently completed two tours and was 'resting' at 13 OTU at Bicester when he just happened to pick up the telephone and receive a call from Pete Simmons, who had been his 'A' Flight commander in 110 Squadron at Wattisham. Simmons had rung to enquire when he was getting some more pilots, adding, 'By the way George, I'm getting some fast aircraft. Do you want to come?' Parry quickly turned down a posting to a squadron equipped with Bisleys going to North Africa and joined Simmons at Swanton Morley.

The CO's promise of 'fast aircraft' had come true, although W4064 left almost as fast as it arrived. After lunch, Geoffrey de Havilland Jr. climbed back into the sleek Mosquito B.IV and was joined by Simmons, who took the right-hand seat for a joyride with a difference. De Havilland Jr. treated his passenger, and the crews watching, to an exhilarating display of aerobatics. When they landed, Simmons was reported to be '...looking a bit green around the gills, but it did not stop him talking about it in the Officers' Mess during lunch!' (Simmons was later killed flying a Turkish Air Force Mosquito.) The sleek new bomber had to return next day to Hatfield, where the first of a paltry 10 Mosquito B.IV bombers was coming off the production lines, for adjustments. Not until July 1941 had it been decided to build Mosquitoes as bombers, and even then only converted photo-recce airframes. A further 60 Mosquito bombers were on order, but they would not start to arrive until the following February. For now, 105 Squadron had to make do with W4066, the first Mosquito bomber to enter RAF service, which arrived at Swanton Morley on 17 November watched by the AOC 2 Group, AVM d'Albiac and his staff; and three other B.IVs: W4064, W4068 and W4071, all of which were delivered at intervals to Swanton Morley by Geoffrey de Havilland Jr. and Pat Fillingham.

'George' Parry and F/L Jack Houlston were sent to Boscombe Down to test-fly the prototype Mosquito and evaluate the aircraft for squadron service. Parry recalls:

Mosquitoes at Swanton Morley. It was on 15 November 1941 that de Havilland chief test pilot Geoffrey de Havilland Jr. landed W4064, the first operational Mosquito B.IV bomber, at the No 2 (Light Bomber) Group airfield, to be received by W/C Peter H. A. Simmons DFC, CO 105 Squadron, and his air and ground crews who were the first to be equipped with the 'Wooden Wonder'. That month the first Mosquito B.IVs came off the Hatfield production lines and 105 and 139 Squadrons were the first two units to receive the type. (RAF Marham)

There were no handling notes; only a few roneoed pages. On 25 November I flew W4057 for the first time, with Houlston in the right-hand seat. After the Blenheim the Mosquito was unbelievable. The maximum recommended speed was 420 mph indicated air speed, but at 20,000 ft this was equivalent to 520 mph. However, the short nacelles caused a bit of buffeting on the tailplane and it also felt tail-heavy. I had to use nose-down to get the aircraft on the deck. We found out why in the Mess. Geoffrey de Havilland was there having lunch. We went up to him and he asked us what we thought. We mentioned the problems with buffeting and he replied that it was caused by the short nacelles; they were going to lengthen them, he said. He looked non-plussed when I mentioned about it being tail-heavy. Then he exclaimed: 'We put 1,000 lb of ballast in for the CoG, and I forgot to tell you!'

Swanton Morley's grass airfield and unfinished state were proving unsuitable as a base for 105 Squadron and so, in early December 1941, they moved to Horsham St Faith, just outside Norwich. For 'George' Parry and his fellow offi-

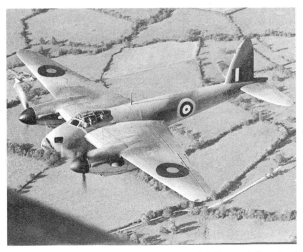

W4051, the prototype Mosquito PR.1 and the last of three prototypes to fly, on 10 June 1941. (The fighter prototype flew for the first time on 15 May 1941.) The PR.1 prototype saw operational service with the Photographic Development Unit, later redesignated No 1 Photographic Reconnaissance Unit, at RAF Benson. The aircraft carried LY-U codes. (via Philip Birtles)

A Mosquito B.IV of No 2 Group in flight in 1943. 105 and 139 Squadrons at Swanton Morley (and later Horsham St Faith and then Marham) pioneered operations with the Mosquito bomber on daring low-level missions throughout Occupied Europe in 1942/43. (RAF Marham)

cers it meant a return to RAF-style barracks after the more palatial accommodation they had enjoyed at Bylaugh Hall, a large country mansion where they slept in large bedrooms with 15-ft-high ceilings and a toilet mounted on a dais in the middle of the floor! On 27 December F/L Parry flew W4066 to an altitude of 30,000 ft. On 5 January he carried out fuel consumption tests in W4068 at a more sedate 10,000 ft.

Mosquito spares at this time were non-existent, although the squadron was expected to become fully operational with 16–18 crews and a dozen aircraft within a six-month period. At least the enterprising crews solved the question of spares, as 'George' Parry recalls:

Roy Maisey, Chief Engineer at de Havilland, lived with us. We piled all the old bits of aircraft into an Anson on 9 January 1942 and I flew it down to Hatfield with Houlston and two others, where we swopped them, with de Havilland's permission, for brand-new parts. On another occasion I flew back with the aircraft filled with timber! Finally, the Air

Ministry wrote and said, 'The degree of serviceability of 105 Squadron is amazing', and thereafter, spares schedules were issued and we had to abide by the rules!

Only eight Mosquitoes had arrived at Horsham St Faith by mid-May 1942, but 2 Group was anxious to despatch its new wonder aircraft on the first op as soon as possible. On 27 May it issued orders for 105 Squadron to prepare four Mosquitoes with bombs and cameras to harass and obtain photographic evidence in the wake of the 'Thousand Bomber' raid on Cologne, scheduled for the night of 30/31 May. S/L Oakeshott, followed later by P/O Kennard, took off from Horsham before the 'heavies' had returned and were followed, shortly before lunchtime the following day, by P/O Costello-Bowen with W/O Tommy Broom and F/L Houlston with F/Sgt Armitage. Oakeshott flew at 24,000 ft over the battered and blasted city and added his four 500-lb bombs to the devastation; but with smoke reaching to 14,000 ft, his F24 camera was rendered useless. Kennard failed to return, his aircraft being hit by anti-aircraft fire. Costello-Bowen and Houlston dropped their bombs from high-level into the smouldering and smoking ruins to prolong the night of misery for the inhabitants and bomb disposal teams, and headed back to Norfolk. In the late afternoon S/L R. J. Channer DFC took off from Horsham and flew in thick cloud to within 60 miles of Cologne, before diving down at almost 380 mph to low-level to take photographs of the damage. Channer quickly realized that this highly successful approach would be particularly effective for future Mosquito bombing operations.

On the evening of 1 June, two Mosquitoes returned to Cologne to bomb and reconnoitre the city. One of the aircraft failed to return. Then, just before dawn on 2 June, 18 hours after a 'Thousand Bomber' raid on Essen, 'George' Parry with his navigator, F/O Victor Robson, flew a lone 2 hr 5 min round-trip to Cologne armed with four 500-lb bombs to stoke up the fires and a camera to observe the damage. However, thick smoke made the latter task impossible. (Robson had come to 105 Squadron from Coastal Command and, according to his pilot, 'At night [he] was like a homing pigeon. No matter how bad the weather, he always pin-pointed exactly.') The Mosquitoes were of course much faster than the 'heavies' and, as Parry recalls, 'We were back having breakfast in the Officers' Mess while the "heavies" were still overhead, heading for home.' His curiosity was taken by a Whitley which had aborted the raid with mechanical problems and was now taking off from Horsham, with its bomb load still aboard:

I looked out the window and thought, it's not going to make it. It didn't. He went off nose-down towards the Firs pub on the road at the far corner of the airfield, and piled into a garage forecourt the other side. Luckily, it didn't explode. I rang the police and they cordoned off the area. Fortunately, the bombs did not go off.

One of the Mosquitoes with which BOAC operated a wartime freight and passenger civil air service between Britain and Sweden. On 4 August 1942 F/L (later W/C) D. A. G. George Parry and his navigator, F/O Victor 'Robbie' Robson of 105 Squadron conducted the first diplomatic flight from Leuchars to Stockholm. (via Ron Mackay)

DK337 pictured at Horsham St Faith on 22 September 1942, showing the damage to its tail caused by light flak. (via Philip Birtles)

W/C Hughie I. Edwards DFC (RAAF).

In June the Mosquitoes of 105 Squadron contin-ued their lone reconnaissance missions over Germany. When, on 8 June, 139, its sister squadron at Horsham St Faith and the RAF's second Mosquito bomber squadron, became operational – on paper at least – 105 Squadron provided crews and some Mosquitoes to add to the new unit's Blenheim Vs sent from 2 Group for training. One of the pilots transferred to 139 was Jack Houlston AFC, who was promoted to S/L. Houlston flew 139 Squadron's first op on 25/26 June, a low-level raid on the airfield at Stade, near Wilhelmshaven, and returned after dark just as bombers for the third in the series of 'Thousand Bomber' raids were taking off for Bremen. Two of 105 Squadron's Mosquitoes flew reconnaissance over the city after the raid and four more went to reconnoitre other German cities to assess damage and bring back pho-tographs.

On 1/2 July 139 Squadron bombed the subma-rine yards at Flensburg in the first mass low-level strikes by the Mosquito. G/C MacDonald and S/L Oakeshott failed to return. Houlston came off the target pursued by three Fw 190s, and F/L Hughes was chased by two more fighters after he had been hit by flak over the target. Both pilots made their exits hugging the wave tops, and applying extra boost, they easily outpaced their pursuers. On 11 July it was the turn of 105 Squadron's Mosquitoes to hit the yards at Flensburg, the raid being laid on as a diversion for the 'heavies' hitting Danzig. P/O Laston made it home with part of his fin blown away by flak, but F/L Hughes' Mosquito failed to return. Sgt Peter W. R. Rowland, in DK296, borrowed from 'George' Parry, flew so low that he hit a roof and returned to Horsham with pieces of chimney pot lodged in the nose. After he had landed Parry barked at Rowland, 'I'm not lend-ing you my aircraft again!'

High-level raids in clear skies were now the order of the day and during July the first 29 'Siren Raids' were flown. These involved high-level dog-leg routes across Germany at night, and were designed to disrupt the war workers and their families and ensure that they lost at least two hours' sleep before their shifts the following

DZ464, a Mosquito B.IV of 105 Squadron, pictured at RAF Marham in 1943. (RAF Marham)

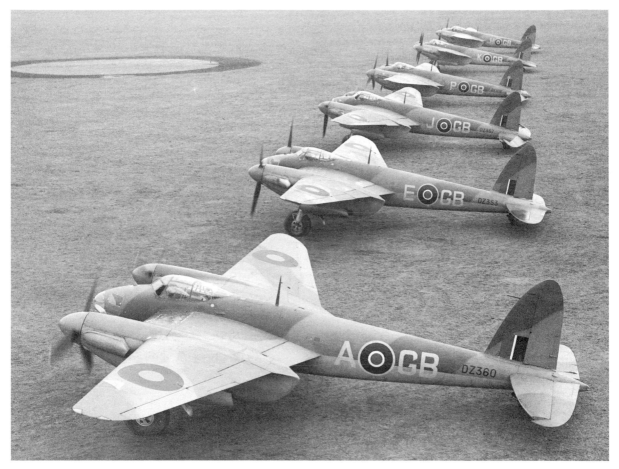

Mosquito B.IVs of 105 Squadron at Marham in December 1942. S/L George Parry recalls that the squadron often made 12-ship formation take-offs from the large grass expanse at Marham, but when this became a little hairy, the practice stopped! (via Philip Birtles)

day. Later that month came something different. George Parry was called into station commander G/C 'Digger' Kyle's office. 'He asked if I would be willing to "have a go" at flying the first Mosquito diplomatic run to Stockholm, to deliver cyphers and mail for the British Embassy.' Parry said he would. DK301 was duly painted overall pale grey and its national insignia and codes removed, while he and Robson caught the train to London to be briefed by Air Ministry and Foreign Office officials. Parry continues:

At the Air Ministry they explained to us what was happening, and then we went to the Foreign Office for their briefing. They said there would be a van coming to pick us up and take us to Liverpool Street. When the van arrived it was filled with about 40 diplomatic

sacks with labels clearly marked 'British Embassy, Stockholm'. What security! I got the driver to roll them together to hide the labels, and 'Robbie' got in the back and I sat up front. At Liverpool Street Station I went and saw the stationmaster and persuaded him to give us a first-class compartment all to ourselves and to make sure we were locked in. Then I rang Horsham and asked for a car to meet us at Thorpe Station, to take us and the bags to the base. As far as I was aware there were codes and cyphers in the bags.

At Horsham the bags were locked in the HQ building overnight. Next morning, 4 August, 'Robbie' and I, wearing our Sidcot flying suits over civilian clothes, boarded our grey Mosquito now loaded with about a 1,000 lb of baggage roped together in the bomb bay and rear fuselage, and prepared to fly to Leuchars for the overwater flight to Sweden. Everyone had been told that we were doing a special test and would be away for 48 hours. One of the ground crew looked at

A Mosquito B.IV of 105 Squadron. This was the first squadron to equip with the Mosquito and their first operation took place on 31 May 1942. The first B.IVs were so scarce that 105 and its sister squadron, 139, often shared the available aircraft for operations from Norfolk. (RAF Marham)

our footware and told me much later he had wondered why we were wearing black civilian shoes.

At Leuchars we rang the Foreign Office for the 'OK' to take off, but they could not apparently raise the Embassy in Stockholm. I had to get there before dark as we had no radio, IFF, or anything else; they had all been taken out to save weight and make room for the bags. After ringing again and getting no definite answer I finally decided I must take a chance and take off. We set off across the North Sea for Stockholm and arrived over Bromma Airport where I cut in in front of a Luftwaffe Ju 52! We landed, and so did the Ju 52. A whole load of Germans came out of the transport and were extremely excited about our Mosquito. We were armed with incendiary devices to set it on fire if necessary, but the Swedes marshalled the Germans into the terminal and locked them in a room. Then the British Embassy staff, tipped-off by the Swedes that we had arrived, drove up and loaded up their cars with the diplomatic bags. A 24-hr guard by men in 'civvies' and armed with concealed revolvers was placed around the aircraft overnight.

We were taken to a large hotel in the middle of Stockholm which overlooked a large lake. We had no money and were not allowed to buy anything but were taken out to dinner at a plush restaurant, where German Embassy staff and spies were pointed out to us by our hosts. We met a squadron leader who had been shot down in 1940 while flying Blenheims in 2 Group and had escaped after being taken prisoner by

falling, unnoticed, out of the column he was in while being marched away to captivity and rolling into a ditch. He got as far as Stettin and got aboard a Swedish collier to Stockholm, where he gave himself up. He was an internee but was being looked after by the British Embassy. He wanted to get home. It was a bit tight and he would have to take turns on the oxygen mask, but I told him he could come home with us in the nose of our Mosquito. Next morning I started up one engine and all he had to do was nip in smartly, but the Swedes were not having it and they nabbed him! (He got back a year later.) On the way home we flew at 500–600 ft over the North Sea because of a weather front, and approaching Scotland two Hurricanes came out to intercept us. I had no IFF, so I opened up and left them behind and quickly landed at Leuchars. (Nine months later, BOAC received Mosquito airliners and flew the route regularly.)

On 25 August 1942 'George' Parry with Robson and F/L Roy Ralston with F/O Sydney Clayton, were detailed to raid two electric power stations, and F/L E. A. Costello-Bowen with F/L Tommy J. Broom a switching station, at Brauweiler, near Cologne:

We took off from Horsham St Faith at 19:30 hrs and went in formation to the Dutch Islands at the mouth of the Scheldt, where we split up and proceeded individually. Not long after crossing the coast and the islands, we were very low and brushed the tops of the trees. A

W/C R. W. Reynolds DSO DFC, takes over command of 139 Squadron from W/C Peter Shand DFC.

In this remarkable oblique view an enemy flak gun emplacement opens up on low-flying 105 Squadron Mosquitoes during an attack on the Stork Diesel Works at Hengelo, Holland in February 1943. The flying debris in the foreground is from a bomb burst through the roof of the Manemeyer electrical and mechanical equipment factory. The train is travelling along the Derventer to Zwolle railway line. (via Philip Birtles)

few minutes later, after crossing over another small wood, an electricity pylon suddenly loomed in front of us. We pulled up, but the starboard engine struck the pylon at its top. Immediately the engine stopped and the propeller stopped. The action of hitting the pylon jammed the controls. We were 80 ft up and there was nothing we could do. We were doing about 240 mph and just had to wait until we hit the ground. I said to Costello-Bowen, 'Well, this is it.' It's a funny thing, but neither of us were worried and were very calm, although death stared us in the face.

We lost height steadily and crossed a couple of fields; then the pine woods loomed up in front. We were bound to crash into them – this was about half a minute after hitting the pylon. Just before we hit the pine trees I instinctively released my safety harness – why I don't know – then we hit and everything went black; no physical pain, just darkness, and I felt myself rolling over and over like a ball. I must have been unconscious for a time. When I awoke, I was covered in branches and bits of aeroplane, and a strong smell of petrol was in the atmosphere. I struggled up and through and was amazed to find I had no injuries, not even a scratch. I must have been flung out of the top of the cockpit as I was right in the front with the nose of the aircraft. It was amazing that the aircraft did not catch fire or the bombs explode. The nose of the aircraft must have passed between two trees – how lucky can you be?

Roof-top attacks on enemy targets were not only daring, they were timed to perfection. Here, factory workers can be seen leaving off at the St Joseph Locomotive Works in Nantes on 23 March 1943 just as two formations of Mosquitoes, led by W/C Peter Shand and S/L Bill Blessing (RAAF) DSO DFC, make their attacks. (via Philip Birtles)

W/C Reg W. Reynolds DSO & Bar DFC, CO 139 Squadron, rests his bandaged hand on the damaged port engine propeller blade (both wounds sustained as a result of a direct hit on the airscrew) and poses for the camera with F/L Sismore DSO DFC in front of DZ601/XD-B following the attack on the Schott Glass Works and Zeiss Optical Instrument Works at Jena, 45 miles from Leipzig, on 27 May 1943. The attack was the last big raid carried out in daylight by 105 and 139 Squadrons. (via Philip Birtles)

Costello-Bowen, though badly injured, and Tommy Broom were very lucky indeed. They later made contact with the Belgian Resistance and were sent down the 'Comete' escape line which ran from Belgium, through France and into Spain. The two airmen arrived in Gibraltar on 21 September, two days short of four weeks since they were posted 'Missing'. Tommy Broom concludes:

I was told 105 Squadron had now moved on to RAF Marham and 1655 Mosquito Training Unit was being formed, and I was posted to it. I enjoyed my leave! My mother and father had never given up hope and were pleased to see me. After a rest as Chief Ground Instructor, I resumed operations once again, with F/L (later AM Sir Ivor) Broom.

While Broom and Costello-Bowen awaited a ship to England from Gibraltar, four of their fellow 105 Squadron crews, based along with 139 Squadron at Marham since 29 September, prepared for a long overwater mission of their own.

F/O 'Robbie' Robson DFC & Bar (left) and his pilot,
S/L (later G/C) George Parry DSO DFC & Bar, who
led the highly successful pinpoint raid by four
Mosquitoes of 105 Squadron on the Gestapo HQ
in Oslo on 25 September 1942. (Victor Robson)

The Norwegian Government-in-Exile in London
had been made aware by reports from the
Norwegian Underground that morale in their
Nazi-subjugated homeland was at a low ebb.
They also learned that a rally of Hirdsmen
(Norwegian Fascists) and Quislings would take
place in the capital, Oslo, between 25–27
September, and it therefore seemed an ideal
opportunity for the Mosquitoes to help restore
national pride. As well as disrupting the parade,
they were to bomb the Gestapo HQ between the
Town Hall and the Royal Palace, which stands on
a hill. The raid would also help flagging morale
in 2 Group, unsure of its exact role in the bomber
offensive and whose four squadrons were expected to operate a mixed bag of Venturas, non-oper-
ational Blenheims, and Mosquitoes, while trying
to come to terms with problems created by the
recent influx of American Mitchell and Boston
aircraft.

The expert low-level raiders in 105 Squadron
were selected and 'George' Parry was picked to
lead the raid, with 'Robbie' Robson as his navigator. The other three crews were: Pete Rowland
with Dick Reilly, Parry's No 2; F/O Bristow with
P/O Bernard Marshall; and F/Sgt G. K. Carter
with Sgt W. S. Young in the fourth Mosquito. A
few days before, on 19 September, Parry and five

other crews had flown the first daylight raid in a
Mosquito to Berlin. None of the six Mosquitoes
were able to penetrate the thick cloud *en route*,
although Parry dropped down through the layers
but did not have enough height with which to
bomb. He finally turned for home and headed
back across the north coast of Germany and into
Holland. At 1,000 ft, just off the Dutch coast, two
Bf 109s 'had a go' at him, as he recalls: 'I did a
steep turn to get away and found myself turning
towards the other, head-on. He had a squirt at me
and got two hits. There was no real damage and I
pulled up into the cloud. Unfortunately, the cloud
soon ran out a mile later, but I got down on the
sea and outran them.' The Oslo raid would be
flown at heights of just 50–100 ft.

On 25 September the four Mosquitoes, their
bomb bays empty, taxied out at Marham and took
off, heading for Leuchars in Scotland, where the
operation came under the control of W/C Hughie
Edwards VC. The raid on Oslo on 25 September
involved a round-trip of some 1,100 miles and an air
time of 4 hr 45 min; the longest Mosquito mission
thus far. 'George' Parry recently recalled the raid:

A photographic still from the attack on the
Gestapo HQ in Oslo on 25 September 1942. 'A'
shows a direct hit on the Victoria Terrasse; 'B' is the
central cupola on which the crews saw the Nazi
flag flying; and 'C' is the university building. (via
Philip Birtles)

We refuelled and bombed-up with four 11-second delayed-action 500-lb bombs and set off at low-level, 50 ft all the way, to Norway. It was like flying down a long, straight road and we were using dead reckoning throughout. We went through the Skaggerak, made landfall at the southern end of Oslo Fjord and flew up the eastern side. We flew up to a police radio station perched on a hill and I was told later I hit the flexible [45-ft-high] radio antenna, although it didn't do any damage to my Mosquito. We had been briefed that there would be 10/10ths cloud at 2,000 ft over Oslo, but it was a lovely day with blue sky. We had also been told there were no fighters to worry about, but the Germans had brought a squadron of Fw 190s south from Stavanger for a flypast during the parade. They had landed at Fornebu and had only been on the ground a short time when we arrived at 3 p.m. over the centre of Oslo. A lookout at the southern end of Oslo Fjord reported us and they were scrambled. Two Fw 190s got into the action. Fortunately, the rest did not get off in time.

The pilot of the leading German fighter was 22-year-old Rudi Fenten, who had temporarily left his unit to train on and pick up the new Fw 190 at Sola/Stavanger. Flying the other Fw 190 was 24-year-old Fw Erich Klein of 3./JG5 based at Herdla near Bergen. Both pilots were very experienced; Fenten had been in the Luftwaffe since 1940, while Klein had joined it in 1937. Fenten at first thought that the twin-engined aircraft flying ahead of him in two pairs were part of the flypast. (The Mosquito was still top-secret and largely unknown to the German units.) Then he realized they were too low and he chased after Carter's Mosquito. Fenten recalls: 'I could see the two men in the cockpit clearly, but I did not want to shoot them themselves. So I shot in the wing. I gave a signal for them to land but they shook their heads.'

Carter's Mosquito had been hit in the port engine. It caught fire and Fenten followed until the aircraft blew up in front of him and crashed into a lake. Carter had not been on the squadron long. S/L Parry adds:

Red tracer was going past me. Some of the Fw 190's shells hit the Royal Palace, although we were blamed for it at the time. I thought it was ground fire during our bomb run and didn't realize he was after me until my No 2 and No 3 overtook me. I was concentrating on 'buzzing' the parade and taking a line south-west over the centre of Oslo for the bomb run. We were travelling at 280–300 mph when I dropped my bombs. The speed the bombs were going meant they more or less followed us. They didn't drop but a few feet. Then they slowed down and hit. It was only after I had dropped my bombs that my navigator noticed a fighter was behind us. I opened up rapidly and shook him off by flying up the valleys at low-level.

Erich Klein, meanwhile, went after Pete Rowland and Dick Reilly. The two aircraft chased around the fir trees north of Oslo for many minutes. Rowland wrote:

Due to inexperience and misguided enthusiasm, I'd pulled up to 300 ft or so in order to observe our bomb bursts, and it was at that instant that Dick spotted a red-nosed Fw 190. We quickly got very low indeed. Klein considered that he had been too close behind to get his fixed-gun platform down and properly aligned on us. In his efforts to do so, he struck a tree. When he eventually broke away we thought he had run out of ammunition, but in fact he had struck a tree with his wing and was forced to return to Fornebu.

Rowland, a post war captain for BEA, learned this at a stop-over in Hamburg in 1963. Klein had later lost a leg in a crashlanding after he was shot down by a P-51 Mustang. In July 1993 Parry met Fenten face-to-face also, when the German flew his light aircraft to Horsham St Faith (Norwich Airport) and they flew a memorable flight around the city! S/L Parry continues:

Some of the bombs didn't explode but I thought it was a remarkably successful raid. It was the first long-distance raid we had carried out. We landed at Sumburgh in the Shetlands where Hughie Edwards was waiting. The first thing he said to me was, 'You were a minute late taking off!' He was a very quiet man. Everything had to be 100 per cent with him. Psychologically, he had to live up to the VC award. I said, 'We made it up on the way.' Then he asked, 'How did it go?' I told him and we waited for the other two crews, who were behind. I was first back to Sumburgh because my aircraft was faster than the others. It always looked covered with oil because I had it specially polished to give me an extra 15 mph.

Rowland adds: 'We arrived at Sumburgh 15 minutes after Parry and Bristow, to be greeted by the squadron commander with relief. He thought that he had lost two aircraft.'

105 Squadron crews gather prior to an operation from Norfolk. (RAF Marham)

George Parry and the other two crews were debriefed and flew back to Norfolk the next morning to rejoin the squadron at Marham. That night, 26 September, listeners to the BBC Home Service heard that a new aircraft, the Mosquito, had been revealed officially for the first time by the RAF and that four had made a daring roof-top raid on Oslo. Next day, when the first photo of a Mosquito was published, along with a caption stating that 'armament may consist of four 20-mm cannon and four .303-in machine guns', Parry flew down to Hendon to travel into London and to Broadcasting House, where he was scheduled to broadcast the story of the attack on Oslo to BBC listeners. He recalls:

It was a bit of a 'thing'. The Air Ministry had cooked up a script. I felt it was not true but they had told me, 'Don't worry old boy, it's for the public. They'll lap it up!' However, I changed it and the broadcast was very different to the hand-out I had been given by the Air Ministry! The BBC paid me five guineas, which I gave to the RAF Benevolent Fund.'

The post mortem and camera pictures taken on the raid revealed that at least four bombs had entered the roof of the Gestapo HQ; one had remained inside and failed to detonate and the other three had crashed through the opposite wall before exploding. On 30 September Parry flew to Newmarket in a Mosquito with F/O Thomas, to meet the people from the Norwegian Embassy. Parry landed on the racecourse runway and was soon in animated conversation with the four Norwegians in a large hotel in the centre of Newmarket. They had been very pleased with the raid and its outcome.

On 6 December 2 Group mounted its biggest operation of the war when 93 light bombers attacked the Philips radio and valve works at Eindhoven from low-level. Although some industrial processes had been dispersed to other sites, Eindhoven was still the main centre, especially for research into electronic counter-measures and radar. The plan was that after rendezvousing with the Venturas and Bostons at a point over the North Sea, the eight Mosquitoes of 105 Squadron and two of 139 Squadron (the latter crewed by F/L Wayman and F/O Clear, and F/O 'Junior' O'Grady and Sgt Lewis) were to trail them to the target despite the fact the Mosquito cruised at 270 mph, about 100 mph faster. S/L Parry, who was to lead the second formation of Mosquitoes behind Edwards' formation, discussed the point with his CO. Both men liked to do things their own way. Parry recalls:

I was happy to go in last, but I wanted us to make our own way. Eddie said things had to stay as they were and we had to fly with the others!

We took off and formed two formations of 10 Mosquitoes behind the Bostons and Venturas, but something went wrong with the timing and instead of being 60 miles behind, we caught them. We came in over the Scheldte at 50 ft and were beginning to wobble a bit flying along at 160 mph, trying to maintain the speed of the leading bombers. We flew through a flock of ducks and one went through my windscreen, split my leather flying helmet, and cut my head. The bird and bits of windscreen fragments hit the armour-plated seat and rebounded into my back. Funny, I didn't feel a thing, but my head went ice-cold. Robbie was cut by flying glass. He thought I was 'out' and grabbed the stick. I recovered and headed inland. Passing Woensdrecht airfield, Fw 190s were taking off. My No 2 and I broke away to decoy them away from the Venturas coming in over the coast behind. I went underneath an Fw 190. He didn't see me.

We caught up with the Bostons and bombed individually. I started a shallow dive on a tall factory building with two gun emplacements on the roof, firing. I released my four 500-pounders and carried on diving until I pulled out at ground-level. We flew out across the town and fields. We were to fly home via Den Helder. I looked at the gaggle of Bostons and Venturas and said to Robbie, 'We'll go home our own way!' 'Junior' O'Grady's Mosquito was hit by flak at Den Helder and crashed into the sea. Nine Venturas and four Bostons also failed to return. The Philips works was devastated, essential supplies destroyed and the rail network disrupted.

On 27 January 1943 Hughie Edwards VC DFC led nine Mosquitoes of 105 Squadron in a daring low-level strike on the Burmeister and Wain Diesel engine works at Copenhagen. Edwards found the target only at the last moment and was on the point of returning, but they hit it and then broke for the sea and home. On 31 January Mosquitoes bombed Berlin for the first time.

Smoke rises from the devastated Philips radio and valve factory at Eindhoven on Sunday, 6 December 1942. (via Philip Birtles)

Both attacks were timed to disrupt speeches in the main broadcasting station in Berlin by Reichsmarschall Herman Goering in the morning and one in the afternoon by Dr Joseph Goebbels. Three Mosquitoes from 105 Squadron, led by S/L R. W. Reynolds and P/O Sismore, attacked in the morning, and in the afternoon three Mosquitoes of 139 Squadron set out. 105 Squadron arrived over the 'Big City' at exactly 11:00 hrs and their bombs rained down, disrupting Goering's speech for over an hour; but the afternoon raid was not as successful and one Mosquito, flown by S/L Darling, was shot down.

The final large-scale daylight raid by 105 and 139 Squadrons was on 27 May 1943 when W/C R. W. Reynolds DSO DFC and F/L Sismore led an attack on the Zeiss Optical Factory and the Schott Glass Works at Jena. The two squadrons then joined Fighter Command and later 8 (PFF) Group for operations with the *Oboe*-equipped Mosquitoes. *Intruder* operations had become something of a speciality and the squadrons' tactics were subsequently adopted by equally brave and dashing young Mosquito crews of 23 Squadron in the Mediterranean theatre.

W/C Hughie Edwards VC DFC (left). An Australian of Welsh ancestry, Hughie Idwal Edwards was 26 years old when he took command of 105 Squadron. He won the VC for his leadership on Operation Wreckage on 4 July 1941 when he led nine Blenheims on an operation to Bremen. On Sunday, 6 December 1942 he led the Mosquitoes as No 2 Group mounted its biggest operation of the war when 93 light bombers attacked the Philips radio and valve works at Eindhoven from low-level. On 27 January 1943 Edwards led nine Mosquitoes of 105 Squadron in a daring low-level strike on the Burmeister and Wain Diesel engine works at Copenhagen. (via Philip Birtles)

A Mosquito B.IV of 105 Squadron is bombed up for a raid. Mosquitoes of 105 and 139 Squadrons were the first to bomb Berlin, on 31 January 1943. (RAF Marham)

Chapter Two

The Pirate Kings

In December 1942 Malta certainly lacked the comforts of home (the billets even lacked windows). Although the siege of the Mediterranean island was virtually broken by the time 23 Squadron arrived from Bradwell Bay, Essex, food and petrol were very scarce. The roads were pitted with partly repaired bomb craters and transport was in short supply. In England the squadron had been issued with 24 new aircraft which, after a chaotic four-week period to equip them for Middle East operations, were flown to Malta via Portreath, Gibraltar and Algiers. The ground crews, meanwhile, had sailed for Malta on the aircraft carrier HMS *Argus*.

Although life on Malta was 'fairly spartan, operationally, one could have wished for no finer situation,' wrote S/L Philip Russell. 'We were within range of Sicily, Italy as far north as Naples, and the North African coast from Misurata to Tunis. The main targets were road and rail traffic, shipping, and the air traffic between Sicily and Tunis. Unfortunately, the ASR launch was restricted to a radius of 40 miles from the island. If one ditched 45 miles out it was a long swim home.'

On Wednesday 30 December, the CO, with F/O G. E. Palmer, led the first 23 Squadron sortie from Malta. To save petrol their aircraft was towed to the end of the runway by tractor. At 03:35 hrs they left Luqa's muddy airfield behind and took a look at Catania, Comiso and Gerbini. However, they did not, as the squadron diarist put it, 'find any joy'. Shortly afterwards they were followed by P/O Williams with Sgt Marston, who went to Trapani, Palermo and Castel Ventranto. They experienced some very inaccurate flak and also returned to report no activity. At 18:45 hrs S/L Philip Russell with Bill Gregory took off to patrol western Sicily. Russell wrote: 'I was immediately impressed by the difficulties of covering airfields and attacking transport in such mountainous country. My fears were later justified by the heavy losses which the squadron suffered, the largest cause being flying into hills or trying to follow a train into a tunnel.' The fourth Mosquito, crewed by a Polish duo, F/L Orzechowski with F/O 'Curly' Sponarowicz, returned to Luqa after receiving some inaccurate flak from Comiso.

The tempo was brisk and the number of sorties flown by the squadron during this period was higher than at any other time of the war, wrote Philip Russell. When Rommel's troops were retreating along the desert coast, on several occasions during the moon period we would fly two sorties each night with a pause for refuelling, rearming and a cup of tea. The sea crossing was exactly 200 miles each way. We cruised at 240 mph. The targets were quite irresistible – long convoys of soft-bellied transports silhouetted on the black tarmac road against the white sand, with the desert moon making it almost as bright as day.

On the night of 4/5 January 1943, 23 Squadron drew first blood in more than one sense. F/Sgt Clunes and Sgt James were one of three Mosquitoes on patrol to Sicily. Before reaching the coast, they encountered a Junkers Ju 52. The slow-flying German transport caused them trouble when it came to making contact, but on the third attempt Clunes put a short burst of cannon fire into the enemy aircraft and started a fire. The

S/L Philip Russell learned to fly with the Leicestershire Aero Club and soloed in a Tiger Moth on 14 February 1937. In April 1937 he joined the RAF Volunteer Reserve and flew Hawker Harts, Hinds and Audaxes. In June 1939 he was commissioned with the rank of pilot officer in the RAFVR. After a spell as a flying instructor with a night fighter OTU, he piloted Mosquitoes in 157 Night Fighter Squadron at Castle Camps, before becoming a S/L and Flight Commander of 'B' Flight, 23 Squadron. He subsequently went with the squadron to Malta, just before Christmas 1942. (S/L Philip Russell)

gunners aboard the Ju 52 returned fire and James was wounded in the ear. Blood was pouring from the navigator's head and so Clunes decided not to press home the attack. He broke off and returned to Luqa with damage to his Mosquito. The second Mosquito returned early with VHF failure but Sgt Olley with Sgt Moss attacked a lit-up building at Comiso and shot-up a battery of searchlights.

On 7 January S/L Jackie Starr and F/O George Lace destroyed an enemy aircraft on the ground at Comiso, and the following night the first air-to-air victory in the Mediterranean went to S/L Philip Russell and P/O E. G. Pullen during a 'routine *Intruder* mission to upset the flying activities at Tunis airfield'. Russell recalls:

Tunis was the main airfield on the African continent for the Germans to use for supplying their armies, and there was fairly continuous traffic between there and their bases in Sicily. There was also heavy traffic on the sea and this was the frequent target of the Beaufort squadrons from Malta. On this occasion as we arrived at the airfield the runway and all other lights were doused, as was normal. We were not shot at, but that was probably because several of their own aircraft were presumably in the circuit and identification would have been difficult.

We were somewhat surprised to find one aircraft with its navigation lights on heading out to sea in the direction of Sicily. Presumably they were on the wrong wavelength to receive a warning from the control tower, or else they were just stupid. (These things did happen.) It was almost like shooting a sitting duck. We came up below and behind, identified it, and one short burst of cannon and machine gun fire, followed by one long burst from 800 yd to point-blank, turned it into a spectacular blaze. It was probably full of fuel for the sea crossing. The aircraft spun four times and went into a near vertical descent into the sea, the wreckage burning for some time on the surface.

After we had shot down the Ju 88 we lost an engine. It was a very hot night and we were flying in shorts. Whilst a Mosquito will fly happily on one engine, extra power is called for on the good engine and it runs hotter than normal. If the coolant boils the engine ceases to function. We flew the 200 miles back to Malta with our eyes glued to the temperature gauge, willing it to stay below boiling. It did – *just*.

Also on the night of 8 January, Peter Wykeham-Barnes and four other Mosquito crews between them flew *Intruder* sorties over Sicily and the road between Sfax and Gabes. The CO made five attacks on a convoy of lorries and Sgt Tibble followed 45 minutes later with seven attacks on the highway. At least eight vehicles were hit. Next day a follow-up raid on the convoy was planned, but the operation was threatened when a severe storm blew up. It was still blowing hard at nightfall when seven Mosquitoes taxied out and prepared to take off. Six got away safely, but Sgt Olley and Sgt Moss' Mosquito crashed just after

Mosquito F.II DZ230/YP-A of 23 Squadron flown by W/C Peter G. Wykeham-Barnes DSO DFC over Valetta in January 1943. (ARP)

take-off and exploded. Wreckage was spread over several fields. The other six aircraft went on the rampage. They found a 'considerable amount of joy', ripping the remnants of the Afrika Korps' convoy to ribbons with their cannon. F/L Neyder with F/O Cornes alone made 16 attacks on the battered column, which was left burning and smoking. (Neyder and Cornes were killed the following month, on 20 February, during a cooperation trip. Neyder had destroyed nine locomotives and seriously damaged another nine during his short career with 23 Squadron.) On 10 January, for the third night running, the convoy was hit again. Explosions were caused all along the route and at Zoura and Misourata.

Philip Russell's most satisfactory 'bonfire' was from two enormous petrol tankers on 16 January near Sfax. 'My claim was confirmed by two other crews who had seen the flames from 40 miles away and had come to investigate. As the German troops became more concentrated towards Tripoli, the flak got very intense and our losses were heavy. They put up a solid curtain of flak – 88-mm and 20-mm stuff – each side of the road.'

Late in the afternoon of Tuesday, 19 January a telephone call from Air HQ revealed that Rommel was on the run, and 14 Mosquitoes took off later in the evening and attacked his convoys on the heavily congested roads between Tripoli and Gabes. In an area between Ben Gardare and Ras Ajedi, the road was left jammed with burning vehicles and fires that could be seen for 40 miles. Johnny Streibel's Mosquito was hit by persistent anti-aircraft fire but limped back to Luqa where he landed with a burst tyre and a hole in his left engine.

On the night of 20/21 January P/O Williams with Sgt Marston destroyed a Ju 88 at Pantellaria during a cooperation sortie with torpedo-carrying

Mosquito F.II DZ228/YP-D of 23 Squadron just below Grand Harbour, Valetta, in January 1943. (ARP)

aircraft (23 Squadron flew 38 such sorties, in cooperation with Wellingtons and Beauforts, between December 1942 and September 1943); but F/S Paterson and Sgt Whitehead's Mosquito crashed into the sea just 70 miles from Malta. Both men were picked up and made PoWs. On 23 January Tripoli fell. Next day an urgent demand for firewood at Luqa was satisfied by the cannibalization of a derelict bus on the aerodrome. This action brought forth from the M/T officer the information that there was a £530 claim on the vehicle. However, Wykeham-Barnes came to a friendly agreement whereby no one said anything and the whole onus of responsibility was put on the Maltese. As the Maltese had already stolen the intelligence officer's entire laundry, the CO was all in favour of blaming them for something!

On 29 January Philip Russell flew G/C Riley, Senior Air Staff Officer (SASO) on Malta, to take a look at Tripoli. Russell recalls:

We landed with some trepidation and I hoped he knew what he was doing. He did, and all was well. We drove into the town in a borrowed Jeep. It all looked rather a mess. In February I happened to be in headquarters when the captain of a merchantman which had just docked, rang up to invite a few officers to dinner. Since it was nearly my birthday, I grabbed the chance. On board the SS *Phemius* in Grand Harbour we had white bread, sugar, butter and beef; all unknown luxuries since we had landed. The skipper was most impressed by the amount we consumed.

On 15 February excellent weather and a full moon enabled 23 Squadron to send off six crews. Four Beaufighters from 272 Squadron and two from 89 Squadron at Takali added to the strength of the *Intruders* on Malta. Russell and Gregory went up to Taranto and attacked two trains after a run down the coast of Italy, and the aerodrome at Grottaglie. F/L Tymm with P/O Topping attacked three trains in western Italy and blasted trucks in sidings. They returned to Luqa with their hydraulics shot away after receiving rifle fire over the target, and they had to land without a tailwheel. (F/L Tymm was killed with Sgt Haley when his aircraft crashed at Luqa while returning from Taranto on 4 June 1943.) Canadian F/O G. L.'Gus' Shemilt with P/O E. G. Pullen shot the port wing off a Ju 88 at Trapani; but F/O Cave-Brown and W/O Westcott were shot down over the aerodrome while providing cover for the other Mosquitoes.

On 18 February Wykeham-Barnes, Philip Russell and several members of 'B' Flight celebrated F/L J. S. M. 'Babe' Barkel's birthday. Two days later several members of 23 Squadron returned from a party given by the Royal Navy, and the calm of the Meadowbank Mess at Luqa was pierced by the sound of singing and cannon-balls being rolled up and down corridors and

down staircases to the accompaniment of Very cartridges and maniacal cries of delight!

On 7 March Peter Wykeham-Barnes with F/O Palmer destroyed a Ju 88 at Catania. In March Philip Russell was 'commandeered by the "Boss-Man"', AVM Sir Keith Park, then AOC Malta:

He wished to attend some high-level conferences (he also wanted to show off one of his Mosquitoes), recalls Russell. I flew him to Telergma (Constantine) on 1 April and, since I was acting as his unofficial ADC, had an interesting dinner with Gen Spaatz and Gen Norstad. Next day I flew the AVM to Algiers and had another interesting meal with AM Tedder and AVM Wigglesworth. I was in good odour because I got him there in impossible weather, whereas another aircraft flew into the Atlas Mountains and killed a lot of 'top brass'.

On 9 April 1943, on the day his CO, Peter

23 Squadron crews in front of S/L Philip Russell's Mosquito, S-Susan, at Luqa, Malta. (Philip Russell)

Wykeham-Barnes destroyed his second aircraft, at Catania airfield, Philip Russell was awarded the DFC:

I had a pleasant note from AVM Sir Keith Park, whom I had chauffeured to North Africa, saying, 'Heartiest congratulations on your award of the DFC. Grand work. Keep it up.' On 16 April we lost an engine after rather stupidly having a go at a destroyer off the coast of Sicily. I told Sgt McManus to feather the engine, but, in all the excitement, he pressed the wrong button and feathered the good engine. There was a sudden dramatic silence, with the sea rapidly approaching. Remedial action was taken a bit smartly and we landed happily on our good engine.

On 24 April I completed my extended tour of 50 operational *Intruder* sorties and was grounded as tour-expired. I was still in charge of the flight and had the dreadful task of despatching crews to various missions and then sitting impotently, awaiting their return. Our losses had been high and new replacement crews were constantly being sent out. With few flying hours behind them and lacking any operational experience, they failed to cope with the difficult operational problems and, one after another, they failed to return. I seemed to spend a great deal of time writing letters of condolence to their relatives. This was not a happy time for me.

In the first three months of 1943 23 Squadron lost five aircraft and crews, while 17 enemy aircraft were claimed 'destroyed'. On the night of 26 April F/L A. J. Hodgkinson DFC* shot down two Ju 88s, which brought Malta's score to 999 'kills'; but he was beaten in the Maltese sweepstake by J. J. Lynch of 249 Squadron, who was awarded the 1,000 Malta victory when he shot down a Ju 52 shortly afterwards. Hodgkinson was later posted as 'Missing', just before notification of his award of the DSO was received.

At the end of April a chance arose for Philip Russell to return to the UK:

de Havillands, who made the Mosquitoes at Hatfield, asked that one of our original aircraft should be flown home to them for examination after several months in the Middle East. Since these planes were made only of wood stuck together with glue, we could understand their interest. So, on 3 May I set off homewards, with Sgt Maxie McManus as navigator. However, when I stopped for refuelling at Gibraltar, I found Wykeham-Barnes wandering about on crutches having broken his leg in some high-jinks party in the Mess. He had set off for home some time earlier and was desperate to get to a new and important posting. So he decided that he would come with me as my navigator, and McManus was fixed up with a berth on a destroyer.

We had only some rather primitive maps between us. After all, we said, over a few beers in the Mess, we really ought to be able to hit England. We decided that if we kept France on our right and then turned a bit more to the right, Lands End should loom up. Unfortunately, the weather over the Channel was horrid and we failed to pick up our landfall. We then had to decide whether we were right of our course and flying up the English Channel, or to the left, in which case we were flying towards the Irish Sea. Eventually I called up for a bearing from anyone who could hear and a very faint-voiced WAAF gave me a bearing of 340°, which indicated that we were indeed in the English Channel. However, land still failed to appear and, since fuel was getting rather low, I climbed to 10,000 ft to improve the R/T range and sent out a Mayday. This brought a controller on the air and, on finding out where we were and what course we were steering, he said, 'Sorry, you have been given a reciprocal bearing. Turn immediately onto 160°.' We wasted no time in so doing and landed safely at Portreath with five minutes' fuel left! The mistake by the WAAF was not uncommon since they twisted their locating set through 360° to line it up on your transmission. You were then either forward or backward – if you see what I mean.

It was just as well that we did not have to ditch. We had enough trouble getting Peter Wykeham-Barnes into the tiny cockpit on his crutches; getting him out of the escape hatch would have been impossible. It was also just as well that I did not drown him since, having later dropped the hyphenated Barnes, he became AM Sir Peter Wykeham with a string of decorations and honours. He went on his way and I flew the aircraft to Hatfield where, having unloaded a very large bunch of bananas bought in 'Gib', I took myself home. My grandfather Wright was in the Regent Road Hospital after an operation. He was very chuffed with the bananas.

After delivering the Mosquito to Hatfield ('it was horrifying to see Mosquitoes being built on the production lines without a nail or a screw being used from start to finish – just bits of timber being literally glued together') and some leave, on 28 May 1943 S/L Russell was posted to No 60 OTU at High Ercall in Shropshire, where he was joined by F/O Gregory, as Chief Flying

Instructor. This unit trained crews to be operational on night fighters before being posted to squadrons:

I have only two clear memories of High Ercall. One was when one of the pilots, having found out that his wife had been unfaithful to him with another pilot, persuaded her to go into the air, quite illegally, and then smartly dived from a great height onto the intersection of the runways on the airfield. I thought that

LAC T. Hamill of Port Glasgow, Scotland, cleans the cannon of a 23 Squadron Mosquito based at Signolla, Italy from September–November 1943. On top of the nose of the aircraft, armourer LAC E. Hurst of Cheadle, Cheshire, feeds the ammunition belt into one of the Browning machine guns. (via Philip Birtles)

this was going a bit far and was awfully messy.

The other was the matter of the cockerel. This creature used to crow outside our quarters and wake us up when we needed to sleep after night flying. One day we caught it and took it up in a Tiger Moth to test its flying abilities. At 2,000 ft we launched him over the side. He glided about for a minute or two very well, but then he looked down, squawked, folded his wings and plummeted down. There was no more crowing.

At Alghero, Sardinia, where 23 Squadron had moved to be closer to the retreating Germans, we received a great welcome – the first crew to return to the squadron – and an enormous party developed. Many of the 'old hands' – Morgan, Waggett, Piggot, Dawson and others – left, tour-expired. The CO of 23 Squadron was now W/C Alan Murphy. 'Sticky' was another one without any fear... Bursting with enthusiasm and a born leader of men, what a fine example he was to amateurs who had to follow him.

After helping in the invasion of Sicily and the subsequent conquest of the island, 23 Squadron had moved to and operated from Gerbini in September 1943, equipped with the Mosquito FB.VI which offered far greater range over Italy. There had been many instances of the sensitive Rolls-Royce Merlin engines being too delicate in the warm Mediterranean skies by day and night, especially when the frequent need arose to fly long distances on one engine with mountains to negotiate or avoid. The consequent overheating could not be lessened by conventional means and led to an agonizing period of suspense when operating near ground-level and having to climb up to 7,000 ft to reach safety. There was little nocturnal enemy air activity and most of the operations carried out consisted of bomb and cannon attacks on any enemy target that presented itself. A great many trains, factories, ships and motor transports were attacked during this period. Following upon the army's advance up Italy in October 1943, 23 Squadron moved to Pomigliano, near Naples. Few operations were carried out before the squadron moved again, this time to Alghero where it would remain for the rest of its tour in the Mediterranean. S/L Russell recalls:

The airfield was not a particularly good one. Scruffy in itself, it also lay right at the foot of some quite high mountains, and considerable care was needed in landing and taking off. We shared the airfield with an

American squadron. We were billeted in an ex-Fascist headquarters – all marble and pretty-pretty, and also damn cold. Food was not too bad and the bartering price with the locals was one egg for two cigarettes. I made an omelette on one occasion with 48 eggs! The surrounding hills were full of armed bandits, and we travelled in convoy and were well-armed when we ventured away from the airfield. Our operational activities were much the same as before but over different territory. On 2 March I carried out a strafing on a railway bridge in the Po Valley with two 250-lb bombs, making four attacks on transport, with one flamer.

I had scarcely properly settled in when I received a signal posting me on 4 March to a Junior Commander's course in Cairo. Back again, I carried out *Intruder* sorties over France and Italy. All these sorties were attacks on surface transport with bombs (which we then had) and cannon. No enemy aircraft were sighted. I don't remember any exciting moments. I was permanently frightened, but I don't recall being *really* frightened.

Typical of these ops was one on 28 March, when Russell and Gregory took off at 19:40 hrs for an offensive patrol to Rimini and Pescara. They made landfall south of Orbetello and set course for Porto St Giorgio, where they hit the coast at Porto Civitanova and turned north. They could see small red beacons on the mountain tops but no 'trade'. Between Porto Civitanova and Fano they saw scattered motor transport lights, but Russell decided to save his ammunition as there were no real concentrations to aim at. South of Pesaro, Russell aimed one of his 250-lb GP bombs at vehicles heading along the highway, but the bomb overshot the target and exploded in line with the road. He aimed a second bomb on vehicles travelling north on a roadbridge north of

S/L Philip Russell (right) enjoying the delights of Cairo while on a course in Egypt. (Philip Russell)

Pesaro. It exploded close to the bridge. After making a series of six cannon attacks on a convoy between Rimini and Pescara, the two men headed home to Sardinia. A heavy burst of flak aimed at them from the Grossetto area exploded harmlessly behind them as they recrossed the coast north of Orbetella.

On 9 April 1944 Russell and Gregory set off on a *Day Ranger* to the Perpignan area. The weather was glorious, with visibility up to 40 miles. Near Beziers airfield they attacked an electric passenger train travelling west, and both men saw strikes on the locomotive and many passengers disembarking at 'high speed' from the carriages. For good measure, Russell attacked factory buildings near Nissan with cannon fire and then sprayed 10 rows of goods wagons and carriages in Narbonne station, seeing strikes 'all over the place'. Then his gun-sight packed up and he turned for home. On 1 May S/L Russell took part in Operation *Dolphin*, which involved blockading Luftwaffe reconnaissance aircraft between Spain and the Balearic Islands. Commencing patrol from Cape Creus to the south, covering an area within 30 miles of the coast to Cape Tossa, Russell and Gregory sighted a motor vessel of about 1,500 tons heading north, close to the coast south of Cape Mongo. Russell let it proceed on its way, for painted on the vessel were Red Cross markings and a Red Cross flag at its stern. The next target they sighted was distinctly hostile. About five miles south when they were off Cape Morfeo they spotted a Ju 188. Russell gave chase, but the Mosquito was unable to make up the distance between them and the enemy aircraft eventually disappeared, heading low over the sea.

At Alghero, an American squadron was the only other allied unit on the island, everyone else having gone up north after the Germans. S/L Russell recalls:

They were a friendly crowd, but with odd habits. When we threw a Mess party and invited them over, we got rather drunk, as usual, and played silly games like rugger in the Mess. Not for them. When *they*

threw a party they invited the entire contents of the local brothel, including Madame.

On one visit to a pub in our local village, Sassari, I must have drunk out of a dirty glass and I had to go to the local medical unit with a horrible throat. Unfortunately for me, the only doctor on the island was American. Diphtheria had been eradicated in the States for some years and he failed to recognize the symptoms, so I was treated for tonsilitis. I was delirious for several days and they had to keep clearing my throat to enable me to breathe. My doctor at home, later, said that untreated diphtheria was nearly always fatal. It almost was.

By this time the invasion of Europe was imminent and it was apparently felt that we would be more use flying from the UK again. We therefore left Alghero and flew our aircraft to Blida, the airport for Algiers, where we abandoned them. We eventually embarked on the SS *Mooltan*; 20,000 tons, a very luxurious liner, previously on the India run and still with her original crew. We duly set off in a fast, unescorted convoy bound for the Clyde. When we were well out in the Atlantic, our steering gear failed and we turned sharply towards an enormous liner in the outside column. Sirens blew and, with life-jackets on, we waited for the big bang. Fortunately, we missed her, slowed to a stop, and sat quietly on the sea watching the rest of the convoy depart over the horizon. We were there for some time, during which we had Sunday Service. Seldom has the hymn, *For Those in Peril on the Sea*, been more enthusiastically sung!

We anchored off Gourock on 29 May, waiting for posting instructions. Eventually, on 1 June, a signal came through to me, as 'senior man' ('Sticky' Murphy having flown home in advance shortly before his wife Jean gave birth to Gail, his only child), instructing the squadron to report to RAF Little Snoring. When I told the gang our destination there was total disbelief, and it was only when we climbed out of the train at Fakenham that the drivers of the buses confirmed that there was indeed such a place!

Little Snoring, despite its name, was one of several airfields in the sleepy backwaters of north Norfolk that were to provide direct support to night bombing or other operations by attacking enemy night fighter aircraft in the air or over their airfields in the Reich.

Chapter Three

Bennett's Brigade

It will be remembered that 105 and 139 Squadrons were the first Mosquito units to join 8 (PFF) Group when they transferred from 2 Group in May 1943. Originally formed from 3 Group, using volunteer crews, 8 Group had started as a specialist Pathfinder Force (PFF) on 15 August 1942 under the direction of G/C D. C. T. 'Don' Bennett, and was headquartered at Wyton. On 13 January 1943 the PFF became 8 (PFF) Group, and 'Don' Bennett was promoted Air Commodore (later AVM) to command it. The tough-talking Australian ex-Imperial

1409 (Met) Flight at Oakington. Bill Woodruff is first in the front row. Second from left is Bob Taylor. Fourth from left is Cunliffe-Lister, the CO and former CO 521 Squadron, Coastal Command, which was used to form the flight. To his left is Braithwaite. (Bill Woodruff)

Mosquito B.IX ML897 of 1409 (Met) Flight, 8 (PFF) Group, lands at Wyton after its 153rd sortie. (via Philip Birtles)

Airways and Atlantic Ferry pilot wanted Mosquitoes for PFF and target-marking duties. The fact that 105 Squadron was commanded by fellow Australian W/C MacMullen whose few Mosquito B.IX bombers were modified B.IVs with *Oboe* radar, which no one wanted, helped him achieve his objective.

Gee-H (from 1944, H2S)-equipped Mosquito B.IXs of 139 Squadron and *Oboe II*-equipped Mosquito B.IXs of 105 Squadron spearheaded the Main Force bombing raids. *Oboe* had first been used on 20 December 1942. 139 Squadron went in with the target-marking Mosquitoes of 105 Squadron, sowing bundles of the thin metal strips called *Window* which produced a 'clutter' of blips on German radar screens to give the impression of a large bomber force. They made diversionary attacks, called *Spoofs*, on other targets to attract enemy night fighters anything up to 50 miles away from the Main Force during the attack.

Bennett's Mosquitoes were to prove so successful that he carried out an expansion of his Mosquito force. Ultimately, 11 Mosquito-equipped squadrons operated in 8 (PFF) Group (the other eight squadrons being equipped with Lancasters). In addition, 1409 (Met) Flight was established at Oakington on 1 April 1943 using Mosquitoes and crews from 521 Squadron, Coastal Command at Bircham Newton. F/L Peter Hall and his observer, Bill Woodruff, were one of the six crews posted to 1409 (Met) Flight. Bill Woodruff recalls:

Our Mosquito Met flights were known as *Pampas*. These were usually required to check the weather in advance of a raid and so they were usually made in daylight. Night flights using 'goose-necks' on the grass at Bircham were fortunately rare. 1409 (Met) Flight's Mosquito Mk Is flew day and night *Pampas* for 8 Group and Main Force commands throughout the rest of the war. We were not armed, but occasionally we carried a couple of bombs in case we spotted a target of opportunity. We carried cameras – one built-in for line overlaps and one hand-held. I understand that some of our photos were of use to PRU – including some of Peenemünde. We rarely encountered flak but were occasionally chased by German fighters. By the use of extra boost – not popular with the engine maintenance crews – we could usually pull away from Me 109s.

Our Mosquito was fitted with *Gee* a day or two before our seventh flight, on 9 May from Oakington; the first one of ours to be equipped. I had been briefed on it and had intended to try it out on the way back. AVM Bennett and his navigator were to fly our aircraft next day to try out the installation. We did a Met recce in the Ruhr and before setting course for home, climbed to about 28,000 ft to find the 'contrail' level. This of course made contrails in the sky and these were spotted by a patrol of four Fw 190s. The '190 was faster than our Mk I and we saw them rather late. Somehow, they managed to remove our tail, and this made continuing the flight somewhat difficult. I was thrown forward onto the floor and became unconscious. The aircraft went into a slow spin (I understand!) and Peter, thinking I had 'bought it', left the aircraft through the roof. This was not the right way out but I was sprawled over the exit hatch; anyway, there was no danger of hitting the tail. I 'came to' after a while and soon noticed that the ground looked remarkably close. The aircraft was still spinning slowly. I was only 21 and not ready to give up. There was a convenient and encouraging hole in the roof and I clambered up through this and, momentarily, sat on the fuselage while I pulled the parachute cord. It seemed only a matter of seconds before I landed in a ploughed field and twisted an ankle. I could see the aircraft going up in smoke a short distance away. It was still daylight. I had landed in Holland some miles south of Den Helder.

Both men spent the rest of the war in Stalag Luft III. Years later, AVM Bennett told Woodruff he was most annoyed at the time to have lost his *Gee*-equipped aircraft!

'Nuisance' raiding had begun in April 1943 and was so successful that by the summer a Light Night Striking Force (LNSF) of Mosquitoes was established. Mosquitoes went in up to an hour before the main attack, descended slowly and released their *Spoof* cargoes of two 500-lb bombs, two target indicators (TIs) or 'sky markers' (parachute flares to mark a spot in the sky if it was cloudy), and bundles of *Window*. German fighter controllers sent up their night fighters, so that when the 'heavies' did arrive, the Nachtjagdgeschwaders were on the ground having to refuel. *Spoof* raiding was first tried by 139 Squadron on the night of 18 November 1943 when flares and bombs were dropped on Frankfurt. Various plain colours with starbursts of the same or a different colour prevented the enemy from copying them. On 26 November three Mosquitoes of 139 Squadron, flying ahead of the Main Force, scattered *Window* on the approaches to Berlin and returned to drop bombs.

Sgt Pete Hardiman, an American in the RCAF who had joined 139 Squadron in September 1942, recalls:

After training by Leonard Cheshire we did mostly low-level marking with pyrotechnic flares, flying to targets at 'zero feet' to avoid radar. We covered most of the major targets in Germany; wherever the Lancs and Halifaxes went. We would arrive over the target about three minutes prior to the first wave, identify the Drop Point and mark it, then stoke up the Drop Zone with remaining flares. They had Lancs carrying flares as back-ups too.

On 1 February 1944 139 used H2S for the first time, marking the target for a raid on Berlin. At this time, 139 Squadron, which had pioneered the use of Canadian-built Mosquitoes, was operating a mix of Mosquito B.IV, B.IX, B.XVI and B.XXs. Pete Hardiman recalls a 'primary marker job' to Hamburg when he flew an FB.VI:

During the photo run I noticed an aircraft off the port side with German crosses. 'Doc' Hemsley, my navigator from Winnipeg, Manitoba, said, 'Don't mess with him. He's an Me 110 night fighter.' Deadly, I thought. After throttling back I fell in behind him to lower my profile. Then I recalled I was flying a Mk VI. I checked the gun-sight and saw his wingspan filling the outer ring, so I fired all guns. He blew up in a brilliant flash. The large blast of the explosion blew us about like a cork in the Atlantic. There was no aerofoil damage and we returned to base to find the paint removed from the entire front of the aircraft, including props, and the radiator intakes full of debris. We had a little problem confirming the 'kill' but as other aircraft had reported the shoot-down, I was later credited with it.

Flying the 'Mossie' was the highlight of my early flying career. It was a fantastic airplane – very fast; even with a full load we could reach 300 mph. The cockpit was not designed for more ease of control, although everything was within easy reach. It was cramped, and to sit for several hours in one place like a crowded dentist's office, was a bit much; but the

Pilot and navigator board their 128 Squadron Mosquito B.XVI at Wyton. (Jerry Scutts)

Mosquito B.XVIs of 128 Squadron taxi out at Wyton at the start of another operation to Germany. (Jerry Scutts)

1409 (Met) Flight Mosquito PR.IX ML897/D, complete with 161 mission symbols. (Jerry Scutts)

thrill outshone any bad points. Some of our missions took 8 hrs; one to Stettin was almost 10 hrs. We had an 85-kt headwind returning west at 15,000 ft. We had a few near misses; had our port engine damaged by flak and were attacked by night fighters while crawling home on one. We made it to Woodbridge and belly-landed there safely. We once set down out of gas near Nairn after a Baltic coast raid with terrible weather *en route* and return.

In November 1943 the prototype Mosquito B.XVI, specially developed for PFF and night raiding, with a pressurized cabin, flew for the first time. The B.XVI was powered by two two-stage 1,680-hp Merlin 72/76s or two 1,710-hp Merlin 73/77s, giving a top speed of 419 mph at 28,500 ft. Its bulged bomb bay could house a 4,000-lb 'Blockbuster', known colloquially as a 'Cookie', or 'Dangerous Dustbin' because of its shape. The B.XVI first flew operationally on 1

January 1944, and 'Blockbusters' were dropped by Mosquitoes for the first time on Düsseldorf on the night of 23/24 February.

The LNSF was expanded and eventually totalled eight Mosquito squadrons. On 24 November 139 Squadron's 'C' Flight B.IVs at Wyton were used to form 627 Squadron at Oakington. 692 Squadron was formed at Graveley on 1 January 1944 and used the B.XVI operationally for the first time on the night of 5 March, on a raid on Duisburg. On 7 April 1944 571 Squadron was formed at Downham Market. A shortage of Mosquitoes meant that 571 had to operate at half-strength for a time. On the night of 13/14 April two crews from 571 and six Mosquitoes from 692 attacked Berlin for the first time, carrying two 50-gal drop tanks and a 4,000-lb bomb. On 1 August 1944 608 Squadron at Downham Market and on 15 September 1944

Mosquito B.XVI ML963/8K-K was delivered to 571 Squadron, 8 (PFF) Group, on 19 April 1944, complete with the bulged bomb bay to accommodate a 4,000-lb 'Cookie'. This aircraft was lost on the night of 10/11 April 1945 during a raid on Berlin. (BAe)

128 Squadron at Wyton, joined the LNSF. They were joined, on 25 October, by 142 Squadron at Gransden Lodge.

Bennett wanted only experienced pilots with 1,000 hours total time for his squadrons. G/C T. G. 'Hamish' Mahaddie DSO DFC AFC, SASO at Group HQ in Huntingdon, was tasked with recruiting volunteer aircrew from the Main Force bomber groups. Sometimes pilots literally came knocking at his door. In June 1944 Philip Back and 'Bing' Bingham, fed up flying Blenheims at Spittlegate and itching to fly Mosquito night fighters, hitchhiked down the Great North Road to his office at 8 (PFF) Group HQ in Huntingdon. Back was educated at Harrow School and had joined the RAF in 1942 on a six-month university course, reading engineering at Corpus Christi College, Cambridge. He and Bingham found Castle Hill House, entered, and knocked on a door marked 'G/C H. Mahaddie, SASO.' Philip Back recalls:

There sat an imposing fellow with many 'gongs'. We saluted. He looked up over his glasses and said, 'What do you want?'

I said, 'We want a job Sir.'

'You'd better sit down. How many night flying hours?' he asked.

'Thirty!' I said.

'Thirty? You mean 300, don't you?'

I simply said, 'Yes Sir!'

He asked us what was going on. When we had finished he said he would see what he could do. Two weeks later we were posted to 1655 Mosquito Training Unit at Warboys!

Back soloed in the Mosquito after only 55 minutes' dual, in August. 'Bing' Bingham was killed on a night cross-country exercise from Wyton on 22 August when his Mosquito hit a hill. Another pilot, who arrived at Warboys in September, was F/O Herbert 'Ed' Boulter. He had grown up in Saskatchewan after his parents had emigrated to Canada, but had returned to England in 1938 and in 1941 had enlisted in the RAF. He teamed up with observer Sgt Jim Churcher. Pilots and navigators were normally put in a large room and told to pair off. Philip Back had met and crewed up with 23-year-old F/O Derek Smith DFC after both men did a dinghy drill session in the Leys Swimming School at Cambridge. Back recalls: 'On the bus back to base he said, "We're crewed up?" I looked at his 'gong' and said, "You bet we are." We became an entity in the air and would fly all our ops together.'

Smith did not learn until much, much later that Back had only 30 hours night flying experience, but he never had the slightest cause to doubt his ability. 'He was a natural who handled the "Mossie" with a skill well beyond his experience and always did the right thing in our more "hairy" moments.'

Derek Smith, having done a trip to Düsseldorf from the OTU in a 'clapped-out "Wimpy"' and then a tour on Lancasters with 61 Squadron, adds:

There was something special about the bomber Mosquito pilot/observer relationship. On my Lancaster tour I flew in a very close-knit crew which was all-sergeant until near the end, but I never formed any lasting relationship as close as I was to have with Phil. In the bomber 'Mossie' we sat side-by-side, almost shoulder-to-shoulder, sometimes for five or more hours, with a lot of decidedly unfriendly citizens down below for most of the time. They were no more friendly to the 'heavies' and although we relied as much on each other, we had so much more space and a little bit of the aircraft which was ours. In the 'Mossie', every move which was made was seen by the other, so maybe it served to weld us closer together as a unit.

F/O McEwan DFC and F/O Harbottle DFC & Bar, watch as their Mosquito, Q-Queenie, is loaded with a 4,000-lb bomb. Note also the 50-gal wing tanks.

Sergeant Charles Parker, a navigator from London, had experienced 'The Blitz' as a 17-year-old and was determined that 'these people had to pay for this', and so had joined the RAF. He crewed up with F/L Patrick James Duncan AFC, whom he had flown with on navigational training flights in Oxfords. '"Dunc" simply said, "Are you willing to risk your life with me, sergeant?"' Parker took one look at his AFC ribbon and said, 'Yes!' At the end of September Duncan and Parker and Boulter and Churcher were posted to 128 Squadron at Wyton, while Back and Smith were posted to 692 Squadron at Graveley on 5 September. The latter crew flew their first op that same night, to Hannover, with a 4,000-lb bomb in the bomb bay. Back recalls: 'The bloody plane shot up about 200 ft when we dropped it – no one warned me!'

Both squadrons were part of the LNSF of 'nuisance' raiders equipped with Mosquito B.XVIs and B.25s in October. All 8 (PFF) Group airmen had to undergo decompression tests, but although the B.XVI was pressurized, crews never used it on operations. Ed Boulter notes: 'You couldn't drop *Window*, and we were afraid to use pressurization in case we were holed. We could still fly at 30,000 ft and above on oxygen.'

Berlin at this time was the 'favourite' destination for the Mosquitoes. 'A' and 'B' Flights at 8 (PFF) Group stations were routed to the 'Big City' over towns and cities whose air raid sirens would announce their arrival overhead, although they were not the targets for the Mosquitoes' bombs. Depriving the Germans of much needed sleep and comfort was a very effective 'nuisance' weapon, while a 4,000-pounder nestling in the bomb bay was a more tangible 'calling card'. The 'night postmen' had two rounds: After take-off from Wyton crews immediately climbed to height, departed Cromer and flew the dog-leg route Heligoland–Bremen–Hamburg. The second route saw departure over Woodbridge and went to The Ruhr–Hannover–Munich.

On 23/24 October 1944 'A' and 'B' Flights at Wyton were assigned different cities: 'A' Flight were given a *Spoof* raid on Wiesbaden; 'B' Flight were allotted Berlin. Boulter and Churcher boarded Mosquito B.25 *D-Dog* and headed for Wiesbaden, while Duncan and Parker went out to their Mosquito for the flight to the 'Big City'. Parker was apprehensive:

The 'Mossie' was considered a 'lady', and as such needed careful handling. Normally, a pilot would do a 'second dickie' flight, but you couldn't do this in a 'Mossie' so Berlin was our first op together. We took off at 17:14 hrs. It was dark until we reached the searchlight batteries. [Altogether, they would fly 20 trips to the 'Big City' and all would follow roughly the same pattern.] Berlin had radar searchlights. We'd be stooging along when the icy-blue searchlight in the distance would suddenly swing over to us, and immediately all the others latched on until we were coned by white light. It was like daylight in the cockpit. Two minutes caught in the beams seemed like two days. I'd duck down. Pat would lose 10,000 ft in diving. Then the flak would get closer. If you couldn't hear it, then it wasn't intended for us – it had someone else's name on it. If you could smell it, well...it was bloody close.

At ETA I said, 'We should be there by now Pat.' He banked and looked down. We were at 25,000 ft and there, only 15 miles in the distance, was the start of the raid, so I was quite pleased we were that close. We didn't have a Master Bomber that night. Another PFF's TIs went down, bursting at different heights. (We seldom got an overshoot on the TIs; normally they slipped back: human nature.) We'd been told to drop our four 500-lb MCs [Medium Capacity] on the green markers. I flicked the bomb selection switch and immediately got down into the glass nose. It was difficult. You could quite easily get snagged on the oxygen knob and the *Window* chute sticking up on the door underneath my feet. *Window* came in a brown wrapper with a loop around it. The idea was to hold the loop while shoving *Window* out. Usually, there were upwards of 50 bundles piled up in the nose and all had to be thrown out in two minutes before using the bomb-sight.

Half crouching, I'd throw out the *Window*, then switch on the Mk 14 automatic bomb-sight. On my knees now, I peered into the illuminated cross, shaped like a sword, the point to the front. The bomb release cable in my right hand was like a bell-push. I gripped it and directed Pat on the intercom: 'Right, right, left, steady, steady...Bombs Gone!' With four bombs you didn't have the gigantic leap you had with a 'Blockbuster'. You didn't wheel away. We still had to fly straight and level for the camera in the rear to take its two photos. Activated by the bomb release it took the first frame, and with the shutter open a time switch shot the second half-a-minute later as the bombs exploded. The flight lasted 4 hr 20 min. When we got

back to Wyton we landed and sat in the cockpit a moment, shook hands and said something like, 'Well, that's the first of many – we hope!'

On a later op, when we were 'windowing' for the 'heavies', seven minutes were allowed because we carried 250 bundles. I felt OK but I heard Pat ask, 'You all right Charles? Your oxygen's off!' I'd knocked the knob to 'Off' with the edge of my 'Mae West' as I clambered into the nose. He turned it back on and I came up gulping for air. OK again, I started back down to the nose. Pat said, 'You going back down there?'

'What do you think we're here for?' I said.

During October, 11 Mosquitoes of the LNSF were lost on operations. New squadrons joined the force, with 142 Squadron reforming at Gransden Lodge on 25 October and flying their first operation when their only two Mosquito B.25s were despatched to Cologne. Berlin was attacked on the night of 30 October and the LNSF returned to Cologne again the following night.

On 6 November 1944, RAF Bomber Command sent out two major forces of bombers; 235 Lancasters of 5 Group, together with seven Mosquitoes, attacked the Mittelland Canal at Gravenhorst, while 128 Lancasters of 3 Group carried out a night *Gee-H* raid on Koblenz. Some 18 Mosquitoes raided Hannover and eight more went to Herford, while 48 Mosquitoes of the LNSF carried out a *Spoof* raid on Gelsenkirchen, to draw German night fighters away from the two Main Force raids. The Gelsenkirchen raid began

A 4,000-lb 'Cookie' is loaded aboard a Mosquito B.IV of 8 (PFF) Group.

A 4,000-lb 'present' for Adolf is manoeuvred into position at Wyton prior to a night bombing operation by 128 Squadron.

Mosquitoes of 128 Squadron equipped with 50-gal wing tanks taxi out for a night raid on Germany.

as planned, five minutes ahead of the two other attacks, at 19:25 hrs. The city was still burning as a result of an afternoon raid that day by 738 RAF bombers. From their altitude of 25,000 ft the Mosquitoes added their red and green TIs and high explosives to the fires. A few searchlights and only very light flak greeted the crews over the devastated city.

The 12 Mosquitoes B.XXs in 608 (North Riding) Squadron began returning over Norfolk shortly before 21:00 hrs to Downham Market. They had to contend with cloud and icing conditions as they descended over the flat landscape. The Canadian-built Mosquito flown by P/O James McLean, a 26-year-old Scot from West Lothian, and his observer, 21-year-old Sgt Mervyn Tansley, from Fulham in London, began to ice up badly. McLean lost control during his descent through cloud and the Mosquito struck overhead electric power cables before crashing into Bawdeswell village church. Both whirling propellers sheered off the engine nacelles and fell into neighbouring gardens, where a tree was cut down as if hit by a chain-saw. The remains of McLean and Tansley were not recovered from the wreckage until nine days later.

On 25/26 November 128 Squadron at Wyton

Mosquitoes of 8 (PFF) Group taxi out for a night raid on Germany.

were part of a force which attacked Nurnberg as a diversion for the 'heavies' attacking Munich. Boulter and Churcher's Mosquito B.XVI held a 4,000-lb bomb, which they released from 25,000 ft. Suddenly, an unseen German night fighter put several shells into the Mosquito. Boulter recalls:

The starboard engine began to run rough. We lost coolant and the engine began to register high temperature and low oil pressure. I feathered the prop. It was all quite 'lighthearted' at this point because the Mosquito could perform marvellously on one engine. However, 20 min passed and the port engine began to behave in the same way! Things were getting a bit hectic! I swopped engines all the way back, feathering one to cool down the engine and then switching to the other when it got hot.

Near the coast of France we were talking to Manston Emergency, and they tried to persuade us to fly 'the 10 miles remaining' (we actually had 25–30 miles to go). It was 4 a.m., 7,000 ft over Dunkirk, and both engines were trailing 40-ft-long flames. A 'Mossie' does not glide too well! I throttled back and we baled out. (Boulter and Churcher were later returned to Wyton.)

On the night of 27/28 November Pat Duncan and Charles Parker went out to their Mosquito for their thirteenth operation. They watched their ground crew winch a 4,000-lb 'Cookie' into the bomb bay. It was almost in position when, CRASH! The back half fell down. Parker recalls:

I did the 100-yd sprint. Pat was more philosophical and stayed put. I stopped. I felt a bit stupid! The S/L 'B' Flight arrived. He told us to take the spare aircraft into the hangar, but we said it hadn't been bombed up. (A 4,000-pounder had to be dropped on the night. We were not allowed to land with one because it would strain the fuselage.) The S/L ordered it bombed up and told me to go to the Briefing Room and work out a direct course to Berlin. I drew up a new course, Cromer direct to Berlin, calculating an extra five knots' airspeed on top of our average cruising speed. Even if we left in the next 10 min we would arrive 20 min after everyone else had left! Pat was halfway up the ladder when I got back to the reserve aircraft. I said, 'Pat, hold it. This is just madness.' In his perfect King's English he said, 'Come on Charles – we're going.'

I am no hero. Flying alone over Berlin was not my idea of fun. Perhaps the thirteenth was at the back of my mind. I argued. We didn't go that night.

On 30 November the LNSF mounted the second major daylight raid of the month when five Mosquitoes from 128 Squadron were part of a force of 20 Mosquitoes from their unit and 571, 608 and 692 Squadrons, despatched to the Gessellschaft Teerverwertung in Meiderich, a suburb of Duisburg. 'Sky markers' defeated the solid cloud cover, and smoke seen rising to 10,000 ft was testimony to their bombing accuracy.

Returning from Berlin on 6 December, F/L Duncan and Sgt Parker encountered severe problems with wind changes and gusty conditions. Low on fuel, they sent out a Mayday call, adding cryptically: 'Gravy is low! Gravy is low!' Charles Parker studied his maps and made his calculations, but the wind played havoc with their Mosquito. He could have sworn it was Grimsby when he saw fishwives on the quay below as they passed over the coast, but it was actually a French port! They finally put down at Friston on the south coast with less than 20 gal of fuel remaining in the 12 tanks.

Another daylight raid was despatched on 11 December when two waves drawn from 128 Squadron raided Hamborn. On 18 December the LNSF, or Fast Night Striking Force (FNSF), as it had become known at Bennett's insistence, was increased when 162 Squadron reformed at Bourn with Mosquito B.25s. Soon it was accompanying 139 Squadron on target-marking duties. Charles Parker recalls:

Bennett thought we should be called the Fast Night Strike Force because we carried a 4,000-lb bomb load to the target – fast, unlike the American B-17s and B-24s. I don't think Bennett had a very high opinion of the Americans. On at least one occasion he ordered Mosquitoes to take off and form up over Cambridge at 500 ft, to show the good folk of that city that there were RAF squadrons in the area besides Americans! Also, if he ever heard squadrons using the American phonetic alphabet (which ultimately replaced the RAF alphabet), a wigging would go to the squadron CO.

FNSF crews practised low-level bombing over the ranges in The Wash, and at Wyton crews used the shooting-in butts. On New Year's Day 1945 the FNSF skip-bombed 15 railway tunnels in the Koblenz area in daylight with delayed-action 4,000-pounders, released from 100–200 ft. A 128 Squadron Mosquito crashed on take-off, killing the crew. Five crews who bombed achieved mixed results. Six Mosquitoes of 692 Squadron bombed tunnels near Mayen, losing one bomber to light flak. Five crews of 571 Squadron were more successful, one bomb totally destroying a tunnel. A record of the bombing was made using cameras mounted in the front and rear of the Mosquitoes to record explosions at the entrance and exit of each tunnel. FNSF Mosquitoes were to fly even lower, sowing mines in the Kiel Canal which they crossed at 50 ft at an angle of about 20°!

By 5 January 1945 Philip Back and Derek Smith in 692 Squadron at Graveley had flown over 30 ops together. The start of January was hectic for them. Derek Smith wrote to his sister: 'We've done three trips in the last three nights to Berlin, Hannover and Nurnberg. It's a nice way of spending New Year's Eve, going to Berlin.

Ed Boulter (left) with Sgt Jim Churcher.

Still, there was a party in the Mess when we got back so we had a slap-up meal and a good time.'

On 5 January Phil Back and Derek Smith set off yet again for Berlin in Mosquito *T-Tommy*. At Wyton Ed Boulter's Mosquito was delayed on take-off by engine problems and ground crews worked on it by torchlight. Just as Boulter reached flying speed the troublesome Merlin misfired and lost power. With a 4,000-lb bomb on board and a faulty engine the Mosquito would flop over on its back and plough in, so the bomb was jettisoned and the operation aborted. On an earlier operation, on 18 December, when their Mosquito hit high-tension cables on take-off, tearing off the Plexiglas nose, Boulter had jettisoned the 4,000-pounder over the North Sea before landing at Woodbridge. 'Churcher felt that "someone was trying to tell us something",' recalls Boulter, 'and after 21 trips, decided enough was enough. He was entitled to call it a day and did so.'

Meanwhile, F/O Back and F/O Smith were experiencing problems returning from Berlin. Back wrote:

We had feathered one engine over Holland due to lack of power and lost some height. At about 27,000 ft the other engine stopped. We discussed baling out but it looked such a bloody long way down and we were over the sea, we decided to try and get down. We could see the lights of Woodbridge. We crossed the coast at about 18,000 ft and requested permission to land. 'What is your trouble *T-Tommy*?'

'We have lost both engines – long pause – "Land, *T-Tommy*."'

We got into the circuit about 12,000 ft on the upwind crossleg – lost all the rest of our height to cross the boundary high and very fast, wheels down and a bit of flap. God knows what our speed was. I know it was over the limits for the aircraft. The next morning I got a bollocking from the engineering officer, for they had found nothing wrong. We were collected on 6 January in the Oxford and the next day I flew back to Woodbridge and flew *T-Tommy* home to

Flt Lt Ed Boulter (left) with his navigator, Chris Hart DFM, in front of B-Bertie at Wyton.

Graveley. A day or two later I got another bollocking from W/C Joe Northrop. I was expecting a Green endorsement in my Log Book and was somewhat miffed at completing a dead-stick landing, in a 'Mossie', at night, losing about 15,000 ft in one enormous circuit and getting the wheels down – and getting my balls chewed up for doing so!

Derek Smith adds: 'It was a remarkable bit of flying and really deserved a medal. I can only think our otherwise amiable Wing CO guessed we had been a little too high!'

The 'Flying Brooms': W/C (later AM) Ivor Broom DSO DFC & 2 Bars with his observer (right), S/L Tommy Broom DFC & 2 Bars. The DSO was awarded for the skip-bombing of railway tunnels in the Koblenz area in daylight on New Year's Day 1945, using delayed-action 4,000-pounders released from 100-200 ft. 163 Squadron was reformed at Wyton on 25 January under the command of W/C Broom.

The monthly squadron parties at Wyton were a great morale boost. S/L Tommy Broom is in the foreground holding a glass.

On the night of 1/2 February 1945, Philip Back and Derek Smith crash-landed at Bury St Edmunds (Rougham), an 8th AF B-17 base, but hit a car as a result of overshooting the runway. The occupants were treated for cuts and shock. Mosquito K-King was written off when it was brought to an abrupt halt by a line of tree stumps. (via Cliff Hall)

During January–May 1945 LNSF Mosquitoes made almost 4,000 sorties over the dwindling Reich for the loss of 57 'Mossies' shot down or written off. The LNSF bombed Berlin on 61 consecutive nights. When, on 14 January, Ed Boulter piloted Mosquito B.XVI MM204 to Berlin, a new navigator, Sgt Chris Hart from Derby, was in the right-hand seat. High winds had grounded the 'heavies' but the 120-kt tailwind got the 'Mossies' to the 'Big City' in record time, although it caused Boulter to overshoot Berlin before he got his bomb load away. England was blanketed by fog. After attempting two beam approach landings over Bedfordshire they were ordered to bale out.

On 25 January 1945 163 Squadron reformed at Wyton under the command of W/C (later AM Sir Ivor, KSB, CBE, DSO, DFC, AFC) Broom. Duncan and Boulter and their navigators were among those posted to the new unit. Broom had instructions from Bennett for 163 Squadron to become operational immediately! He was just one day out. Duncan was promoted S/L and CO 'B' Flight, and his navigator's commission was awarded. Parker's first application, while in 128 Squadron, had been turned down. 'W/C Burroughs had berated me for having leather arm pads on my battledress (I wasn't the only one) and for not having my battledress blouse buttoned at the back to my trousers! This would have severely restricted my movement in the Mosquito.' Parker was finally commissioned after a recommendation by G/C O. R. Donaldson, DSO, DFC, his previous station commander, SASO, at 8 Group.

On the night of 28/29 January 163 Squadron flew its first LNSF operation when four Mosquito B.25s dropped *Window* at Mainz ahead of the PFF force. On the night of 29 January Philip Back and Derek Smith in 692 Squadron flew their fortieth op, with their second mission to Berlin in 48 hr. Smith wrote:

Our own 'drome at Graveley closed down and we were diverted to Bradwell Bay. Bradwell closed in and

128 Squadron celebrate VE-Day at Wyton with visiting Russian general staff. A/C 'Don' Bennett is seen with glass raised above the head of one of his two children. G/C D.F.E.C. 'Dixie' Dean DSO DFC, station commander, is in the foreground looking to his right. A Pathfinder demonstration was given, but only after the Soviet Embassy allowed one Russian general to fly in a Lancaster – provided it was piloted by 'Don' Bennett. The other general and some of the six colonels flew in another Lancaster.

Coltishall advised, 'Land where you can.' We went into a Yank 'drome, at Hethel, near Norwich. They gave us a great time. A Jeep wherever we wanted to go, pineapple, ice cream, whisky, cigs' and tobacco, and they would not let us pay a cent. We spent the night at Phil's place. They gave us a Jeep to take us the 12 miles and fetched us the next morning. [Philip Back wrote in his Log Book: '10/10ths Hospitality!'] On the morning of 31 January it was back to Norwich by car and there we were picked up by a Yank lorry. Weather was u/s and we were unable to go back to Graveley. 'Flicks' in the evening and drinks in the Club. We showed some of the boys over the 'Mossie' at midnight. On the morning of 1 February we flew back to Graveley.

We went back to 'The City' again that night. It was an easy trip, but we had our starboard engine out after we crossed the coast. Fog had closed down the whole of 8 Group, and we were left virtually to our own devices to find a clear field. We saw Drem lights. [Bury St Edmunds (Rougham); an 8th AF B-17 base.] Phil took his chance (there wouldn't be a second one), hopped over a Fortress in the approach and made a perfect touchdown, apart from being halfway down a

1,400-yd runway. We overshot and hit a car. The occupants were cut and shocked. Phil was OK. I had two or three cuts. *K-King* was written off when we were brought to an abrupt halt by a line of tree stumps. Next day we travelled to Cambridge by train and got back to Graveley by car from there.

In February the LNSF flew 1,662 sorties, and in March 163 Squadron alone visited Berlin 24 times. On 6 March the 'Wooden Wonder' made its last daylight raid when 24 Mosquitoes, led by *Oboe*-equipped aircraft of 109 Squadron, bombed Wesel. On 14 March Philip Back and Alex 'Sandy' Galbraith RNZAF, Joe Northrop's navigator, were posted to 139 Squadron. Philip flew his fifty-first op on 25 March and would fly nine more before the war's end.

Meanwhile, the largest operation ever on Berlin had occurred on the night of 21/22 March when 138 Mosquitoes attacked in two waves. Only one aircraft was lost. The last attack on the

128 Squadron air crews and WAAFs celebrate VE-Day, 8 May 1945, at RAF Wyton. Ed Boulter is pictured second from left, front row.

'Big City' by Mosquitoes took place on the night of 20/21 April when 59 Mosquitoes raided the German capital. On the night of 2/3 May, Boulter (who had flown 19 operations to Berlin), Duncan and Parker all flew their fiftieth operations when they took part in an attack, by 116 Mosquitoes from eight squadrons in 8 (PFF) Group, on Kiel. Appropriately, they had the honour of flying on this, the last Bomber Command raid of the war.

Ely Cathedral, a reassuring wartime landmark for homecoming bomber crews, was the setting for a special RAF service on 15 August 1992 marking the foundation of the Pathfinder Force 50 years earlier. Mrs Lys Bennett, widow of the late AVM 'Don' Bennett, was in the congregation with about 800 former air and ground crews. The Rev Michael Wadsworth, who lost his father in Pathfinder operations over southern Germany in 1944, gave the sermon. He said that of 93 seven-man Lancaster crews posted to the unit between June 1943 and March–April 1944, only 17 survived. 'Nevertheless, there was a strange alchemy about bomber operations,' he said. 'They were a special breed.'

The memorial stained glass window in Ely Cathedral commemorates 8 Group.

Chapter Four

This Special Breed: John Clark

Despite the intensity of raids, 'Don' Bennett's LNSF Mosquito squadrons had the lowest losses in Bomber Command (one per 2,000 sorties). John Clark, a Scottish navigator, tells the story of his ops, starting at 1655 MTU:

RAF Warboys was just like so many other airfields in wartime – some Nissen huts and hangars strung together by concrete paths. There were so many aircraft flying that day it seemed as if the whole of East Anglia was one large airfield. I was told to report to an assembly hut, or Briefing Room, the next day. There were about 20 of us, of whom half were pilots, half navigators. For some it was their second tour of operations. For a few it was their third tour. DSOs and DFCs seemed to be commonplace among them. Not a few had what was known as an 'operational twitch'. Their eyes and heads involuntarily flicked from time to time. I stood well back in deference to all this array of talent. I was, and felt, a very 'sprog' sergeant.

A group captain, with so many gongs displayed on his chest that he must have been flying one wing low any time he took to the air, jumped up on a table and addressed us in no uncertain manner. We were, he said, a specially picked lot and would augment the LNSF which was already causing the 'Hun' night fighters a few headaches. He warned us, however, that their flak was more accurate than it had ever been. The Germans knew they were losing the war but they were going down fighting, especially since they had been presented with unconditional surrender terms. He made the analogy of a wounded animal being more vicious when hurt. As an afterthought he tossed in the information that we would be carrying no guns whatsoever. We would have to rely on our speed to keep clear of trouble. A gasp of incredulity greeted this revelation. After a few more remarks of this nature he announced that he wanted us all crewed

up within three or four days. It reminded me of those announcements in the quality newspapers: 'The engagement has been announced, and a wedding will take place.' It was going to be a whirlwind courtship.

I was still standing at the back of the Briefing Room when a squadron leader, complete with 'operational twitch', came up to me. He had a scar, which he must have collected on one of his previous operations, across his forehead, and a DSO and DFC Bar across his chest. He looked me up and down. 'You've been saying nothing all this time, but I think you've been taking it all in. I like that. Think about it.'

I did. A cat, so legend states, has nine lives. I wondered how many he had and how many he had used up so far. Just then a little warrant officer, the only non-commissioned pilot in the room, came over to me. His shoulder flashes identified him as a New Zealander. His accent was as sharp as his profile. 'I hear you're a Scot. Will you be my navigator?'

For some reason which I could never explain, I answered, 'Yes.' We shook hands on the deal and introduced ourselves.

'I'm Bill Henley,' he said. 'I've been instructing for the last 18 months. This will be my first tour on ops.'

'Same here, only I haven't been instructing. You could say I've been like a spare one at a wedding – just hanging around. Let's have a beer and talk things over.'

We popped up to the bar in the Sergeants' Mess and gave each other a potted history of our service careers so far. He came from Auckland and had a brother who had been killed in the fighting in Crete in the Middle East campaign. Good God, I thought. Is no family going to be untouched by this war? I had just heard that my sister, who had become a driver in the ATS, had nearly been drowned driving a DUKW from the Ayrshire coast to the Isle of Arran.

I pulled a bit of a face. 'Too bad about your

John Clark.

B.XVI K-King of 571 Squadron photographed by the incomparable Charles E. Brown during a test flight from Hatfield on 30 September 1944. Major repair work on the aircraft had recently been completed, following damage sustained on operations. It returned to 571 Squadron in October.

brother. Let's try to get you back to New Zealand in one piece when this war is over. Who knows, we may get our commissions, and a gong to go with them.' What a load of bull, I thought. Still, it was better to look on the bright side. 'By the way, I've got to report for *Gee* training this afternoon. I've never used the thing before.'

He smiled. 'And I've got to familiarize myself with the Mosquito. I've never flown one before.'

A week or so later I joined Bill at Wyton, a permanent station with brick buildings and tarmac roads which seemed to ooze luxury compared with the muck and mess of Warboys. I walked round the aircraft we had been allocated to make our first familiarization flight together.

'She's got beautiful lines, hasn't she?' I observed. 'Except for this extended belly, which makes her look pregnant.'

'Yes,' Bill replied. 'Pregnant with celestial fire. It's extended so that it can carry the 4,000-lb bomb. The bomb looks like an extra large can of beans, and the casing is just about as thick as a bean can. The rest of

it is all explosives. We'll have to handle it rather carefully – no belly landings – and if we drop below 4,000 feet, we're liable to get our tail blown off.'

'Are we? So now you tell me!'

I clambered up the steps after him, into the cabin of the aircraft. 'They don't give a navigator much room to navigate.' I looked at the foldaway navigation table complete with anglepoise shaded orange light on my right, as I sat on the rather uncomfortable seat with part of the bomb bay under it. 'I've got to get us to Germany – and back – using this,' I said, pointing to the table. 'I see I'm considered more expendable than you.' At the back of his seat, armour-plating rose above his head. In my part it stopped at my waist; the rest of the space above the armour-plating was crammed with Bendix radio and LORAN. The *Gee* box was positioned behind the pilot's seat and was easily accessible.

The ground crew, who had been standing patiently, waiting for us to get settled, folded the telescopic ladder, stowed it away and slammed the main door shut. I in turn fitted the floor under my feet, slipping my

S/L McKay DFC and his Australian navigator at Oakington late in 1944. (John Clark)

Oakington 1944 showing aircrews of 'A' Flight, 571 Squadron with S/L McKay DFC (centre, hands on knees), in front of L-London, a Mosquito given to all new crews. When Henley and Clark flew L-London on their first operation, it had already done 120 ops and 'knew its way there and back'. (John Clark)

parachute and navigation bag behind my legs. This routine was going to take some getting used to. With the aid of the ground starting 'ack' the two engines coughed into life. The ground staff waved us off the dispersal pan and in no time, it seemed, we were lined up, looking down the runway. Bill pushed open the throttles and the two Merlin engines took us by the seat of our pants and pulled us down the runway.

Then it happened. The aircraft swung to the right. Fortunately, our wheels were off the ground and by a quick piece of avoiding action, we missed a hangar and pointed our nose skywards.

'Sorry about that.' It was Bill's voice over the intercom. 'It's never done that before, and I'll make sure it doesn't do it again.'

I tried to be jocular. 'That's what the man said when his horse dropped dead. Anyway, why worry? We missed the hangar by about 500 yd.' What a lu-lu of a take-off! I wondered what kind of driver I had chosen – or had he chosen me? As the months rolled on, Bill was as good as his word. Our aircraft never again swung on take-off.

One morning, the whole of the OT Course was summoned to present itself in the Briefing Room. The group captain with all the medals on his chest strode in and, without preamble, congratulated us on having completed the course. It was too bad that we had lost one crew during that time. It was unusual at an OTU. There had been no case of 'OTU-itis'. Our postings were on the notice board outside the Crew Room. We were being spread among the other Mosquito squadrons in 8 Group. He left as abruptly as he had arrived. 'What on earth is "OTU-itis"?' I asked a seasoned-looking navigator.

'Well, to put it crudely, some of these intrepid birdmen like to wear a brevet.' He pointed to his wings. 'And pick up a few free beers in their "local". However, when the chips are down, they suddenly discover that they have an incurable disease which their great uncles, or some other relative in the family, had picked up fighting in the Afghan wars or somewhere else in the British Empire. They call off flying before they have to face the flak and the fighters. The powers that be treat them pretty roughly. They're stripped of their rank and brevet, then their documents are stamped "LMF" – Lack of Moral Fibre. They usually become shit-house cleaners-out.'

We found that along with another crew we had been posted to 571 Squadron at Oakington, halfway between Cambridge and Huntingdon, where we would share the airfield with No 7 Squadron Lancs.

The next day we presented ourselves to the squadron adjutant of 571. Evidently our credentials

had gone before us. We had been allocated to 'A' Flight; the other crew to 'B' Flight. We were introduced to the 'A' Flight commander and his Australian navigator. 'Ah yes, you're the new boys. We'll put you on ops tomorrow night.' He looked at his navigator. 'How say you, Blue?'

'Yes, the usual treatment. Blood them early. They can take the old lady L-London for their first trip.'

He sounded quite laconic about it, as if he were allocating us an ice-cream cart for a day's 'jolly' at some fairground. Didn't he realize we had waited years for this minute?

'That's all right,' he continued, 'she'll get you to the target and back. She's done it over a hundred times. Yes, I know what you're thinking, mate.' He eyed me as he said it. He looked a jovial person with a twinkle in his eye. I reckoned he'd have difficulty squeezing into the aircraft. He was unlike his skipper who had, like Shakespeare's Cassius, a 'lean and hungry look'. He continued, still looking at me. 'You think it's your job to get to the target and back. Well it is, but she'll help you.' He spoke about the aircraft with as much reverence as an Aussie could about anything.

The flight commander took up the conversation, which was very one-sided. 'OK, you chaps. Get settled in and find your bearings. You can do a night flying test tomorrow morning and do some practice bombing at the same time. I'll fix it.'

'They don't waste any time, do they?' said Bill as we left the Flight Office. 'I suppose it's better than biting our nails up to our elbows waiting for our first trip.'

Next morning we were taken out to a dispersal pan where L-London stood. She was painted all-over black and the flight commander's navigator hadn't exaggerated when he said she had completed over 100 trips, if the bomb insignia stencilled on the side of the aircraft were to be believed.

'There's no practice bombing; it's been scrubbed,' said the 'Chiefy' who was waiting for us. He and Bill discussed a few technical points before Bill signed the Form 700, accepting the aircraft.

After an impeccable take-off we headed for the Norfolk coast. I undid my waistband harness and, with a bit of difficulty, crawled underneath the dashboard on my side, to check the course-setting bomb-sight which jutted out over the Perspex nose. There was also a bomb 'tit' hooked innocuously on the side of the fuselage, and the fuse-setting switches which activated the three fuses on the 'Cookie'. I glanced through the two Perspex panels set in either side of the nose. The propellers were churning the air at what seemed only a few inches from my earholes. If one of those props detached itself and flew off, I would be like a piece of corned beef – all ground up. Rubbish!, I thought. They'll fly forwards, not sideways. Anyway, they won't fly off. I clambered back to my seat. We joined the circuit and I took a *Gee* fix as we passed over one of the hangars. I registered it in my 'memory box' between my ears – just in case.

'Everything OK?' asked 'Chiefy' when we got our feet on the ground again. We gave him the thumbs-up sign. 'We'll see you later,' we added.

'It's your first trip, isn't it? Good luck. She'll get you back.' He nodded at the aircraft.

Bill looked at me. 'No messing. Briefing is at half-past three with take-off about half-past five. In between those times we get supper – bacon and eggs, I'm told.'

'Hmmm. It's almost worth going for that alone.'

At the appointed time we assembled in the Briefing Room. We immediately felt isolated from the outside world. Special policemen stood at all the entrances with revolvers hanging from their waists. On a raised platform at one end of the room, some sitting and some standing, were the commanding officer, the flight commander, the intelligence officer and the Met officer. On the wall behind them, illuminated by strong lights, were maps of the UK, France and Germany. Superimposed on them were tapes indicating our route out and back.

'OK chaps, settle down.' It was the intelligence officer. 'Your target, as you can see, is Gelsenkirchen.'

'Where the hell's that?' I muttered. A Canadian sitting next to me leaned over and whispered, 'It's in the Ruhr – the "Happy Valley" in other words, just north of Essen. It'll be a doddle.'

Reassured on that point I concentrated on what the intelligence officer was saying.

'We're taking you west of London, then over France to Germany. You'll attack the target from the south-west to take advantage of the winds on your leg into the target. The raid is of a diversionary nature. The "heavies" are bombing here.' His pointer jabbed at a different spot. 'Because it is a diversionary attack you will *Window* most of the way into the target – navigators please note.'

'Jeeze,' said the Canuck out loud. 'Why don't you stick a brush up our ass, then we can sweep the floor when we crawl through to the bomb-sight to drop our "Cookie".'

The remark received a ripple of laughter which the intelligence officer ignored. 'The target will be marked by *Oboe* markers, so I'll be looking for some good photographs on return.' He waffled on for some time about searchlights, flak, etc., and was followed by the Met man who assured us that the airfield would be wide-open on our return and that the winds were in fact blowing from the south-west. The CO affirmed that the 'Graveyard' airfields of Woodbridge and Manston would be wide-open for any aircraft that couldn't make it back to base. 'However, I'll be waiting for each of you here. Good luck!' he wound up.

As it turned out we sat waiting for an hour-plus, looking at each other and the wall opposite, each minute seeming like an hour. Now I knew in some degree what the soldiers of the First World War must have felt like when they knew they were going 'over the top' when the whistle blew. Bill produced a shiny black pair of sheepskin flying boots. 'I got them in New Zealand and decided I wouldn't wear them till I did my first op.' They looked pretty swep-up compared with my battered old escape-type boots, so-called because there was a single-bladed knife in a small pocket in the leg of one of them. The idea was that, should I have to bale out and resort to walking back, I could cut the leggings off and make them resemble civilian shoes.

After what seemed like aeons of time the WAAF orderly came round the rooms to tell us that the flight trucks were waiting for us. We climbed aboard, stopping at the Crew Room to pick up our parachutes, 'Mae Wests' and escape packs; then, crew by crew, we were dumped at our respective aircraft. I made a cursory check of the fuses on the bomb while Bill did the rest of the checks; then I followed him, navigation bag slung over my shoulder, into the cockpit. It seemed to get smaller each time I got into it, especially with the bundles of *Window* stacked all over the place. How we would get off the ground with 100-gal drop tanks fixed underneath each wing and a 4,000-lb load of explosives underneath us I refused to contemplate, consoling myself with the thought that it had been done many times before. Bill, with the aid of the ground crew, started the engines and I switched on my navigation light, spreading my charts over the navigation table. The other aircraft were 'crocodiling' their way to the end of the runway. It was comforting to see we were not alone. Their navigation lights were shining and they were being given a green flare from a caravan at the threshold of the runway. Our turn came. Bill gave the engines everything they had and trundled off.

'Come on, you son-of-a-bitch, get airborne,' I heard myself muttering into my face mask as old *L-London* bounced once, then twice, then bounced no more. We were off the deck. I noted the time in my Log. We passed over a railway line which ran at right angles to

Rooney caricature of John Clark. (Ann Solberg Clark)

the runway. There was a train puffing sedately along the track. We must have missed it by 10 or 20 ft. I don't know if we frightened it but it certainly frightened us.

We turned on-course, climbing steadily, listening subconsciously to the beat of the props and the throb of the engines. The blue flames of the engines spurted from the exhaust stubs in an asymmetrical pattern. While they were alarming to look at, it was very reassuring to see them. I checked our course on the climb. We were bang on track. I turned the light down on my navigation table and looked outside again. 'Here comes Eastbourne and Newhaven, and there's Brighton on our right. We'll be crossing the coast in a few minutes. I'll switch off the navigation lights.'

We levelled off at 25,000 ft. Although we were over France, heading for Germany via Belgium, I still had the feeling we were over enemy territory in spite of the fact that we were passing over places occupied by our own troops. Northern France and Flanders were covered by a layer of stratus cloud. Probably it was best that way; so much killing and death had taken place there over the years. The cloud cleared as we approached the Ruhr Valley. We seemed to be alone, with no other aircraft around, but when we turned in on our long run-up to the target the flak and searchlights opened up on us. I gave Bill his course to fly after we had dropped the bomb, then folded away my table.

Now to get rid of this *Window*. I adjusted the wooden chute. Breaking open two bundles of *Window,* I placed them in the chute and pressed it down through the floor and through the trapdoor of the outer fuselage. Unfortunately, in my haste and the confined space, I found I had pushed the 'V'-shaped chute out into the outside air, with the 'V' scooping up the air instead of sucking it out. A 300+ mph gust of air blasted the whole cockpit with silvery metal strips of paper. I quickly remedied the situation, chucking down the remaining bundles which slipped out of sight into the night air.

'What on earth's going on?' asked Bill. He looked like a mock-up of Santa Claus sitting in a heap of glistening metal.

'I'll clear it up after we've got rid of the bomb,' I said. It would have been quite funny if we hadn't been flying in one of the most heavily defended parts of Germany. I disconnected my intercom, dived under the sea of tinsel, and replugged it into a socket in the nose of the aircraft.

'How do you read me?' I asked.

'Five by five. How me?'

'Ditto. We seem to be on track. The red TIs have

gone down on time. Remember to fly straight and level for half a minute after the bomb's gone – photographs, remember. I'm fusing the damned thing now.' I pushed the fuse switches. 'Bomb doors open – confirm?'

Bill parroted the phrase back to me. I watched the TIs as they came closer. I was told later that there was flak and searchlights all over the place, but I didn't notice any. My eyes were riveted on the TIs as they started to slide down the wires of the bomb-sight.

'Left, steady!' Bill nudged the aircraft to the left so that the TIs came back to the centre of the bomb-sight.

'Steady, steady, we're nearly there.' As the TIs reached the crosswire I pressed the bomb tit.

'Bomb gone! Bomb doors closed.' It was like reading from a prepared script. The first part of the script was totally unnecessary as the aircraft reared up like a startled horse as the 'Cookie' fell away into the night sky.

'Hold that course,' I said as I waited for the camera lights to wink. There were flashes on the ground below. Which one was ours? Only the 'boffins' at base could say.

'OK, the camera's worked. Head for base.' My mouth and throat were dry and devoid of all saliva. Whether it was the tension of it all or the oxygen blowing into my mask, I didn't know, but I made a mental note to carry some chewing gum on our next trip. How totally impersonal it all seemed. I didn't really think of the German civilians who would be on the receiving end of the load of explosives I had released on them. For the first time I noticed the flak sparking around. None, as far as I could see, had hit us. My sympathies, if I had any, were for Bill who had to sit like an automaton, viewing the whole scene and having to follow my instructions. There was no automatic pilot fitted to the aircraft. He had to fly it manually.

I scrambled back to my seat and looked ruefully at the sea of tinsel covering the cockpit. I gathered most of it up and stuck it down the chute as we flew over Holland. I reckoned I was going to have some explaining to do to the ground crew when we reached base. I turned to the *Gee* box. The two matchsticks, or, to be more correct, the two blips, were flickering brightly on their time bases and getting stronger the nearer we got to England. I took a fix and gave Bill an alteration of course. We were going to come in over the Cromer beacon.

I turned on the navigation lights and switched from the main tanks to the outer drop tanks. Bill always liked to keep 25–30 gal in each outer tank, which he used for landing. I stuck my forehead against the *Gee* box visor again and started to home in on the two coordinates I had memorized. I was very tired, although we had been airborne for less than four hours.

Visibility was very good, and every airfield in East Anglia seemed to be flashing its green Morse code beacons giving its identity. We joined our circuit and came in over the runway threshold onto a very nice three-pointer landing. I noted the time in my Log.

At the dispersal pan the ground crew undid the catch of the outer fuselage and set the telescopic ladder in position. 'Watch out!' I yelled, as I lifted the trapdoor in the floor. They got a deluge of tinsel on their heads. It blew away in the early November breeze which drifted across the airfield. I hurriedly explained the reason for the loose *Window* which seemed to have covered everything. They took it in their stride and assured me I had not been the first navigator to make that mistake. Bill was telling the ground crew that as far as he knew we hadn't been hit by flak. I interrupted him. 'A very gentle christening, don't you think?'

'Tell that to my grandmother – you weren't sitting where I was.'

There was a moral there somewhere, I felt. Just then the crew truck drew up. We piled aboard and headed for the debriefing. A mug of coffee heavily laced with rum – a double shot for me as Bill didn't drink it – beckoned. At the debriefing the other crew, who had joined the squadron at the same time as we had, were having some difficulty deciding where they had dropped their bomb. The navigator had a rather glazed look in his eyes. His Log Sheet and charts looked as if they had been stuffed in his pockets at some point on the trip. He stated, categorically, that no TIs had gone down and that he had dropped his load 'by guess and by God' at his ETA over the target. On a replot of his navigation it was decided – and later confirmed by his photographs – that he had done some 'TNT ploughing' on the North German Plain. How he had managed it no one could understand.

I felt quite an 'operational type' after the trip. It had been pretty easy going as far as I was concerned, and I felt quite chuffed when the flight commander took us to one side and congratulated us on the photographs we had brought back.

Ground crew manoeuvre a 4,000-lb 'Cookie' into position. (Jerry Scutts)

Chapter Five

On Ops

John Clark's story continues:

As things turned out it was four nights before we again went through the ritual of a bombing trip. This time it was Hannover, with a nice civilized take-off time at six o'clock. Then followed two more trips in succession to Hannover. On our third trip we flew into a cone of searchlights quite early; Bill, who could raise or lower his seat, decided to do the latter until we had passed through them. There was no flak; an indication that fighters were on the prowl. I looked back into the night sky. We weren't making any contrails and I told him so. A few minutes later we were shrouded in darkness again, except for the dim amber light which shone on my navigation table.

Bill raised his seat so he could better spot any attack which might come from a night fighter. In doing so his oxygen tube was pulled out of his mask and fell to the floor. At first, neither of us noticed it; then the aircraft started to wallow all over the sky and went into a steep dive. I looked up and saw that Bill's head had sunk onto his chest. He was rapidly passing out. Then I spotted the oxygen tube lying on the floor. I grabbed the control column with one hand and steadied the aircraft. With the other I ripped off his mask and my own and quickly fastened mine to his face. At the same time I switched the oxygen to emergency and stuck the tube, which was lying at his feet, into my mouth. There was nothing in the rule book about this, I thought. What a carve-up! We readjusted our masks and attained some degree of normality. We had overshot our turning point and were out of the main stream of bombers. I gave him a course to fly direct to the target.

The aircraft was climbing again to our bombing altitude when the first burst of tracer bullets flicked past our wings. A fighter was on to us. 'He's a bloody poor shot, whoever he is,' I mumbled. 'Perhaps it's because we are climbing that he didn't give us the knockout punch.' Bill, as so often happened, didn't say anything. I stuck my nose into my charts and tried to ignore it. After all, that was Bill's department. He seemed to be tossing the Mosquito all over the sky. However, I couldn't ignore the second attack; the tracer bullets seemed to be going in one side of the wings and out the other. The engines were maintaining their steady beat, as did the propellers. I glanced at all the luminous dials on the dashboard and they were remaining steady. Then I noticed our green navigation light shining from our [starboard] wing-tip. I looked past Bill's head and saw the red one shining on his side. He was busy with the evasive action.

'Hell's bells, Bill. We've got our nav lights on! No wonder the bastard is picking on us. He must think we're crazy. We must have knocked them on in that mix-up with our oxygen masks.'

I quickly switched them off and returned the oxygen supply to normal, while Bill pulled the engine throttles back through the 'gate', where he had thrust them at the first attack. After all, it was like driving a car at full speed with the choke out: it didn't do the engines any good at all.

'Do we press on or abort the trip altogether?' I asked.

'The engines seem to be OK and we aren't losing any petrol. Any sign of that fighter?' asked Bill.

'Not that I can see. Let's carry on.'

We dropped our 'egg' and came back via the Cromer beacon, as usual. On the dispersal pan I moved to the grass verge, spat out the chewing gum which I had rolled around in my mouth since take-off, and at the same time stripped and wiped the curd which had formed on my lips. I lit a cigarette. Hell, it tasted good. Bill came over to me. He had been discussing the damage with a rigger. We had collected quite a few bullet holes in the wings, but nothing vital had been hit. 'We were lucky,' I remarked.

'Yeah, we'll need a lot more luck before this tour is over. Thanks a lot for noticing the oxygen tube. I was pretty 'gaga' by that time.'

I made light of it. 'If you go – we both go; whereas if I catch a packet you can always get back to England using that little information card I give you before each trip, and which you slip into the top of those shiny black flying boots of yours.'

I had just finished lunch the next day when Bill came over to me. 'We are on the Battle Order for tonight, Johnnie. Briefing is at three o'clock.' At the appointed hour Bill and I presented ourselves for briefing.

'Ye Gods,' muttered Bill. 'Do you see where we are due to go tonight? Berlin.' The route tapes were pinned to the map.

'So, it's the "Big City" tonight,' drawled the Canadian at my elbow. 'With *Spoof* attacks on Hannover and Magdeburg, I wonder where the "heavies" are going tonight? Is this your first to the "Big City"?' I nodded. It was funny how everyone took the same place at briefing. Still, it was more comfortable that way.

The intelligence officer soon filled us in on where the 'heavies' were bombing that night. They were coming in on a nothern route and were going to saturate Potsdam. We were going to bomb the centre of Berlin, with a view to drawing off some of the flak and searchlights from the Main Forces. The Germans may have had a 'busted flush', to use the Canadian's poker language, but they were still a force to be reckoned with; a fact which the paratroopers' disastrous landing at Arnhem was but one example. Their fighters, flak and searchlights were others. That we were winning no one doubted, but it was going to take a big heave yet. The Germans were fighting for their lives with their own lives.

We were given our time on the target, which would be marked by the H2S Mosquitoes of 139 Squadron. H2S was airborne radar. *Oboe* aircraft couldn't mark as far as Berlin. Their activities were confined to the Ruhr and its environs, although their range was extending as the armies on the ground advanced. The *Oboe* marker was very accurate and very 'hush-hush'.

'You'll find the flak and searchlights really concentrated around the "Big City",' remarked the intelligence officer. Cold comfort for us, I thought, as the briefing progressed. When it ended I turned to the Canadian. 'You been there before?'

He nodded. 'Two or three times, and as yet not a scratch to show on us.' He pointed to his pilot. 'We're hoping our luck lasts.'

We got airborne just after five o'clock, thanks to the short days at the end of November. Running up to Hannover, the *Gee* blips grew fainter and eventually guttered out like two spent candles. After collecting our share of flak over that city we pointed our nose towards Magdeburg. There was no need to navigate to it as the Americans had been there during the day. The place was still burning. We turned towards the north-east and headed for the 'Big City'. The TIs went down on time and I noticed another bunch on my left. Potsdam was being marked for the Main Force of 'heavies'. They were operating much lower than we, the Mosquitoes. Then the searchlights came into play. First the bluish ones, operating singly and radar-controlled, wandered haphazardly, or so it seemed. Suddenly, one of them darted sideways and caught a Lanc in its beam. The Lanc dived and wriggled left and right, but hadn't a hope as 20 or 30 other searchlights immediately lit the sky around it. It was caught in a wigwam of light. Then the sparks of flak began to burst around the aircraft. Some of the flak shells must have hit the starboard wing, for within a minute flames were rolling over the wing and the Lanc started to spin round and down ever so slowly, I thought. I heard myself yelling into the microphone which was clamped to my face, 'Bale out, you stupid bastards. You haven't a hope. Don't you know you're on fire?'

As if they had heard me, the silk parachutes began to appear in the searchlight beams. I started to count them – one, two, three – and then no more. Four hadn't made it. As if to underline the whole affair which was unfolding, the aircraft seemed to disintegrate as it went down. The three parachutes hung like stationary mushrooms in the cone of light. Just then there was a flash and what looked like an explosion. Two aircraft must have collided in mid-air. There would be no parachutes coming out of that, I reckoned.

As we were running up to the target a bunch of searchlights caught us. It had been sheer good luck on their part that they did so, since all the pale blue ones were latching onto the Main Force on our right. I was completely blinded by the light and couldn't see the TIs, far less bomb on them. 'I've overshot the TIs — we'll have to go round again,' I said into my mike, adding automatically, 'Bomb doors closed.'

'Oh, bloody hell,' replied the somewhat strained voice of Bill. 'Which way do you want me to turn the damned thing?' It was the first and only time I had ever heard him swear. After a moment's thought I replied, 'Make it a wide right turn. All the others will be making a left turn after dropping their loads. We don't want to run into any of them.' Bumping into another aircraft's slipstream was no fun either, as I had found out over Hannover when we had been attacked

Mosquitoes of 8 (PFF) Group stand idle, waiting for the next operation.

by night fighters. Our right turn seemed to fox the searchlights. Presumably, they had anticipated we would be making a left turn, heading for home. Anyway, we lost them, and were shrouded in darkness again.

I resolved to concentrate on the markers and ignore what was going on around me. This I found rather hard to do; it was difficult to tell which were bombs bursting and which were aircraft either on fire or blowing up. It seemed to me that Dante had underestimated his description of Hell. I went through the patter on our second run-in, dropped the TIs, waited for the photographs, then headed for the Cromer beacon and home. 'Sorry about the run-in to the target. I couldn't see a thing; the searchlight blinded me,' I said rather lamely.

'Not to worry Johnnie, we're still in one piece. It was a good idea of yours to make a right turn – it caught the Jerries on the wrong foot.'

I didn't explain to him that I had been thinking more of the aircraft following us than of the German defences.

We landed safely. Bill, following the laid-down instructions, opened the bomb doors at dispersal before cutting the engines. I was doing my usual – having a pee and spitting out the wad of chewing gum which had kept my mouth moist during the trip – when an armourer of the ground staff approached me. 'I say sergeant, come and see this. It looks a bit queer to me.'

'Nothing wrong I hope?' We ducked into the empty bomb bay together.

'Do you know where you collected that?' He pointed to the whole side of a flak shell embedded in one of the main spars.

'Over the "Big City" I suppose,' I answered. Bill had joined us and was looking curiously at the splinter. 'I never felt a thing hit us during the whole trip. It must have gone through the bomb doors or the fuselage. Isn't there a hole somewhere?'

'That's what's making me wonder. There's not a mark on the outer skin of the aircraft at all,' replied the armourer.

I looked at Bill and found him gazing at me. 'Are

you thinking what I'm thinking?'

I shrugged. 'I don't know, but I reckon we could only have collected it after I'd dropped the bomb and before you'd closed the bomb doors – a matter of seconds.'

'That's what I thought,' said Bill. 'Thank God the bomb had gone.' We turned to the armourer, who was looking as if he had seen a couple of ghosts. 'Yes, a matter of seconds – the difference between the quick and the dead.'

At the debriefing my Canadian oppo said, 'I hear you went round the target twice tonight?'

'That's right. I liked the look of the place,' I answered, dryly.

* * * * *

Being on a squadron was to be quite remote from the rest of the world. Time passed quickly, except for that gap between briefing and take-off, which seemed an eternity. Bill, thanks to his magpie instincts, had a gramophone and a large pile of records. At first he and I sat on our beds listening to the records; then one or more crews engaged in flying on the same trip would slip into our room and listen to Bing Crosby, Vera Lynn, the Ink Spots *et al.* Singing the sentimental songs in vogue at that particular time took our minds off the trip that lay ahead. Usually, one of the tunes swung around in our heads subconsciously while we were airborne. To get the wrong tune didn't help when you were waiting to be pounced on over Germany. Once Bill remarked, 'I've never heard a nightingale since I came over to the "Old Country".' Ann Shelton had just warbled out about the one that sang in Berkeley Square. 'There's still time,' I answered.

Someone else joined the conversation. 'Can anyone tell me why we are doing formation flying on our night flying tests? It frightens me fartless all this tucking up to one another. At least at night I can't see you lot. This formation lark puts you too close to me.'

We found out pretty soon. Seemingly, the CO hadn't gone batchy as we had thought. We had done a trip to Hagen and another to Berlin, and were waiting to take off again to the 'Big City' when we were summoned to the Briefing Room at 8 o'clock one morning and told we were going to take part in a bombing raid on some coking plant at Duisburg. It was going to be marked by *Oboe* aircraft. The idea was that we were going to form in pairs behind the markers, then when they opened their bomb doors we would open ours, and when we saw their bomb drop, we'd press the bomb tit and release ours. That meant that upward of two-dozen 4,000-lb bombs would hit the coking plant together. In order that those following would see when the marker bomb was released, the formation would step down 50 or 100 ft behind the aircraft in front. It also kept the following aircraft out of the slipstream of those ahead. It worked like a charm, except that the likes of us, who were in the middle of the formation, found ourselves flying through a cascade of 4,000-lb bombs. Those, allied to the numerous flak bursts, combined to make us long for the cloak of darkness. No wonder the daylight boys reported heavy flak. To our knowledge, the idea was never repeated. What the effect of it was we never found out – Berlin was a 'piece of duff' by comparison.

I decided one thing after the trip and discussed it with Bill.

'Do you think you could wind the aircraft up 1,000 ft above our flight-planned level on our next op?' Bill looked at me and I explained my reasoning. 'That sounds like good common sense,' said Bill. 'I think I can. It'll keep us out of the others' paths.'

'Good. I'll speak to the photographic section about our change of altitude, then they can adjust the camera for the extra 1,000 ft.' Apparently, I hadn't been the first to think of the idea. The corporal winked and smiled. 'You've decided to join the other clever buggers up top. I don't blame you.'

The next night we flew to Osnabruck, bringing our tally of ops into double figures. We completed the trip and we went on the beer with the boys the next night. The day following the flight commander wanted us in his office. We laid on all the bullshit we had ever been taught – marching in, saluting, and banging our feet in the approved manner.

'What in God's name are you playing at? Sit down,' came the laconic request from the flight commander. His Aussie navigator had his ample bulk parked on the seat in the corner of the office. 'By the look of them they must think they're going to be put on a fizzer,' he said. 'Park your asses on these chairs.' A burnt matchstick protruded from the corner of his mouth. We sat on the edge of our chairs, not quite knowing what was coming.

'You've been posted,' said the flight commander.

We looked rather crestfallen. 'Cheer up. I've been asked to supply two crews for 162 Squadron which is starting up at Bourn.' He doodled with a pencil on the blotting pad in front of him. 'It's being reconstituted as a Pathfinder Mosquito squadron. I was warned that they didn't want any rubbish, so it's quite a compliment to you both.'

'Yeah,' added his navigator. 'They don't want kangaroos that can't jump. You're good "press on" types with lots of ops left in you.'

'It's a bit of a shoestring airfield compared with

Bombs arrive for a Mosquito of 8 (PFF) Group.

here,' broke in the flight commander, 'but you'll get used to it. By the way, I've recommended you both for commissions.'

They wanted their pound of flesh, however, and a week before Christmas 1944 we were detailed for a trip to Hanau. We took off, in heavy fog, dropped our 'Cookie' on the target and returned with some degree of apprehension gnawing at us. We needn't have worried for a wind had picked up, blown the fog away, and substituted snow and sleet instead. We landed safely. We left the next day, 18 December. The Canadian navigator and his pilot were the other crew who were posted. After a lot of asking and swearing we found the adjutant's office. He was in a complete muddle. I noticed he was wearing wings above his breast pocket which I found reassuring. I reckoned if he could have jumped into an aircraft and got the hell out of the place, he would have been a happy man.

'What a shambles the whole thing is,' he said. 'It's a silly question I know,' remarked Bill, 'but there are aircraft here for us to fly, I suppose?'

The adjutant looked up from his jumble of papers. 'Yes, that is one thing that is not in a muddle. There

are a lot of brand new Mk 25 'Mossies' in the hangars or on dispersals waiting for you. We've got to get operational in a couple of days. That's an order from God himself.' He jerked his thumb in the vague direction of Huntingdon. We presumed he was referring to our intrepid AOC.

'By the way, there's a meeting of all you members of the squadron in the Briefing Room at six o'clock tonight, so don't get ideas of going out on the piss to Cambridge or the Caxton Gibbet. See you then.'

We nodded, left him to untangle his knickers, climbed aboard the 30-cwt truck and directed the driver. The billets were warm, even if they were a bit rudimentary. NCOs and officers mucked in together, at least as far as living accommodation was concerned, and we were all on 'Bill and Ben' terms within the hour.

The CO looked as if he had just left the Upper Sixth. His display of 'gongs' disproved that. Our flight commander, on the other hand, wouldn't have looked out of place in a comfortable chair by the fireside, wearing a pair of slippers. He must have seen 30–35 summers – aged by our standards. The rest of the bunch seemed to be a cross-section of the Commonwealth and the Colonies. Besides members from every county in Great Britain, there were Australians, Canadians, New Zealanders, a South African; 'Ossie', a Scots tea planter from Ceylon, and a sugar planter from Jamaica. There was even a Czech. How he arrived in the squadron only he knew. We were going to meld into a new squadron. All of us had flown on ops before. It was satisfying to know that Bill and I were no longer 'sprogs' but had several trips under our belts.

We were operational in two days, but without night flying tests on our aircraft. The foggy weather precluded that. We were called to briefing one afternoon just about three days before Christmas. We had to do a *Spoof* raid on Cologne. The 'heavies' were going to bomb it again an hour or two later, the idea being to help cut the jugular vein feeding the Ardennes offensive. Apparently, it was far more ferocious than had been anticipated at first, and had caught the Allies on the wrong foot. When the intelligence officer said we would drop *Window* on our way into the target, Bill smiled at me and asked if I was going to make a Father Christmas of him again.

Just after six o'clock we groped our way onto the runway and got airborne safely. The fog had been swirling across the field in banks; sometimes it was clear, sometimes it cloaked everybody and everything. It had been an on-off trip from the start. The Met men could give no assurance about the fog, either on take-off or return. The 'heavy' boys were going to follow us after an interval, so that each time our trip was delayed, the Main Forces had to fall back in time.

The weather over the target was pretty bloody. Snow showers drifted across the Cologne area and it seemed as if the defences hadn't much heart for putting up a barrage. It must have been cold and bleak on their gun-sights that night. I threw the *Window* out on the run-up to the target, making sure the chute was positioned correctly, and dropped four 500-lb bombs on the TIs which had been put down by the *Oboe* markers; then headed for base. Before we crossed the coast at Cromer we heard over the R/T that all was not well. All the fields were out owing to fog, although some aircraft had got into Wyton which was still producing some holes in the fog. But many were running around East Anglia like scalded cats. I used this expression to Bill. He glanced in my direction. 'Have you ever landed at an airfield using FIDO?'

No, have you?' Woodbridge and Manston had it. Flicking through the sheets of flimsies I was reading, I said, 'There's one at Foulsham.' FIDO [Fog Investigation and Dispersal Operation] consisted of two raised pipes running either side of the runway and well back from it. There was a crossbar at either end and the theory was that oil was injected into the pipes, which had holes in them, at various intervals. The oil was then set on fire and the resultant heat lifted the temperature and with it the fog that blanketed the runway. It was a dangerous and expensive way of getting aircraft down in foggy weather.

I glanced at the petrol gauges. We still had plenty of juice left. If the worst should happen and we couldn't get into Foulsham, we could always head south. 'Let's have a stab at Foulsham.'

We crossed the coast, and I didn't have to give Bill a course to steer as we could see the red glow of the burning oil that showed we were on track for Foulsham. From the chatter on the R/T it was evident we were not the only ones with the idea. We joined the queue circling the airfield, being tossed around by the turbulence of the upcurrents from FIDO. At least, we hoped it was the upcurrents and not the slipstream from some other aircraft which had forgotten to switch its navigation lights on. At last our turn came, and Bill pointed the aircraft's nose at what seemed to be a raging inferno. He kept the gyro compass lined up on the main runway. It was no easy task as the nearer we got to the flames the more the turbulence tossed us around. When we had almost given up hope of getting down we burst through the fog and saw the runway ahead of us. Bill had more nerve than I would ever have had. I would have overshot and abandoned the landing. He pulled back on the steering column and we thumped onto the tarmac. The flames from FIDO were licking up on both sides of us but, although dazed by the experience, we obeyed the R/T injunction from the control tower to clear the runway as quickly as possible as there were other aircraft following on behind us. With the aid of a 'Follow Me' van and the torches wielded by ground crew, we got to an overcrowded dispersal pan and cut the engines. We found that our aircraft and the ground crew were covered in thick oily flecks of soot.

'It sticks like shit to a blanket,' said one of the distraught ground crew, whose face looked as if he had been made up for a Black and White Minstrel Show.

Bill phoned base to say we were safely down, and we slept where we could find a place on the Mess floor. Next morning, in gin-clear conditions, we flew over to Bourn. As we rumbled down the runway at Foulsham we caught a glimpse of a Fortress lying across the FIDO installation. He hadn't quite made it.

* * * * *

It was Christmas Eve 1944 and only the Scots and a few Commonwealth personnel were left on the air-

Oboe-equipped Mosquito B.IX LR504 of 109 Squadron after its 190th sortie, at Little Staughton on 1 March 1945. (via Philip Birtles)

field, with a skeleton staff of admin people to keep the place ticking over. I hitchhiked to Peterborough, then stood in the corridor of a crowded, dirty train all the way to Edinburgh. We had the usual wartime Scots New Year. My sisters and my father guessed I was flying on operations but didn't mention it to my mother. At the end of my leave I caught the Colchester night train from Waverley Station, which was looking even dirtier than on those occasions earlier in the war. I knew I'd be flying that night and would need my wits about me. I got a cup of tea from the engine driver of the train which connected with the Colchester one, and arrived back at base about midday. Bill, who had spent his leave with some distant relatives of his in Kent, told me he had done the night flying test without me, and that we were due in the Briefing Room at three o'clock.

It was the long slog to Berlin again. We were airborne just before 18:00 hrs. I tried to ignore the searchlights and box barrage flak over the target, concentrating on my charts illuminated by the small navigation light which stretched over them. We dropped our bombs, got our photographs, and headed for home. I turned the oxygen up; it perked me up quite a bit. While we were emptying our bladders at the edge of the dispersal pan after landing, Bill remarked, 'That was our thirteenth trip.'

'Oh was it? Superstitious are you?'

'No, I just thought you'd like to know.'

I spent the next night drinking beer in the Caxton Gibbet with the rest of the squadron who weren't flying that night. Bill, ever diligent, told me the next day that we were on the Battle Order and had to report to briefing at six o'clock that night. The target turned out to be Hannover. 'Christ, not that bloody place again. It's been burning for days,' said the Canadian out of the corner of his mouth.

At 20:45 hrs we got airborne and climbed to our cruising altitude via the Cromer beacon. There were quite a few snow clouds around but the steady beat of the engines and the propellers was reassuring. I switched the taps from the 100-gal drop tanks to the main fuel supply. The change-over went smoothly and after crossing Holland we saw Hannover burning long before we got there. We knew it was no *Spoof* fire as the Germans needed every bit of fuel they could get their hands on for domestic use and for armaments. I moved the wad of chewing gum to the other side of my mouth as I pointed out the blaze to Bill. 'There's the target. Seems as if we're only going to stoke up the blaze and turn over the rubble. I'll get up to the nose and prime the bombs. You OK?'

'Yes. Just awaiting your directions. They may have lost their night fighters but their flak looks pretty hot.'

I glanced around. The sparks from the 'ack-ack' peppered the sky. What was it some cynic had said: 'The flak was so thick I cut my feet walking on it.' Hell knows what the Yanks thought looking at all the black powder-puffs of smoke that those sparks left in the sky. Still, that was their pigeon. We did not attract any searchlights and in the anonymity of darkness we dropped our bombs on the target, then headed for base.

I don't know how long it was after we left the burning city that it happened. It may have been two minutes; it may have been 10. The aircraft gave a lurch and the engines began to splutter. I quickly raised my eyes from the navigation table and looked at Bill, who was scanning the dials on the dashboard in front of him. 'What the hell's the trouble?'

'Quick, switch on to the drop tanks again.'

I switched the levers over and the engines coughed a bit, then resumed their steady beat. 'No fuel starvation there,' I muttered. The fuel in the 'drops' we worked out at between 55 and 60 gal. Not enough to get us back to England. 'Just in case, make the heading 250°. We don't want to ditch in the North Sea in this weather. That heading should take us towards Holland and Belgium.'

I tried the port engine's main tank again, but the engine spluttered and died almost at once. Bill had put the aircraft into a nose-down attitude to keep up the speed and prevent it from stalling while we switched tanks.

'Let's have it on the "drop" again,' said Bill

When the port had picked up we tried the starboard one, with the same result. Bill sucked in his breath. 'I'll keep it on the starboard engine until it dies on us, then go on the port one. I'll keep the speed up by losing height.'

We were down to about 18,000 ft from our original 26,000 ft. Although outwardly calm, we knew that when the petrol in each of the drop tanks had gone we had to go as well. It was galling to us to know that although we were sitting on plenty of 'juice', we couldn't get to it. The flak had seen to that; it must have cut the pipes from the main tanks, as the gauge showed that we still had plenty of fuel in them. We settled on the starboard engine only until it packed up, our reasoning being that we wouldn't be chopped to pieces by a whirling propeller when we baled out, as the escape hatch was situated on the starboard side under my feet. We sat and waited for it to die on us. Each minute took us nearer the Allied lines and away from Germany. Their citizens, so we had been told, were not averse to hanging any aircrew from the nearest tree or lamppost, if aircrew dropped among them.

The port engine was purring away by now. We would have to get out soon. Neither of us showed any panic even though we felt it. It was the waiting that was the worst aspect of the whole thing. If we could have jumped and got it over with we would gladly have done so, but every minute we stayed in the air meant we got nearer to safety and freedom. We were caught between instant action and playing the waiting game. We knew we were going to 'hit the silk', as the Yanks said, eventually.

I started to get ready to jump, clipping on my chest parachute. I realized I hadn't had it checked since I drew it from the Parachute Section at Wyton several months previously. I hoped it would open when I pulled the D-ring. Then I smashed my elbow through the *Gee* box radar tube, realizing after I had done it how stupid a thing it was to do. After all, if the aircraft was going to crash, the *Gee* box would be mangled up with the rest of it.

Bill made one transmission on the R/T, giving our call-sign and saying we would be baling out in the next few minutes. Bloody hell, was this really happening to us? I turned and bent down to lift the floorboard under my feet so that I could get to the outer door. It had a pedal attachment to it. One press of the foot on the pedal and the whole door was supposed to jettison. Nothing happened. I pressed again, then realized the door was jammed. In leaning forward to reach the handle to release one side of it, I caught my parachute D-ring in the edge of my folded-up navigation table. The result took me by surprise. A small spring or something forced out the pilot 'chute and the main canopy spilled out in front of me. I gathered up the folds of the 'chute in one arm, edged round the hole where the floor had been and faced the tail of the aircraft. I didn't want to break my back when I dropped out. Then I told Bill about the outer door having jammed. 'I'll have to unhook it and let it swing in the wind. What height are we now?'

Bill grunted. '10,000 ft, and all the needles are knocking on the stop.'

'I'd better go now and leave you some time to get out.' I pushed the lever holding one side of the door. It

B.XVI RV297/M5-F of 128 Squadron taxis out at Wyton for a raid on Berlin on 21 March 1945.

swung open. I looked at the dark void under my feet. I noticed flames flickering from the starboard engine. 'Hell – we're on fire! I'm on my way now. Good luck. See you back at base.' Sheer bravado on my part, as I didn't think either of us would make it.

'Hey!' Bill shouted. 'You've got your oxygen tube and intercom flex caught between yourself and your parachute!'

I raised my thumb in acknowledgement, unhooked one side of my 'chute with one hand and tore off my helmet and oxygen tube. My other hand was clutching my spilled 'chute. I stuck my legs into the black void under me and slipped off the edge of the floor into the night.

After landing, I gathered my parachute and dusted the snow off my battledress. I was in Holland. Almost at once, two British soldiers approached me and ordered me to put up my hands. Apparently, I'd landed in a minefield and they didn't believe I could have come from this direction! I suppose the frozen ground kept the mines inert!

Eventually, I was flown to Alconbury and thence returned to the squadron at Bourn. I removed the sym-

bolic axe from my pillow, put there by the other crews. After all, I hadn't got the 'chop' yet. My back was acting up a bit and my testicles felt as if they had been thumped by a truncheon. I was told Bill was in hospital in Belgium with frostbite in both feet. His flying boots came off when his 'chute opened and he had to walk quite a way through the snow in his stockinged feet before he met up with the 2nd Army. Consequently, he lost the skin off both his feet. I remembered the pride and joy Bill had for his shiny black boots he had brought all the way from New Zealand. The adjutant had offered to fix me to fly with another pilot till Bill came back, but I said, 'Like hell you will.' The thought appalled me. 'I'll wait for Bill to get out of the "boneyard".'

Bill arrived a week or so after me. He seemed more perturbed about losing his flying boots than by the frostbite. We compared notes. He gave me the impression that he was highly delighted that I had insisted on waiting for him to return. I brushed his remarks aside by mangling part of the marriage ceremony by saying, 'Till death us do part.'

Bill and I didn't get off the ground until the middle

of February, although we did a couple of air tests combined with practice bombing, just to break us in. When we finally presented ourselves at briefing, we found that our usual place had been left for us. Some faces were missing, and we would never see them again. 'Hiya flight sergeant,' I said to the Canadian. 'It's an honour to have you sitting next to me, *Sir*.'

'Spherical objects to you,' came the reply.

'My, you've improved your language, too!'

'Like hell I have. Look at where we're going tonight – Dessau. That's south-west of Berlin – it's like an elephant's foreskin: a bloody long haul.'

We kept the idle banter going while the various bigwigs had their say.

As we climbed from the runway, Bill switched on his microphone. 'Nervous?' he asked.

No more than usual,' I replied. 'It's a pity we didn't land a short trip, though, to break the ice. How are you?'

'I'll have to get used to these boots I've been issued with – otherwise I'm OK.'

We chattered on much more than usual until it came to changing the fuel intake from the outer drop tanks to the main supply. We were both listening to the throb of the engines and the beat of the propellers. Everything went according to the text book. By the time we had crossed the Dutch coast we were behaving like an experienced crew and not like a couple of scared rabbits.

We dropped our bombs on time and headed for base. We had encountered flak over the target and were skirting Hannover and the flak barrage that rose so accurately from there, when our starboard engine started vibrating, sending shudders through the aircraft. 'Curse that damned place Hannover,' I thought.

'I think its the prop that's copped it,' said Bill. 'The engine revs seem to be all right. I'm going to feather it.' He pressed the button. The engine went dead and the prop rigid. The aircraft stopped vibrating, and Bill started slowly to lose some height and to keep the forward speed up.

'Shall we head for home or what?' he asked.

'I don't think we should head for base as the Met men said there was a cold front line squall stretching across the North Sea. We would have to go through it. That would be no fun with both engines, but on one – well, it's anyone's guess.' I had hoped we would fly over the top of it.

'Where to, then?' His voice was as sharp as a pin.

'Manston in Kent. That way we'll fringe the south end of it, I hope.'

'St Elmo's Fire was flickering its blue veins across our Perspex windscreens when we dipped into the cloud. We were tossed around like a bottle on a surf-pounded beach. Lightning hit the cabin repeatedly, followed by thunder almost immediately. How the aircraft stuck together only God and the manufacturers knew. We bounced out of the storm as quickly as we had gone in. We landed on our one engine. The starboard prop had a jagged hole in one of its blades and was twisted like a badly broken leg. The fact that it and the lightning storm hadn't broken up the aircraft was a tribute to the people who had built it as much as to Bill, who had kept the thing in the air until we reached this graveyard called Manston. We could find no other damage.

I turned to Bill. 'I'm going to report sick. My ears are all bunged up and I have a bad cold. At least, that's my story. It will get us off flying for a week or so.'

'You do that Johnnie. I'll back you up if necessary.'

We were both rattled and twitching a bit, and we knew it. There was nothing wrong with my ears. Strange, I reflected; had anyone suggested three or four months before that I would be contemplating doing such a thing, they would have received a rather dusty answer in reply. However, once I had stepped into the Clearance Centre I felt ashamed. Aircrew were lying on stretchers. They had burns, flak wounds, arms bandaged and legs in splints. I felt a complete fraud. I said to Bill, 'Come on, let's go to the Mess.'

Back at Bourn, a 'Wing Ding' had been laid on in the Mess. What started off as a civilized party developed into a real 'thrash'. 'Ossie', the Scots tea planter from Ceylon, climbed onto the bar counter.

'Right!' he bellowed. 'I think we all need a bit of practice at landing on FIDO. I'll be the controller.' Newspapers and magazines were confiscated from the lounge, rolled up and placed in almost parallel lines on the highly polished Mess bar floor. Tins of Ronseal were sprayed on the papers. 'Let's make it realistic,' said someone. 'Get the feather cushions from the lounge and we'll have 10/10ths feather visibility.'

The idea was to slide down the polished line between the burning papers and have the air full of feathers at the same time. 'Ossie' bellowed out the time-honoured phrase, 'Come in Number One, your time is up!' Whereupon the CO whipped down the burning line of newspapers on his bottom and crashed into the stove at the other end. The atmosphere of the burning papers plus the clouds of feathers made the bar almost untenable.

It could have been worse. They could have burned the place down. At one party a bunch of aircrew from another squadron had found a pile of bricks, sand and cement. Contractors were building an extension to the

Mess. The chaps used the lot and bricked up the CO's car which was parked outside. The contractors had been reported as saying that they hoped they were better flyers than they were bricklayers.

At briefing the following afternoon my Canadian oppo flopped into the seat beside me. 'Jeeze! Look where we're going tonight – way down south,' he said. I followed the tapes on the Master Plan. It looked a little place south-west of Berlin called Erfurt. Why it was going to receive the heat-treatment from us was explained by the intelligence officer. It was a centre for light engineering, and in order that we hit it fair and square we were going to go in at 7,000 ft; abnormally low for us. No flak or opposition was expected. We duly bombed Erfurt and left it blazing. I saw what I took to be a church steeple tumble into the flames and secretly hoped that the few faithful left in that town were tucked up in their shelters and didn't suffer the indignity of dying in the House of God.

On the way back, over Holland, we spotted what we thought was a jet aircraft boring its way through the atmosphere. It was heading straight for us. It rose level with us and continued on upward, arching northwest on its sightless way towards England. It was a V2. I quickly spotted the place from which it had been launched. I was not the only navigator to do so, and I understood the place was located the next day and bombed out of existence.

We were full of coffee and rum when 'Ossie' and his navigator arrived at the debriefing, having bombed the town by themselves, as they had been about an hour behind us. They, like us, reported no opposition. 'By God,' 'Ossie' said in his blunt way, 'I can't see that town contributing much to the Nazi war effort now. It was burning beautifully when we attacked.' He gave a graphic description of the carnage we had created. The powers that be hadn't thought so, however, and we did two more trips to Erfurt with similar results. Each load we dumped on the place contained one long-delay bomb which must have disturbed the residents for many hours after the raid. We puzzled over our trips there, as it stretched our flying endurance quite a bit. It wasn't until after the war that I saw films of the gas ovens in the concentration camps, with the trade plates on them stating that they had been built in Erfurt.

* * * * *

Returning from leave, Bill and I congratulated each other on winning our 'gongs' [DFCs]. Bill's commission had come through a week or two beforehand, so we were feeling pretty much on top of the world. We were preparing to get our heads down knowing we would be flying the next night, probably to Berlin. We'd done 15 trips to the 'Big City' so far. The Air Council seemed bent on sending Mosquitoes to Berlin every night and we were told, when we turned up for briefing the next day, that our target was the usual. We were to go over the target on our tod. Ten past three in the morning was our time.

That night was a night to remember. As we flew over north Germany, heading for what had been Hamburg and before we turned and pointed our nose at Berlin, we could see the whole of Heligoland, Denmark and south Norway, with the moon reflecting off the North Sea which looked like polished steel against the dark ground. The searchlights caught us, followed by the flak. We ran the gauntlet. I dropped our bombs and we emerged unscathed.

On landing back at base we had our routine pee. The pee tube in the aircraft froze up if we used it. We were then driven to an Intelligence hut where a group descended on us. They were tired and jaded, unlike us. We had been flying on oxygen for $4^{1}/2$ hours, then jacked-up with coffee heavily laced with rum. That, and the knowledge that another op was behind us, made us feel like spring lambs, which was more than could be said of the Intelligence mob. We dictated our report and headed for the billet. We crept into our beds and went out like lights.

Life went on as if the war was going to last for ever. Things were changing a bit, however. At each briefing to the 'Big City' (where else?), we were issued with a plastic label which we hung around our necks. It was imprinted with a Union Jack and stated in Russian that we were Englishmen. We were told that if we were shot down and didn't finish up a mangled heap, we were to raise our hands above our heads. What would happen if we landed among a bunch of fanatical Germans was never mentioned. As most of the Russians, so the story went, couldn't read, it was a case of heads you win, tails I lose – and a lump of lead was waiting for us wherever we landed. When I strung one of these labels, complete with white tape, around my neck, I felt like an evacuee from the 1940 era.

The Allies had crossed the Rhine and had fanned out over Germany. The 'Huns' were still fighting, albeit in their own Fatherland. We did get a break and bombed Nurnberg one night. Strange to think it was in that city that the Nazis' evil dream had all started which turned the world upside down. Then we bombed Berlin again. It was our last trip there, and we discarded our plastic labels with the Union Jack and switched our efforts to Munich, with just one break in

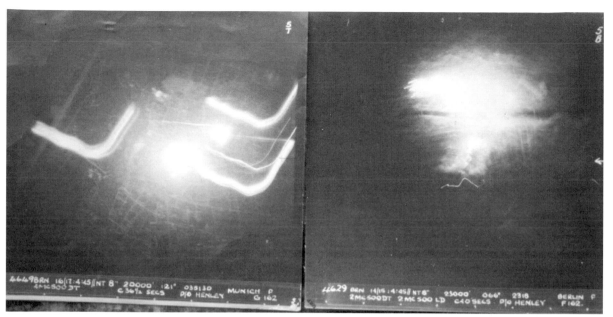

(Left) Munich pictured from 20,000 ft on the night of 16/17 April 1945, when P/O Henley and John Clark flew to the city. (Right) Berlin shudders under the impact of bombs and flares on the night of 14/15 April 1945. This photo was taken from P/O Henley and John Clark's Mosquito at 23,000 ft while the raid was in progress. (John Clark)

Kiel. Why Kiel, no one knew; not even the intelligence officer. We were sent back to Munich as a farewell punch. Perhaps we were helping the Yanks. We didn't know.

Bill and I compared notes. We had completed 40 trips; 18 of them had been to Berlin during the non-stop bombing of that city by Mosquitoes. We were told that Mosquitoes had visited the 'Big City' nearly 40 nights on the trot. We had grown older, if not wiser, during that time. Any other target offered to us had become quite a novelty.

One night, after a late trip to Munich at the end of April, we were walking back to our billets with bed very much in our thoughts. 'Listen,' I said, and held my finger to my lips. 'You said you had never heard a nightingale when we played that record of the one that sang in Berkeley Square. Well you're hearing one now.' Through the stillness of the morning one was singing as if there were no tomorrow. 'Now you can tell your folks back home that you have heard one.' We stopped and listened. All thought of sleep had left us.

Chapter Six

The U-Boat Killers

An armourer holds a 57-mm shell fired by the Molins cannon carried on the Mosquito FB.XVIII 'Tsetse', also armed with four .303-in Browning machine guns. (Jerry Scutts)

On 22 October 1943 two Mosquito FB.XVIIIs, which had a 57-mm Molins cannon in place of the conventional four 20-mm cannon, arrived at Predannack and were issued to 248 Squadron, engaged in anti-shipping operations in the Atlantic. The squadron was equipped mainly with the Beaufighter, but earlier that October, five Mosquito crews and 34 ground crew from 618 Squadron had been transferred to fly and service the new aircraft. The 618 Squadron crews were an ideal choice for maritime operations, two having commenced operations on Mosquito FB.XVIIIs two days earlier when S/L Rose DFC DFM and F/O A.L. Bonnett (RCAF) attempted to track a U-Boat in the Bay of Biscay. On 4 November Rose was killed by return fire from a trawler in the second of two attacks on the vessel. Three days later Bonnett scored hits on a surfaced U-Boat heading for Brest. The enemy submarine crash-dived, spurting clouds of yellow and black smoke. Although this debut by the Mosquito in coastal strike operations did not prove tangible evidence, the Kriegsmarine was nevertheless forced to provide escort vessels for its U-Boats from then on.

Conversion from the Beaufighter moved on, and by 1 January 1944 248 Squadron had 16 Mosquito FB.XVIII 'Tsetses' and four FB.VIs available for fighter reconnaissance and support for anti-shipping operations in 19 Group, Coastal Command. On 20 February 248 Squadron flew their first interception and anti-shipping patrols in the Bay of Biscay. On 10 March four FB.VIs escorting two FB.XVIIIs tangled with four Luftwaffe Ju 88s flying top cover for a German naval convoy. One of the Ju 88s was shot down on fire and two 'probables' were claimed. Meanwhile the Mosquito FB.XVIIIs went after the German ships. They damaged a destroyer and shot down one of the Ju 88s. Coastal Command Liberators waded in and continued the attack on the convoy.

On 1 April nine Mosquito FB.VIs and FB.XVIIIs took off for a coastal patrol. One crashed into a hill on take-off but the other eight engaged a German convoy escorted by eight Ju 88s. They made damaging runs on the ships and shot down two of the Junkers, but two Mosquitoes were also lost. A third Mosquito was written off in a crash-landing back at base. At the end of the month 248 Squadron ground crews began fitting drop tanks in place of bombs below the wings of the Mosquitoes as the role of the squadron changed to land targets in support of the coming invasion of France. The squadron flew five operations on D-Day, 6 June 1944, being employed on anti-shipping, escort and blockading sorties in support of the seaborne

attack forces off the Normandy, Brittany and Biscay coasts. In a fitting finale, Mosquitoes covered 31 anti-flak and rocket-armed Beaufighters in the Biscay area. One of the Mosquitoes destroyed a Ju 188 which dared to interfere.

On D-Day +1 a Mosquito FB.XVIII of 248 Squadron attacked a U-Boat, firing a dozen 57-mm shells into the submarine, which was forced to crash-dive, leaving a pool of oil and a single crewman on the surface. The Mosquito's cannon jammed and the crew were forced to make a series of dummy runs on the fleeing vessel, which escaped. On 10 June 248 Squadron shared in the sinking of *U-821*. Attacks on U-Boats were the order of the day throughout the summer of 1944, using wing-mounted 25-lb Mk XI depth charges for the first time on 22 June, and also A.VIII mines, in addition to more conventional bombs, cannon and machine gun fire. Also during June, 248 Squadron was joined at Portreath by 235 Squadron, equipped with the Mosquito FB.VI.

The Mosquitoes also flew escort for the

Mosquito FB.XVIII NT225 of 248 Squadron, in D-Day invasion stripes, with four .303-in Browning machine guns and two 57-mm cannon for anti-U-Boat operations. On 7 June 1944 a Mosquito NF.XVIII of 248 Squadron attacked a U-Boat, but the cannon jammed and the crew were forced to make a series of dummy runs on the fleeing vessel, which escaped. On 10 June 248 Squadron shared in the sinking of U-821. Attacks on U-Boats were made with bombs, cannon, A.VIII mines, and machine guns; and, from 22 June, with wing-mounted 25-lb Mk XI depth charges. (Alan Sanderson)

A 235 Squadron FB.VI of the Banff Wing attacking shipping off the Norwegian coast on 19 September 1944. On 9 April 1945 a 235 Squadron Mosquito sunk U-843 and shared in the destruction that same month of four more U-Boats. (BAe via Philip Birtles)

A Banff Wing Mosquito fires its cannon and rockets out to sea at a range during a night firing test. On 26 October 1944 the Mosquitoes used rocket projectiles for the first time. (G. A. B. Lord)

A briefing by G/C Max Aitken in 1944. The information on the blackboard has been censored. (G. A. B. Lord)

Beaufighters and intercepted missile-carrying Dornier Do 217s which attempted to sink Allied shipping using Henschel Hs 293 glider bombs. In September, enemy activity in the Bay of Biscay had decreased to such an extent that Coastal Command felt secure enough to post its two Mosquito squadrons north to Scotland. The final sorties were flown on 7 September; then 235 and 248 Squadrons landed at Banff to form the Dallachy Wing together with 333 (Norwegian) Squadron. The Wing's Mosquitoes and Beaufighters were used in attacks throughout the remainder of the war on targets in Norwegian waters.

The first Mosquito anti-shipping operation to Norway took place on 14 September 1944, when 29 Mosquitoes and 19 Beaufighters attacked shipping between Egero and Stors Toreungen Light. On the 17th they hunted U-Boats, and on 21 September six Mosquitoes and 21

Beaufighters sought shipping in Kristiansund. The Dallachy Wing brought the month to a closing crescendo on 30 September with a *Rover* involving 17 Mosquitoes and a dozen Beaufighters. Three days earlier, Mosquitoes were fitted with eight underwing rocket rails to accommodate 25-lb solid armour-piercing or 60-lb semi-armour-piercing, high explosive projectiles. A month later, on 26 October, the Mosquitoes used rocket projectiles for the first time.

During October 143 Squadron, Coastal Command, which was equipped with Beaufighters at North Coates, shed its virtual OTU status and moved to Banff to convert to the Mosquito as part of the Banff Strike Wing, commanded by G/C Max Aitken DSO DFC. On 7 November 143 Squadron entered the fray for the first time since relinquishing its Beaufighters when two Mosquitoes flew a patrol off the coast

of Norway. In November the Mosquitoes of the Banff Wing operated in increasingly larger formations of up to two-dozen aircraft.

George Lord, a pilot in 248 Squadron at this time, who had sunk two U-Boats and seriously damaged another during a tour of ops in Hudsons in North Africa, has vivid recollections of Mosquito shipping strikes:

We took off usually in the dark, to arrive over our targets soon after first light when possible. We flew in a loose formation, usually without navigation lights, at a nominal 50 ft above the North Sea. We had a primitive low-level altimeter with a tolerance of about +/- 17 ft when set at 50 ft. Not much of a margin, flying in the dark on instruments, no autopilot, and occasionally hitting the slipstream of someone ahead, unseen. The altimeter had three lights – red, green and amber – one above the others. Green was a datum, red if you went below, amber if you went above. With the long rollers of the North Sea the three lights usually flashed continually in sequence all the way across, so

G/C Max Aitken, CO Banff Wing. (G. A. B. Lord)

Mosquitoes of 248 Squadron en route to Norway. G. A. B. Lord is flying V-Victor, its tailwheel unretracted, at about 50 ft above the sea. (G. A. B. Lord)

that our actual height above the sea must have varied down to something like 30-35 ft, all at some 220 kts cruising speed! Not much room for error!

We remained at low-level until either in sight of the Norwegian coast or if we knew we had been detected by enemy radar or aircraft. It was worse when we had to fly with a gaggle of Beaufighters (including some 'Torbeaus'), whose cruising speed was 180 kt. The 'Mossie' with a full warload was staggering a bit then, and rather unpleasant in turbulence or someone's slipstream when you couldn't see the chap in front.

We flew the FB.VI fighter-bomber with two Merlin 25s. It had four 20-mm cannon and four .303-in Brownings in the nose, with four rocket rails and drop tanks under each wing. Initially, the rocket heads were 60-lb explosive heads, used in the desert for tank-busting. It was found these exploded on contact with ships and did only superficial damage. Moreover, if there was a 'hang-up', the rule was not to attempt a landing back at base but to bale out, because the slightest jolt once the rocket was armed would cause the head to explode, with disastrous consequences for the aircraft and crew. The 25-lb armour-piercing heads we used, if fired at the correct range and airspeed and angle of dive, would enter the ship's hull above the water-line, continue through the hull and out the other side under-water, leaving the remains of the cordite motor burning in the ship and making a hole some 18 inches or more in the far side of the hull for the sea to pour in. Meantime, there was a chance the rocket motor would have ignited fuel or ammunition in the ship.

These attacks were all at low-level, ending almost at ship-level. It was easy to almost overdo it by concentrating on aiming at the target and firing at the right moment. On one occasion, my navigator yelled 'Pull up', and we just missed hitting the ship's masts! When there was a formation attack one sometimes suddenly saw another aircraft shoot across our line of fire, attacking from a different angle.

When a number of our aircraft were involved the usual practice was to split into three sections of, say, three aircraft each. One would be top cover to watch out for any fighters; one would be anti-flak (the most dangerous, going in first to silence the anti-aircraft guns – hopefully!); the third was the section making the actual attack – also pretty dicey. The idea was to rotate the order to give everyone a fair chance of survival (we had a rate of about one in five), and obviously the favourite was to be top cover and the worst to be anti-flak. An unusual hazard flying low-level along the Norwegian coast and into the fjords was shore-based artillery firing at us, and the first one

Mosquito FB.VI HJ719 fitted with Rolls-Royce Merlin 25 engines. (ARP)

On 27 September 1944 Mosquitoes were fitted with eight underwing rocket rails to accommodate 60-lb solid armour-piercing HE projectiles, as used in tank-busting. But when it was found these exploded on contact with ships and did only superficial damage, they were replaced with 25-lb semi-armour-piercing warheads, which could enter a ship's hull above the water-line and punch a large hole out the other side, leaving the remains of the cordite motor burning in the ship (with a chance that it would ignite fuel or ammunition). (G. A. B. Lord)

Arming a Mosquito of the Banff Wing. The first Mosquito anti-shipping operation to Norway took place on 14 September 1944. (G. A. B. Lord)

De-icing a 248 Squadron Mosquito the hard way during the winter of 1944/45. (G. A. B. Lord)

knew of it was when a huge plume of water rose up in front of us! If we had flown into it, it would have meant almost certain death.

George Lord flew an armed recce on 3 November and another on the 4th. Low cloud prevented bombing and he attacked a motor vessel alongside the quay at Floro with cannon and machine guns. Flak was intense and his mainplane and tailplane were holed. Frequent snow and hail dogged ops on 8 and 9 November when the Mosquitoes skirted Ytteröene, Marstein and Askvoll. On 21 November 42 Beaufighters and a dozen Mustang III fighter escorts were joined by 32 Mosquitoes in a shipping strike at Aalesund. Their quest to sink a U-Boat nearly bore fruit on 29 November when a 248 Squadron FB.XVIII scored several hits with 20-mm cannon.

On 7 December 25 Mosquitoes of the Banff Wing and 40 Beaufighters of the Dallachy Wing, escorted by three 'Finger Fours' of Mustang IIIs of 315 (Polish) Squadron flying to the rear, were despatched to Gossen, a German fighter airfield in Norway. F/L Konrad Stembrowicz, one of the Mustang pilots, who flew 13 such escorts from Peterhead, recalls:

As we approached the coast of Norway one of the Mosquitoes had an engine-out and it turned back. I nodded towards my No 2, F/O 'Danek' Nowosielski, who turned and followed to escort him home. It wasn't what I intended but it was very noble of him. Very soon afterwards our radios were jammed by the Germans, and all I could hear was one long whistle. Then 15 Fw 190s and Bf 109s appeared at 5,000 ft from behind the small white clouds. They attacked the Mosquitoes and the Beaufighters and we went after them. I saw a '109 attacking and went after him. It was a short combat. I destroyed one '109. He flew through my hail of bullets and a grey stream of smoke appeared. I was hit by four rounds in my wings but they all passed between the petrol tanks! We lost F/O Andrzej Czerwinski. [Altogether, the Mustangs downed four fighters and two more collided. Two Mosquitoes were among the four aircraft that failed to return.] When I broke off I found myself alone, so I flew back with a lonely bomber.

In 1946, Stembrowicz flew Mosquitoes from

G/C Max Aitken DSO DFC points out a spot on a map of Norway. On the far right is W/C G.D. Sise DSO DFC, a New Zealander and CO 248 Squadron. W/C R. A. Atkinson DSO DFC, Australian CO 235 Squadron (killed in action when cable across a fjord cut off his wing during an attack), is to Aitken's right. (G. A. B. Lord)

Aston Down and would delight in sneaking up on the tails of Meteors for mock dogfights! Later, he flew Mosquitoes in No 5 Ferry Pool.

On 12 December the Mosquitoes were escorted to Gossen again, but no fighters were seen. Four days later the Mosquitoes winkled out a merchantman and its escort, lurking in Kraakhellesund, and made two attacks, the first in line astern! Two of the Mosquitoes were shot down. On 19 December Mustangs escorted them to Sulen, Norway, but again no fighters appeared. On Boxing Day 1944 a dozen Mosquitoes flying at very low-level destroyed two motor boats in Leirvik harbour but had to contend with attacks by two-dozen Luftwaffe fighters. Each side lost one aircraft. On 11 January F/L N. Russell DFC and another Mosquito pilot shot down a Bf 109 during an anti-shipping strike in Flekkefjord by 14 Mosquitoes and 18 Beaufighters. The Mosquitoes returned to Leirvik harbour on 15

January 1945. This time they destroyed two merchantmen and an armed trawler before fighting their way back across the North Sea, pursued by nine Fw 190 fighters. Six Mosquitoes failed to return to Scotland.

In February 1945 235 Squadron fired its rockets in anger for the first time and delayed-action bombs were dropped in a narrow fjord off Midgulen. They rolled, 'Dam Buster'-style, down a 3,000-ft cliff and exploded among the ships below. The Mosquitoes began to widen their horizons and, operating independently of the Beaufighters now, ranged far and wide over the Norwegian coast seeking specific targets. On 7 March 40 Mosquitoes attacked self-propelled barges in the Kattegat with machine guns, cannon and rocket fire. A dozen P-51 Mustangs provided top cover and two Warwicks of 279 Squadron were in attendance to drop lifeboats to ditched crews if called upon. The enemy fighters were

An airborne lifeboat carried under a Vickers Warwick. (G. A. B. Lord)

Mosquito FB.VI RS625 with 100-gal drop tanks, rocket projectiles, and an F.24 camera in the nose. This aircraft served with 143 Squadron, Coastal Command, based with the Banff Wing in Scotland, and was used on anti-shipping strikes off the coast of Norway. Normal armament comprised four .303-in machine guns, four 20-mm cannon and eight 3-in rocket projectiles. (via Philip Birtles)

248 Squadron Mosquitoes make rocket attacks on a motor vessel in Dalsfjord on 23 March 1945. (via Alan Sanderson)

Opposite: *On 30 March 1945 24 Mosquitoes, led by W/C Simmonds and covered by eight other Mosquitoes, made a lo-lo-level rocket attack on chemical sheds and enemy shipping moored at Menstad quay at Porsgrunn-Skein, as the remarkable stills (opposite) shot by a photo-recce Mosquito show. The black cloud was caused by a Mosquito which crashed after hitting overhead electricity cables. Two of the three merchantmen hit by over 120 rocket projectiles can be seen quite clearly burning and emitting heavy smoke. (via Alan Sanderson)*

noticeable by their absence, but on a similar strike five days later, the force was intercepted by eight Bf 109s. The Mosquitoes shot down one of the enemy machines for no loss to their number.

On 12 March 44 Mosquitoes and 12 Mustangs flew an armed reconnaissance over the Skagerrak and Kattegat and flushed out a formation of Bf 109s. One was shot down and the other claimed as a 'probable'. On 17 March 31 Mosquitoes devastated shipping at Aalesund using cannon and rocket fire. Six days later, rocket-firing Mosquitoes of 128 and 143 Squadrons made short work of an enemy ship at Sandshavn. On 27 March a freight train near Naerbo was attacked. On 30 March facilities at Porsgrunn came under attack by 24 rocket-firing Mosquitoes, covered by eight more which remained on station on the lookout for enemy fighters. None appeared but the 'Mossies' provided accurate suppression fire against gun positions in the sides of the fjord. The attackers flew so low that they crested the wave tops, and one Mosquito struck an overhead electric cable on land. But the attack was devastating once more: three merchantmen were holed by over 120 rocket projectiles.

New crews replaced those lost. Among them was F/Sgt Colin R. Smith, a navigator in 248 Squadron and his pilot, F/L Peter McIntyre, whom he had teamed up with at the OTU at East Fortune in the autumn of 1944 on one of only two Mosquitoes (the rest were Beaufighters). Smith recalls:

Both of us came from a farming background. I was just 18 years old in September 1939 and 'Reserved Occupation', working on my father's fruit farm. I was finally accepted for pilot training in 1941, but sent home on deferred service again until 1942. Peter was also 'Reserved Occupation', coming from a farming background in Aberdeenshire, and had then done his flying training in Pensacola, Florida, before injuring his back badly playing rugby.

The first day on the squadron we were not flying, and so I went on the roof of Flying Control to see the 'famous' formation of three Mosquitoes take off on the runway at the same time. G/C Max Aitken was watching too. He turned round and said to me, 'They are a beautiful sight, aren't they?' He added, 'You're new at the Banff Wing?' I said I was. He then said he believed all pilots and navigators should be commissioned officers, as in the American air force, and

would recommend me if I went and saw him after I'd done a few operations.

April dawned, and with the war almost over, the Mosquito crews had yet to get a confirmed U-Boat 'kill' all to themselves. All that was about to change on 9 April when 37 Mosquitoes of 143, 235 and 248 Squadrons were despatched to Norway. Colin Smith recalls:

9 April was my most memorable day. It began with the morning briefing for a wing sweep through the Skagerrak and Kattegat, looking for enemy shipping to attack.

We were told that our Mosquito, Q-Queen, was unserviceable, but as our new W/C, Jackson-Smith, wasn't flying that day, we were told we could have his K-King – a brand new aircraft. When we read for take-

F/Sgt Colin R. Smith, navigator, 248 Squadron, who with his pilot, F/L Peter McIntyre, made a memorable attack in K-King *on U-Boats in the* Kattegat *on 9 April 1945. (Colin Smith)*

off it refused to start for some minutes. When we were finally ready, all of the others were airborne and heading for Peterhead to get in formation. We had some difficulty getting off the runway, nearly removing the top deck of a passing bus! We flew flat-out to catch up and take our position in the formation. We went through the Skagerrak without seeing anything and were heading back to Banff when we saw three U-Boats line astern on the surface of the Kattegat, coming from Denmark and heading for Norway. We did not hear any order to attack but when the leading aircraft in our formation attacked the leading U-Boat, Peter decided to attack the middle one with our rockets and cannon. He scored direct hits and the U-Boat blew up. We normally flew at about 50 ft to beat the German radar but we were well below this; probably only about 20–25 ft. As we passed over the U-Boat, straight into the explosion, we were hit by some debris and it knocked out our starboard engine. We had been told that in the event of serious trouble, not to try to get back to base but to make for neutral Sweden. So

we announced over the wireless we were making for *Brighton,* code-name for the day for Sweden. We did not hear any reply. It would seem we were transmitting all right, but our receiver was out of order.

We set off for Sweden on a course I had given and managed to gain several hundred feet. We passed over what I believed to be the Swedish coastline when some anti-aircraft guns opened up. It brought immediate panic from Peter, and even though I had been pretty sure I knew where we were, I began to worry a little. He shouted, 'This isn't Sweden; it's Norway! And you know what the Germans are doing to PoWs.' (It was rumoured that they were castrating Allied aircrew.) It *was* Sweden. The Swedish AA gunners must have been practising as the shells did not burst near us. We limped on and some minutes later I recognized a viaduct that was marked on my map. It gladdened my heart, for I knew we were spot on course for an airfield I had headed for. Peter immediately brightened up and told me to get rid of the ARO, which was secret.

On 2 May 1945 27 Mosquitoes were despatched on anti-U-Boat operations in the Kattegat, and two U-Boats were attacked. This photo was taken by a 248 Squadron Mosquito during the attack. (via Alan Sanderson)

Mosquitoes attack an enemy convoy in the Kattegat on 4 May 1945. (via Alan Sanderson)

We came upon the airfield and he made a perfect one-engined landing far superior to the practice ones he had made at home. I pressed the two small buttons on my right which destroyed the IFF and *Gee* box. When we got out of the aircraft, Peter got down on his knees and kissed the ground. He got up, put his arm around me and said, 'Good old Smitty. You knew where you were all the time, didn't you?' I didn't say anything. A Swedish Air Force officer with a revolver in his right hand wasn't taking any chances, but he shook hands with us with his left. 'Welcome to Sweden,' he said, in perfect English.

During McIntyre and Smith's internment the Mosquitoes sank a fourth U-Boat, on 19 April, and would sink six more, including four on one day, 4 May, before the war ended. McIntyre and Smith returned to Leuchars aboard a BOAC DC-3 after internment at Falun. Colin Smith recalls:

In Sweden I had changed about £25 into Swedish Krona and had bought silk stockings for our sisters and girlfriends. I also purchased an unabridged copy of *Lady Chatterley's Lover* (which was banned in Britain at this time). The book, printed in English, made me so very popular back at Banff, until I was foolish enough to lend it to a WAAF who didn't return it! We were sent to the Air Ministry in London to be interrogated, then back to Banff to be rekitted. On home leave we experienced VE-Day, 8 May 1945.

Chapter Seven

'Wooden Wonders' of the 'Winged Eight'

America wanted Mosquitoes, but Robert A. Lovett, Assistant Secretary of War for Air, suspected that Britain wanted to keep them all because 'it was the one airplane that could get into Berlin and back without getting shot down.' Maj Gen Henry 'Hap' Arnold and other USAAF officials saw the Mosquito for the first time on 20 April 1941 at Boscombe Down. The prototype, painted bright yellow, and which had first flown at Hatfield a year before, gave a dazzling performance in front of the Americans whose country was not yet in the war. Gen Arnold's aide, Maj Elwood Quesada, no doubt excited by the Mosquito's rolling climbs on one engine, recalled: 'I was impressed by its performance [and] the appearance of the aeroplane...all aviators are affected by the appearance...an aeroplane that looks fast usually is fast, and the Mosquito was...It was highly regarded, highly respected!'

On 4 December 1941, three days before America declared war on Japan, a request was sent to Britain for one airframe, this to be evaluated at Wright Field.

In the summer of 1942, Col Elliott Roosevelt brought two squadrons of F-4 Lightnings and a squadron of B-17F 'mapping Fortresses' to Britain. The President's son was preparing his group for the invasion of North Africa and was to work with the RAF until ready. Given a Mosquito B.IV for combat evaluation, Roosevelt discovered that the aircraft outperformed his F-4s and had five times the range. The first of the Canadian-built Mosquitoes had already given demonstrations at Wright Field. It

was so good, Gen Arnold ordered that no US aircraft were to be raced against the Mosquito, to avoid embarrassing American pilots! Arnold asked that Mosquitoes be obtained to equip all American photo-reconnaissance squadrons in Europe – almost 200 aircraft for 1943 alone! In 1943 30 Mosquitoes were diverted from British production after the Canadian allocation of 120 for the Americans had been reduced to just 60 B.XXs because of RAF demands. These, plus 11 Canadian-built F-8 models, were delivered to the 802nd (later, 25th) Bomb Group at Watton. However, these were not as popular with the pilots and navigators as the British-built Mosquitoes, and they were soon reassigned to a bomb group in Italy.

The 802nd, with the 7th Photographic Group, became part of the 325th Photographic Wing, commanded, since August 1944, by Col Elliott Roosevelt. Many personnel who were transferred into the 802nd BG had to be retrained. Mechanics who had never seen a Mosquito night bomber, attended a two-week course at the Rolls-Royce engine school in Derby. Others attended the airframe school at the de Havilland factory in Hatfield. Most of the aircrew, many of whom were P-38 Lightning pilots from the 50th Fighter Squadron in Iceland, and who were used to the P-38's contra-rotating propellers, had never experienced the take-off and landing characteristics of the Mosquito bomber; especially its high landing speed and tendency to swing on take-off. They had also to remember to open the radiator shutters just prior to take-off to prevent the engines overheating.

Above *Mosquito PR.XVI NS591 of the 25th BG lands at Watton, Norfolk on 22 February 1945. The group's Mosquitoes were used in a number of roles, including agent dropping (code-named Redstocking, in the hope that the German Abwehr would think they were connected with Bluestocking weather missions). (via Philip Birtles)*

Left *Col Leon Gray, who assumed command of the 25th BG on 23 September 1944, and Gen James E. Doolittle, Commanding General, 8th AF, confer at Watton. Elliott Roosevelt described Gray as the most outstanding photo-reconn pilot of the war. (via George Sesler)*

Opposite right *Mosquito PR.XVI MM384 comes to grief at Watton. (via George Sesler)*

Mosquito PR.XVIs used a two-stage, two-speed supercharger that would cut in automatically at altitude. The superchargers were independent on each engine and a small difference in adjustment caused one to change gears hundreds of feet before the other. The resulting 'bang' and surge of power to one engine could wrest control from the unwary pilot and give the impression that the aircraft had been hit by flak. Several Airspeed Oxfords and three dual-control Mosquito T.IIIs were assigned for training.

The 652nd Bomb Squadron (BS) was equipped with the B-17 and B-24, while the 653rd Bomb Squadron used Mosquito T.III and PR.XVI aircraft on meteorological flights, known as *Bluestockings,* gathering weather information from over the continent. The 654th, or the 'Special Squadron', flew day and night *Joker* photo missions and scouting sorties just ahead of the main bombing force, transmitting up-to-the-minute weather reports back to the task force commander to prevent him leading his bombers into heavy weather fronts. The D-Day invasion

was determined by intelligence gathered on *Dillies* (night photography missions of coastal defences). A local storm front, forming suddenly east of Iceland on 5 June, and monitored by the *Bluestockings,* postponed the invasion for one day until 6 June. On *Joker* missions the Mosquitoes dropped 1,000,000-candlepower-type M-46 flash bombs to illuminate and obtain evidence of enemy troop movements and bridge construction conducted under the cover of darkness.

The Mosquito was also used on *Skywave* long-range navigation missions using LORAN (the RAF did not begin using the LORAN system to any extent until after the end of the war); daylight missions code-named *PRU,* using still and motion-picture photography; and H2X *Mickey* flights. Mosquitoes brought back bomb-approach-strips, or target run-ups, which were used to brief the key radar navigator-bombardier of the bomber mission and to sight the bomb target through the overcast during the actual bombing. Three *Mickey* sorties flown at night failed to

Above *A 492nd BG Mosquito taxis out at Harrington in May 1945. After 3 May 1945, Redstocking missions became an all-492nd BG operation. (Andre Pecquet)*

Opposite above *All-black Mosquito pictured at Harrington. On 13 March 1945 covert operations using the Mosquito moved from Watton to Harrington, but overcrowding and maintenance and political infighting deteriorated to such an extent that RAF ground personnel had to be brought in to maintain the aircraft, and OSS subsequently regained control over all Mosquito covert operations. (Art Cannot)*

Opposite middle *All-black Mosquito PR.XVI TA614, pictured at Harrington in May 1945. At Harrington, 25th BG pilots and navigators flew the aircraft until enough 492nd BG personnel were available. A 492nd BG pilot and navigator carried Cmdr Simpson on the group's first communications mission, on 31 March 1945. (Marvin Edwards)*

Opposite below *Mosquito PR.XVI RG157/Q, pictured at Harrington in May 1945. (Marvin Edwards)*

Below *A 25th BG Mosquito starts its port engine at the B-24 Liberator base at Attlebridge, Norfolk, prior to a Red-Tail mission with the 8th AF in 1945. Some 74 Mosquito Red-Tail missions (so named after the aircrafts' red tails, painted to distinguish them from enemy aircraft) were flown from bases in East Anglia, each carrying the command pilot of 8th AF bombing missions. (via Mike Bailey)*

return and later, four P-38 Lightnings were assigned to escort the H2X missions going in at high altitudes.

American Mosquitoes accompanied Project *Aphrodite* and *Anvil* pilotless drone operations using war-weary B-17s and PB4Y-1 Liberators respectively. Each aircraft was packed with 18,000 lb of Torpex, a nitroglycerine compound, and was flown to a point over the English coast or North Sea where the pilot and co-pilot baled out, leaving the drone to fly on and be directed onto its target (normally a V1 or V2 site) by remote control via a Ventura 'mother ship'. Strike analysis depended upon the films brought back by the accompanying Mosquitoes to determine the success, or failure, of the mission.

Each *Aphrodite* and *Anvil* mission was preceded by a *Bluestocking* weather reconnaissance flight over the target by a 653rd BS Mosquito. After the drone was airborne, a Mosquito in the 654th BS joined the mission carrying an 8th Combat Camera Unit (CCU) crewman. The mission was to fly close to the drone and to photograph its flight and its effects. These photographs were used to analyze all angles of the flight and to improve methods and equipment used on such missions. Some of the 8th CCU cameramen came from the Hal Roach Studios in Hollywood, where they trained alongside movie stars making training films, such as Ronald Reagan (the Administrative Officer), Alan Ladd, Van Heflin, John Carroll and others.

On 4 August 1944, of four *Aphrodite* B-17s, or 'Babies', despatched to *No-ball* sites in the Pas de Calais, one crashed in England, killing its pilot; the second refused to dive over the target and was destroyed by flak; the third overshot and the fourth undershot. On 6 August two *Aphrodite* drones crashed and exploded. The missions were photographed by S/Sgt August 'Augie' Kurjack and Lt David J. McCarthy in 25th BG Mosquitoes. Kurjack ran about 50 ft of movie film of the crash in England. McCarthy's Mosquito, flown by Lt Robert A. Tunnel, picked up some flak and flew home on one engine.

The US Navy's first Project *Anvil* mission went ahead on 12 August. Some 21,170 lb of Torpex was distributed throughout the PB4Y-1 Liberator, together with six demolition charges

each containing 113 lb of TNT. The pilot for the *Anvil* mission was Lt Joseph P. Kennedy Jr, at 29, the eldest son of Joseph Kennedy, the former US Ambassador to Britain, and who had flown a tour of missions from Dunkeswell with VB-110. 'Bud' Willy was co-pilot. Their target was a secret weapon site at Mimoyecques which concealed a three-barrelled 150-mm artillery piece, designed to fire 600 tons of explosives a day on London.

A Mosquito flown by Tunnel, with McCarthy in the right-hand seat, followed behind the formation of two Ventura 'mother ships', Kennedy's Liberator, a navigational B-17, a P-51 Mustang and a P-38 Lightning. The mission proceeded satisfactorily to Blythburgh when, at 1,500 ft, two explosions ripped the Liberator asunder. McCarthy reported:

We had just decided to close in on the 'Baby'. I was flying in the nose of the plane so that I could get some good shots of the 'Baby' in flight ahead of us. The 'Baby' just exploded in mid-air. As we heard it I was knocked halfway back to the cockpit. A few pieces of the 'Baby' came through the Plexiglas nose and I got hit in the head and caught a lot of fragments in my right arm.

McCarthy crawled back to the cockpit and lowered the wheels. Tunnel concludes:

I didn't get a scratch but I was damn near scared to death. The Mosquito went up a few hundred feet and I didn't get any response from my controls. I was setting to reach for my parachute but decided to check the controls again. This time they responded and I decided to try and make a landing. One engine was out and the other was smoking. We were near a field so I headed straight for it. We made a good landing and then the second motor cut out. I had just enough speed left to get the Mosquito off the runway, but I couldn't taxi onto a hardstand.

I'm sure glad that the pictures of our previous mission were good because I don't think we're going to get that close to the 'Baby' again.

A dozen drone missions were flown before the British advance overran the Pas de Calais area. Several attempts were made to convert Mosquitoes into 'mother ships' but they were not used operationally.

On 13 August Dean H. Sanner and Kurjack filmed the flight paths of *Disney* glide bombs released from under the wings of B-17s at U-Boat pens at Le Havre, France, and photographed any damage to the submarine pens. The 18-ft-long, 2,000-lb bombs, powered by a rocket motor in the tail, had been invented by Capt Edward Terrell RN and were designed to pierce 20 ft of concrete before exploding. The first was not going to hit anything, so Sanner broke off the pursuit and climbed back to follow the second glide bomb. At the Initial Point the second bomb was released and he zig-zagged back and forth considerably to hold the faster Mosquito behind the slower glide bomb. As Sanner flew over the bomb it exploded. The blast blew him out of the aircraft. His cameraman was killed. Sanner suffered a broken leg and injuries to his right arm and was captured within the hour. He finished the war in Stalag Luft I.

In September 1944 the Allies attempted to capture bridges on the Rhine in Holland at Veghel, Grave, Nijmegen and Arnhem, using Britain's 1st and America's 82nd and 101st Airborne Divisions. Operation *Market-Garden* was planned to cut off the Germany Army in the Belgian sector and save the bridges and the port of Antwerp for the American army units and British XXX Corps advancing north from the Dutch border. Claude C. Moore, a Mosquito navigator, recalls:

On the night of 16 September three 'Mossie' crews were called in and told that we would go out early next day at staggered intervals. No details. One plane was to take off at 2 a.m., one at 4 a.m., and one at 6 a.m. Next morning, just before take-off, we were given the details – the Nijmegen-Arnhem area. Find the base of the clouds in the area. How thick and how low. Go down to the deck if necessary. Radio back that information.

We were the last flight, at 6 a.m. Jimmy Spear was the pilot. The sky was already light when we left. It was only a matter of minutes from Watton to Holland. We skimmed across at 2,000-3,000 ft. Soon we were at the target area, which, I learned later, was where the parachute drops were made and the gliderborne assault troops were landed. There were large clouds, intermittently broken, so we descended. At around 500 ft we were finding the base of the clouds. Apparently High Command was not waiting for our information; there were planes everywhere. I had never seen so many fighters up close. Below us, above us, around us, on every side they were climbing, diving, milling like a swarm of angry bees. They were really beating the place up.

We reported thick, low, occasionally broken, white clouds and smaller, grey puffs of clouds, and gave the cloud base as approximately 400-500 ft. The smaller, grey puffs of clouds were spaced all around. Only, I finally realized, they weren't small clouds. They were shell bursts. We were being shot at.

I was startled to see a plane coming off the deck, climbing straight at us and closing – a snub-nosed, radial-engined plane. From the markings and the silhouette I took it to be from Hermann Goering's own elite group – cowling painted in a distinctive yellow-and-black checkerboard pattern. 'Focke-Wulf 190' flashed through my mind. 'Damn,' I thought. 'This is it!' I'm sure that, mentally, I was frozen in space. But the next thing I knew, the snub-nose had zoomed past us. I did a double-take. It was a P-47 Thunderbolt.

We stayed in the area a little longer, made a few more weather reports, then headed back to Watton. At the base we were debriefed. We went over to the Combat Mess for breakfast and settled into the day's routine.

On 18 September the Germans counter-attacked and forestalled an American attempt to capture the bridge at Nijmegen. Just over 100 B-24 Liberators dropped supplies and ammunition to the American Airborne forces at Grosbeek, in the Nijmegen-Eindhoven area. Five Mosquito weather scouts were despatched to Holland. 1/Lt Robert Tunnel and his navigator-cameraman, S/Sgt John G. Cunney, failed to return. Both men are now interred in the American War Cemetery at Neuville en Condroz, Belgium.

Bad weather during Operation *Market-Garden* made regular air reconnaissance over the Arnhem bridge impossible, so on 22 September three 25th BG Mosquitoes were despatched. Lt 'Paddy' Walker's navigator, Roy C. Conyers, recalls:

We were to dip as low as possible to try to establish by visual observation who controlled the bridge, the Germans or the British. I thought that this regularity was crazy and mentioned it to Edwin R. Cerrutti, 654th navigator. His only comment was that the German Command wouldn't believe that we were that stupid.

As 'Paddy' Walker flew over the north end of the bridge just below the fog, at under 500 ft, he and

Roy Conyers could see Germans running for their anti-aircraft guns. Walker remembers:

Ground fire began almost immediately. This continued as we flew over and past the other end, on towards the coast. Tracer fire could be seen coming up around us and the plane was hit. I saw the left wing drop tank disintegrate, and jettisoned both. The right engine was shut down and the propeller feathered. The fire went out, but the engine was inoperative. I was flying as low and as fast as possible to get out of range. As we crossed the coast additional fire was received, spurts of water coming up near the plane from the barrage; however, we were not hit. After we got out of range, I climbed up into the weather to gain enough altitude to make an emergency Mayday radio call, to get a 'steer' to the nearest base where the weather was suitable to land. We steered to Bournemouth. My Mayday call was answered by the sweetest girl's British accent – 'Tommy' Settle, a beautiful blonde WAAF at Tangmere. During the days that it took to repair the plane she and I became better acquainted.'

On 25 September another *Bluestocking* mission was launched as evacuation of the surviving paratroops from Arnhem began. 1/Lt Clayborne O. Vinyard and his navigator, 1/Lt John J. O'Mara, took off at 01:26 hrs in fog so thick they could only see 300 yd in front. They flew too deep into Germany, reaching the Frankfurt area before turning back. They descended to 18,000 ft, but a night fighter got on their tail and shot them down. Both men baled out and later joined Dean Sanner at Stalag Luft I.

Some 352 Chaff (*Window*)-dispensing sorties, code-named *Gray-Pea* (after Col Leon Gray, who assumed command of the 25th BG on 23 September 1944, and Col (later Gen) Budd Peaslee), were carried out by Mosquitoes of the

653rd and 654th BSs using an electric dispensing mechanism in their bomb bays. Capt Roy Ellis-Brown DFC, was returning from a 'chaffing' mission for 8th AF bombers to St Vith and Abois when he spotted a flight of P-51 Mustang escorts below him. 'One of these jocks called me and said, "Don't worry old boy, we will protect you on the way home." 'I replied, "Thanks, I'll slow down so you can give me cover!"' Feathering one engine and pulling full power on the other, the Mosquito pilot dived and performed a slow roll past the Mustang formation, pulling up in front. 'I then called the leader and said, "Sorry old chap. Will have to cut in the port engine as the 'Mossie' rolls a bit on one fan. Also have a hot date tonight!"' Ellis-Brown restarted the engine, and as he opened the throttles his observer reported that the Mustangs' engines were smoking as they tried to catch up. 'As I landed, the P-51s overflew the base at low-level, in a beautiful beat-up. I think we made our point.'

Another extrovert was F/O Vance 'Chip' Chipman, a former racetrack driver from Chicago who had joined the Royal Canadian Air Force when war started in Europe. To some he was '...a strange chap in USAAF uniform with both RAF and USAAF wings. His chest was splattered with combat decorations and he sported a long handlebar moustache. In a crisp British accent he introduced himself, mentioning that he would be assisting in Mosquito pilot training.' On 1 November, during an H2X photography mission to Schweinfurt, Chipman's Mosquito was shot down by enemy fighters. He became a prisoner of the Germans, although he once tried to escape by stealing an Me 109. He was recaptured before he could start the engine.

On 6 November 1944 Otto Kaellner's Mosquito crashed in England following a *Mickey* night radar-mapping mission using the H2S radar system to Cologne. *Mickey* flights were temporarily suspended and, beginning on 19 February 1945, the 654th BS switched to light weather missions. On 24 March, a daylight mission was tried. A Mosquito piloted by Lt C. B. Stubblefield and his navigator-radar operator, 1/Lt James B. Richmond, flew ahead of the 8th AF bombers, escorted by eight P-51 Mustangs from Wattisham. They would be led to the

Opposite above *25th BG Mosquito PR. XVI NS651/F crashed at Watton on 5 March 1945. (via Ken Godfrey)*

Opposite middle *25th BG Mosquito PR.XVI NS774. This aircraft crashed at Watton on 25 March 1945. (via Ken Godfrey)*

Opposite below *PR.XVI NS748 lost its tail and rear fuselage in this crash at Watton in April 1945. (via Ken Godfrey)*

German fighters as they started their climb to attack the bombers. Unfortunately, the Mosquito was shot down by a 9th AF P-47. Stubblefield was killed and Richmond was made a PoW.

Next day 1/Lt Bernard J. Boucher and his navigator, Louis Pessirilo, were killed during a *Bluestocking* mission over Germany. Five other Mosquitoes on weather reconnaissance returned safely. On 3 April six *Gray-Pea* Mosquitoes were detailed for Chaff-screening for the 8th AF, five more scouted for the B-17s, and seven flew weather-reconnaissance over the continent and seas around Britain. Lt Col Alvin E. Podojski, pilot and group deputy commander, and Capt Lionel A. Proulx, navigator, were leading a flight of four Mosquitoes on a *Gray-Pea* mission over Kiel when they were attacked by German fighters. Their Mosquito received damage and they limped to Sweden.

Some 74 Mosquito *Red-Tail* sorties (named after their red tails, so coloured to distinguish them from enemy aircraft) were flown from bases in East Anglia, each carrying the Command Pilot of 8th AF bombing missions. On 4 April 1945 1/Lt T. B. Smith and Col Troy Crawford, CO 446th BG, were shot down by B-24 Liberator gunners who mistook their Mosquito for an Me 262 as the formation headed for the jet airfield at Wesendorf. Crawford was captured but was freed later by some Germans who realized that Germany had lost the war. He returned to the USA.

By early 1945 several anti-Nazi agents were ready to be parachuted into Germany from American aircraft, but there were problems. In France agents had successfully used the long-established, but weighty, S-Phone device; but making air-to-ground contact with the agents once they had landed in Germany was more difficult. A large and heavy suitcase was highly suspicious and safe houses were few and far between. And anyway, the S-Phone had an effective range only up to 10,000 ft – well within reach of the German flak batteries.

Stephen H. Simpson, a Texan scientist with the honorary rank of Lt Cmdr, and Dewitt R. Goddard came up with a transmitter-receiver system so small that it could be easily carried by the agent in the field, yet could transmit a radio beam so narrow that it was practically immune to detection by the German 'Gonio' (Radio-goniometry) vans. The new system was named *Joan-Eleanor*, after both a major in the WAC and Goddard's wife. The *Joan* device, which beamed UHF transmissions and weighed only 4 lb, was carried by the agent. The *Eleanor* receiver set was housed in the host aircraft and used a wire recorder for capturing the ground-to-air conversations.

Goddard and Simpson's invention was modified and installed in a Mosquito after all unnecessary equipment – even the IFF device – was removed. An oxygen system was installed in the bomb bay and adapted to accommodate the *Joan-Eleanor* device and an operative. Eventually, five Mosquitoes were made available for *Joan-Eleanor* and agent-dropping missions, the latter being known as *Redstockings* in the hope that the German Abwehr would think they were connected with *Bluestocking* weather missions.

On 22 October the first test flight was made

Flight Officer Vance 'Chip' Chipman poses with the pet monkey he bought in London. Chipman was a former race track driver from Chicago who had joined the RCAF when the war started in Europe. On 1 November, during an H2X photography mission to Schweinfurt, Chipman's Mosquito was shot down by enemy fighters, and he became a PoW. He once tried to escape by stealing an Me 109, but was recaptured before he could start the engine.

with Steve Simpson and his equipment in the rear fuselage. On 10 November 1944 the first agent, code-named *Bobbie,* was dropped during the night at Ulrum on the German border with Holland. *Bobbie* was Anton Schrader, a 27-year-old Dutch engineer, the son of a Netherlands governor-general in the Dutch East Indies. An agent was given a line of 100–150 miles, anywhere along which he could use his radio. He was never to use it in the same place twice. He should broadcast from a 50-yd clearing in a forest because the spreading frequency waves would be quickly absorbed by trees and shrubbery. The BBC would broadcast an innocuous sentence – 'Mary needs to talk to you Thursday the 10th.' – at a pre-arranged time. This meant a mission would fly the line on that date after midnight and call continuously. When the agent responded he was acknowledged and the aircraft continued for 20 miles. The point was then orbited at a radius of 20 miles as the Mosquito flew in a 40-mile circle above 30,000 ft. By using direction finders in the Mosquito, the contact man located the point from which the agent was transmitting. By using synchronized instruments the contact man in the plane could direct the pilot.

Simpson's first two attempts to contact *Bobbie* failed. Both missions were flown in Mosquito NS676, the second of two Mosquitoes supplied by the RAF, crewed by Capt Victor S. Doroski, pilot, and Lt Bill Miskho, navigator. On the first try the Mosquito's elevator controls jammed and control of the aircraft was wrenched from Doroski's hands. On the second effort *Bobbie* could not be contacted.

On 22 November Simpson made a third attempt to make contact with *Bobbie*. Mosquito NS707 was used as NS676 had been badly damaged on landing after the abortive second trip. As they crossed the Dutch coast, Doroski lost height, and the *Redstocking* Mosquito started circling at 30,000 ft at a pre-set time and at an established rendezvous point to enable Simpson, crouched in the bomb bay, to record the conversation on the wire recorder. There was no response from *Bobbie*. Simpson ordered Doroski down to 20,000 ft in an effort to pick up the agent's signal, but still there was no response. Below the Mosquito there unfolded a barrage of fireworks.

The aircraft shuddered with each burst. Simpson shouted on the intercom, 'We're in a storm, Captain. You'd better get us out of here!'

'Commander, that's no storm. We're being shot at!'

Doroski climbed back up to 30,000 ft and cruised around the area again. At midnight Simpson finally made contact with *Bobbie*. Through heavy static the agent informed Simpson that he was 'quite all right'. He said that a Panzer regiment was headed towards Arnhem and pinpointed a railway bridge over the Ems Canal at Leeuwarden. If Allied bombers destroyed the bridge, he said, they would paralyze traffic from this key junction into Germany. *Bobbie* finished abruptly. 'I am standing here near German posts. It is very dangerous.' Simpson said goodbye and told Doroski to head for home. (Doroski was subsequently lost on a night photography *Joker* mission on 8 February 1945.)

On 12 December the seventh mission in contact with *Bobbie* was flown. Simpson's pilot was 'Paddy' Walker; Capt Bill Miskho flew as navigator. *Bobbie* told Simpson that the IX SS Panzer Division was in a rest camp in the area but had been ordered to move in 48 hours. He added ominously that, '...it is almost impossible as all railroads, cars, trucks and buses have been taken over and are moving troops and supplies. Something big is about to happen.' The message was clear and in English. After receiving and recording the full communication from *Bobbie* the Mosquito headed for Watton. On arrival, the recording wire was transported to London and reported to Secret Intelligence, but the significance was not realized. On 16 December Field Marshal Karl von Rundstedt's Panzer divisions attacked the Allied front-line in an area of the Ardennes where American units were in rest and rehabilitation. The German offensive achieved complete surprise and caused widespread confusion, and a salient, or 'bulge', was opened. The Ardennes Offensive had proved that the German Army was yet capable, and agents were needed in Germany.

Bobbie was later apprehended by the Abwehr who used him to transmit deceptive intelligence, but by a pre-arranged code OSS knew that he had been 'turned' and contact missions continued to

Above 25th BG Mosquito NS595 crashed at Watton on 9 March 1945. (via Ken Godfrey)

Below 25th BG Mosquito NS590 lost its starboard engine in a crash-landing at Watton on 5 May 1945. (via Ken Godfrey)

Southern Belle, a 25th BG weather-reconnaissance Mosquito crashed on 28 May 1945. The 653rd BS used Mosquito T.III and PR.XVI aircraft on meteorological flights, known as Bluestockings, *gathering weather information from over the continent. (via Ken Godfrey)*

be flown regularly by the 25th BG. However, the stripped-down Mosquito flew above 45,000 ft to avoid German night fighters and interceptors. Two months later *Bobbie* returned to England equipped with a German radio, having persuaded the Abwehr that he would make a good double agent!

On the night of 1/2 March 1945, an A-26 Invader dropped two agents near Berlin (the Mosquito could carry only one agent). On 12 March a *Redstocking* Mosquito successfully established contact with one of the agents by using *Joan-Eleanor*. On 13 March operations moved to Harrington, where 492nd BG *Carpetbagger* Liberators, commanded by Col Hudson Upham, were used on covert missions. B-24 and B-17 night leaflet crews arrived from Cheddington at the same time, and chaos ensued. Mosquito maintenance suffered drastically and, eventually, RAF ground personnel were brought in to maintain the aircraft. OSS regained control over all Mosquito operations and 25th BG pilots and navigators flew the aircraft until enough 492nd BG personnel were available. A 492nd BG pilot and navigator carried Cmdr Simpson on their first communications mission on 31 March 1945.

On 12 April 1945 President Roosevelt passed away in Warm Springs, Georgia. His son was relieved of his command and a recommendation for a Presidential Citation for the 25th BG was discarded. Requests for awards for the 325th Photographic Wing, signed by Elliott Roosevelt, were returned, stamped 'Denied.' After 3 May 1945 *Redstocking* missions became an all-492nd BG operation. Animosity between Upham's bomb group and OSS reached a peak and negotiations at the highest level were held in London to resolve the matter. The outcome was that the 492nd BG extended its B-24 operations to include central Germany and beyond; and as Lyon had proved unsuitable for *Carpetbagger* operations, new bases were established at Bron Field, Dijon in France and at Namur, Belgium. OSS were anxious to despatch their growing number of anti-Nazi agents to Germany. *Carpetbaggers* flew 11 *Redstocking* missions (and 12 communications missions from England, only two of which were successful). Between 19 March and 28/29 April 1945, 31 successful *Joan-Eleanor* missions and 47 unsuccessful *Redstocking* sorties were flown.

* * * * *

First Lieutenant Andre E. Pecquet was posted to the 856th Squadron as a *Joan-Eleanor* operator on 21 March 1945, after decompression testing in London. He recalls:

My departure from London was delayed because Cmdr Simpson lacked personnel, and the few people working under him were too busy to be able to train anyone.

Mosquito PR.XVI NS619 of the 25th BG at Watton, still in its PRU Blue colour scheme and wearing RAF roundels. (via Steve Adams)

Also, the *Joan-Eleanor* project was transferred around the 19th from Watton to Harrington, thus creating additional work. Cmdr Simpson did not receive adequate co-operation from Harrington. Due to the lack of experienced ground crews, the maintenance of the Mosquitoes was also poor.

Jean M. Nater was also posted to the 856th Squadron as a *Joan-Eleanor* operator, where he met Andre Pecquet and Calhoun Ancrum:

Pecquet told me some harrowing details of his work with the Maquis in the Vecors. He had flown also and trained with Mosquitoes. He had been with US armour, so he wore his hat on the left side of his head. [Pecquet had been born in France in 1912, and in 1940 was one member of a French AA battery credited with 17 aircraft shot down. He served with the US 11th Armoured Division and had trained as an OSS paratrooper at Ringway.] We often spoke French together. He really didn't like flying in Mosquitoes. It upset him, but he did it.

Calhoun Ancrum was a quiet, serious young man.

He spoke several languages, Russian included. He had flown a couple of successful *Joan-Eleanor* missions but he never talked about these, nor about himself. Stephen Simpson showed me the *Joan-Eleanor* equipment, how it was used, some of the technical details (in very general terms); and he told me of his own experiences as a *Joan-Eleanor* operator over Germany. He noted that the equipment worked well but that it could be improved. He was particularly dissatisfied with the wire recorder. 'The spools can work loose, then you have wire all over the place,' he said. And he was unhappy with the cramped space for the *Joan-Eleanor* operator behind the collapsible fuel tank in the bomb bay. Further training was undertaken by George Fogharty, another quiet man.

I met the 'Mossie'. It was an impressive machine. Small, slim and sleek. Our models, mostly older photo-recce veterans, had been stripped of all arms and armour and the bomb bays had been stripped of bomb racks. Navigational equipment was left intact and there was a tail-warning radar to tell the pilot if there was anything on his tail. To fit in the *Joan-*

Eleanor operator, his radio receiver and wire recorder, our squadron riggers had adapted a small hatch on the starboard side of the fuselage just aft of the wing. They had fitted a makeshift seat close to the bottom of the fuselage; this was hinged and held together with parachute elastic cords so that you could pull it down to sit on. Great in theory, but when you shifted your backside, the seat tended to collapse. Imagine yourself all togged up in an electric flying suit covered with a pile-lined flying suit, wearing felt flying boots, a chest-pack 'chute and an emergency oxygen flask strapped to your leg; hunched over in a crouch in front of a radio with dials and an antenna which had to be rotated and a wire recorder which was apt to shed a spool! It was not very comfortable. The thing that bothered me most was the long-range bomb bay fuel tank. It was just forward of me and my gear, looking much like the rear end of an elephant backed up against a low fence. Because the Joan-Eleanor operational flight usually lasted between five to six hours, the ground crew would top up the tank to its full capacity.

As we climbed fast up over the Channel, the fuel would expand and be sucked into my compartment, where it would bubble in the bottom of the glass camera port just under my feet. Being on oxygen, you couldn't smell the stuff. The mere sight of it forced you to make an important decision: tell the pilot and have him abort the mission; or tell him, adding that you'll stay for the ride. As we gained altitude and reached our operational altitude of about 35,000 ft, the temperature inside the fuselage was about –20°, and the danger of an internal explosion was greatly diminished.

Jean Nater flew on two 'live' high-altitude training flights: one in an A-26C Invader, and a second on 19 April, in a Mosquito. He managed to contact and record messages from an 'agent' somewhere on the ground. Meanwhile, on 23/24 April, Andre Pecquet flew his first mission, to *Farmer-Chauffeur;* a 6 hr 50 min flight in a Mosquito flown by Lt Knapp with his navigator, Lt Jackson. Pecquet recalls: 'The first two hours

H2X-nosed Mosquito PR.XVI NS538/F of the 25th BG taxies past a B-26 Marauder at Watton. (via Steve Adams)

were unpleasant as liquid gas, due to some leak-age, was floating all over my compartment. I made contact with both *Farmer* and *Chauffeur.*'

Nater's first operational flight was scheduled for the night of 24/25 April. Nater says:

Although the war in Europe was visibly coming to an end, it was still almost dogma among Allied commanders that the German Army, particularly the *Waffen SS,* would mass in southern Bavaria and the Austrian Alps for a Wagnerian final battle. If we could get agents into the Alpine Redoubt, we would be well-placed to defeat Germany's final stand. Our target this time was south of the Munich area. After a light supper (belly gas is to be avoided at high altitude in unpressurized aircraft) we were kitted up and taken out to Mosquito PR.XVI NS707, waiting on the runway. The pilot was 1/Lt James G. Kunz, whom I knew, and the navigator F/O Bob Green, recently assigned to the squadron and on his first mission.

I was helped to squeeze into my compartment. The hatch was closed and I locked it from the inside and quickly tested the *Joan-Eleanor* equipment. I had been issued for the first time with silk gloves to wear under my heavy, heated flying gloves, and these made it much easier to manipulate the *Joan-Eleanor* gear. As usual, the 'Mossie' got off fast. We flew south over the Channel and over France began steadily climbing to our operational altitude. Cold, noisy, but steady. I turned on my tiny lamp (no gas bubbling in the camera port, thank God) and tested the equipment again. The intercom was on and I could hear the pilot checking our position. Kunz said, 'We're at altitude, but still some way to go.' Time went by. Suddenly, I heard a French-accented voice asking us to identify ourselves or 'We will open fire.' Kunz cut in: 'That's French AAA – I won't answer them. They'll open fire, but the bursts will be way, way below us.' Then he announced, 'We can see the bursts below us.'

It was dark and I was cold. Kunz suddenly announced, 'Tail radar has gone on! I'll do a quick 360.' A '360'? I soon learned what it meant. We turned sharply and I was pushed down into my bench. It collapsed. Still we went around. We levelled out just

Lt Kingdom Knapp taxies out Mosquito PR.XVI NS725/F at Harrington. (Andre Pecquet)

as quickly. Kunz said, 'Jesus! Something's flown past us! It had a tail light! Maybe it was one of the new Messerschmitts we've heard about!' Was it true, or was Kunz just keeping me awake?

At about 22.00 hrs Kunz said, 'Time's right; we're on target. Do your stuff Jean. I'll fly a large figure-of-eight.' So it began. I turned on the *Joan-Eleanor*. There was static in my headphones. The set was working. I began turning the antenna. It was functioning. I began calling the agent's code-name, repeating it twice and then identifying myself with a name I had been given. I repeated this procedure several times in German. If the agent was at the rendezvous, at this time, remembered the code-name, his transmitter was working, and there was no German military within 50 yds, he must hear me and respond. Silence. Nothing. I tried again and again. Green checked our position. We were where we were supposed to be. Kunz changed the flight pattern. Around and around and back and forth we went for 15-20 min. Nothing. Kunz suggested we return to base. I made one more call. No answer. I agreed with Kunz. I was sweating and cold.

My altimeter stayed at 35,000 ft for a long time before moving down. Kunz told me we were deep into France so he'd come down lower. I must have fallen asleep. The bouncing and whipping of the aircraft woke me. The altimeter had us at 5,000 ft. I asked Kunz where we were and he replied, in a tone of great relief, that we would be crossing the Channel soon, then he'd go down lower. I watched the altimeter come down and then level out at 1,000 ft. Despite the bouncing and shaking, I felt much better. The altimeter started down again, to 500 ft. In my mind's eye I saw the water below and the cliffs of Dover before us. The altimeter went below 100 ft and then lifted. 'We're over the coast,' said Green. We climbed to 3,000 ft. Smoother, much smoother.

About 10 min after crossing the coast, one of the engines began to miss and the aircraft shuddered. Kunz ordered Green to switch on the reserve fuel. I assume he complied, but the engine did not pick up. Instead it started to shake itself loose. Kunz began calling for an emergency landing. Two stations answered him and gave him a 'fix' so the navigator could work out a course. Kunz told them that we were at 'Angels Three'. Then he saw the port engine begin to burn. He ordered us to bale out. 'Green's out! Jean, Jean, when are you going?' I told him, 'I'm going!'

In theory, the *Joan-Eleanor* operator was to 'kick out the hatch' and go out head first, but going out into the roaring darkness head first was something I could not do. I went out feet first and got stuck in the hatch with my legs banging outside on the fuselage. My 'chute had stuck on the hatch frame. I tried to disengage it with my hands. As I did so I smelt smoke. I was terrified that my searching fingers would spill the 'chute inside the aircraft. 'Relax,' I thought. Then I was outside on my back, the aircraft going away from me with the port engine burning. I pulled the rip-cord. A long, strong tug on my shoulders and body and a God-given quiet. My 'chute had opened!

Jean Nater landed near an ammunition depot not far from Farnham and was taken to RAE Farnborough. Kunz was alright, but Green was missing. Kunz told Green before he baled out that he had not done up the legstraps of his parachute harness. Green pulled the harness up between his legs but probably went out without buckling the legstraps.

After a brief physical examination, Kunz and Nater joined the search for Green in the open, partially wooded countryside. They found his open 'chute high in a tree. His body was found the next day. At Harrington, Kunz told Nater that the port engine had been retrieved by RAF engineers and taken apart. A steel projectile had pierced the jacket of the supercharger and lodged there, effectively sealing the jacket. Over England, the projectile had worked loose, causing the carburettor to explode. Kunz reasoned that the 'projectile' could only have come from the 'aircraft which had been on our tail while we flew over Germany'.

* * * * *

On 27/28 April 1945 Andre Pecquet flew his second *Farmer-Chauffeur* mission, with Lt Knapp and Lt Jackson. 'Gas again leaked all over the rear compartment but stopped after an hour. The weather was very bad during the 7 hr 40 min flight and we flew at 32,000–35,000 ft. No contact with either team was made in spite of a thorough search over a wide area.'

On 30 April Jean Nater flew his last Mosquito operational mission. He recalls:

We staged at either Dijon or Lyon, and had a light but excellent dinner in some OSS-recquisitioned French country manor house. This time our target was in the Breganz area. The flight from the OSS French base to the target area and then to Harrington took 5 hr 25 min. Over the target at 35,000 ft we flew figures-of-eight and I called someone on the ground. I called and called. There was no answer.

Time was running short so we turned for home. Not long after this, there was smoke in my compartment. I immediately informed the pilot. He confirmed that he and the navigator could also smell smoke. I then noticed that some liquid – probably gas – was bubbling in my camera port. I told the pilot. He asked, 'Do you want to bale out?' What a question at 35,000 ft! It would mean turning on the emergency oxygen flask strapped to my leg, getting out of that damned hatch, and then free-falling for a count of 10! I asked the pilot where we were. 'Over the Alps,' he replied! Visions of mountain peaks, snow and ice. 'No, not this time,' I told the pilot. I would stay…

In time the smoke disappeared and the camera port cleared. The only instrument I had was the altimeter. When I could see it going down to 3,000 ft, staying there for a while while we turned, the engines changing their tune, feeling the flaps come down – then I knew we were home!

On 1 May 1/Lt Andre Pecquet flew another mission in search of *Chauffeur*, with Lt Kunz and navigator Lt Edwards, but the interphone, VHF and radio equipment 'blew out' and they were compelled to return after 40 min. Pecquet recalls:

We tried another plane, but because of several mechanical defects we were unable to take-off. The plane was repaired, but while taxiing we discovered that one engine was out of order. By then it was too late for a fourth attempt. This was my last mission. The surrender of Germany took place a few days later.

The 25th BG expected to be sent to to the Pacific, but soon orders arrived to return their Mosquitoes to the RAF. Lt Warren Borges wrote: 'We came home...after flying our beloved Mosquitoes into a field ('Boondocks' – the grass was two feet high!) in Scotland – what a sad day!!?'

Quietly, without ceremony or flag-waving, the Americans' involvement with the Mosquito was over.

Crews and Joan-Eleanor *operators at Harrington, 1945. L-R: Lt Green (killed 24/25 April 1945); Lt Calhoun Ancrum (Joan-Eleanor operator); Lt Kingdom Knapp (MIA Korea in an A-26); unknown pilot; 1/Lt Andre E. Pecquet (Joan-Eleanor operator). (Andre Pecquet)*

Chapter Eight

Night Fighting

While American Mosquitoes, and for that matter, B-17s and B-24s of the 8th AF, were waging war on Germany from bases in East Anglia with their brothers-in-arms, the RAF's four-engined bomber force, British civilians continued to 'take it' from a number of night raids by the Luftwaffe on towns and cities in East Anglia. Following an attack by 234 RAF bombers on the old Hanseatic city of Lübeck, Hitler had ordered a series of Terrorangriff (terror attacks) mainly against cities of historic or aesthetic importance, but little strategic value. In Britain they became known as the *Baedeker*

raids, after the German guide books of the same name.

Despite its historical significance, the cathedral city of Norwich made a tempting target for Luftwaffe raiders ever since the first *Baedeker* raid on the Norfolk capital on the night of 27/28 April 1942. The 28 Luftwaffe raiders were met by nine Beaufighters, 10 Spitfires and three AI.V radar-equipped Mosquito NF.IIs of 157 Squadron based at Castle Camps. Meanwhile, 20 Ju 88s of Kampfgeschwader (KG) 30 laid mines off the coast. The enemy was picked up on radio at 20:15 hrs and although radar con-

Mosquito F.II DZ716/UP-L of 605 Squadron prepares to start engines prior to another night operation over enemy territory. (via Philip Birtles)

tacts were made, the defending fighters failed to shoot down any of the raiders, which, from 23:40–00:45 hrs, rained down 41 tonnes of high explosive and four tonnes of incendiaries onto the city of over 126,000 inhabitants, causing the deaths of 162 people, injuring 600 more and damaging thousands of buildings. Reports spoke of some of the bombers machine gunning the streets. The raid was the first sortie by I/KG2 since converting to the Do 217E. The 'Holzhammer' unit, plus IV/KG30 and II/KG40, all based in Holland, would venture to England many times over the next 12 months.

'Ack-ack' batteries were drafted into and around Norwich and the fighter defences gradually improved. The Mosquitoes suffered particularly from problems with cannon flash and exhaust manifold and cowling burning. On 19 May a 157 Squadron Mosquito lost an engine and crashed at Castle Camps, killing both crew. 'A' Flight in 151 Squadron at Wittering had received its first Mosquito NF.II on 6 April ('B' Flight had to wait until later to replace its Defiants). 151 was commanded by W/C I. S. Smith DFC, a New Zealander, and the station commander at this time was G/C Basil Embry. The latter narrowly avoided a collision with a Dornier 217E-4 on the night of 1 May. On 29/30 May F/L Pennington, who had flown 151 Squadron's first patrol, on 30 April, put several cannon shells into a Dornier Do 217E-4 before receiving return fire, and P/O Wain damaged a Do 217E-4 of KG2. Both attacks took place over the North Sea while the bombers were *en route* to raid Gt. Yarmouth. On 30 May, another Dornier of KG2 was almost certainly destroyed south of Dover by S/L G. Ashfield in a 157 Squadron Mosquito from Castle Camps.

264 Squadron at Colerne had operated Defiant night fighters since early 1942 and on 3 May it received its first Mosquito. The squadron flew its first operational sorties on the type on 13 June, and the first Mosquito 'kill' occurred on the night of 30/31 July when a Ju 88A-4 was destroyed. Meanwhile, on 24/25 June a 151 Squadron Mosquito destroyed a Do 217E-4 of II/KG40. On 26/27 June F/L Moody of 151 Squadron from Wittering destroyed Do 217E-4 U5+ML of 3./KG2, flown by Fw Hans

Schrödel, when He 111 pathfinders, Ju 88s of KüFlGr 506 and Do 217s of I, II, and III/KG2 raided Norwich. On the night of 28/29 June an *Intruder* Mosquito of 264 Squadron, piloted by F/O Hodgkinson, forced down Uffz Rudolf Blankenburg over Creil as he made for home in a KG2 Do 217E-2 after a raid on Weston-super-Mare.

During July–August III/KG2's much reduced bomber force continued to send single aircraft on daylight low-level or cloud cover 'pirate' sorties against selected targets in Britain. They also made several small-scale night raids, during which they began to encounter, in increasing numbers, the Mosquito night fighter. Although 157 Squadron at Castle Camps had been the first to become operational on the Mosquito NF.II, the enemy continued to elude them. To their chagrin, by the end of July 1942 151 Squadron Mosquitoes had destroyed four more machines. On 21/22 July P/O Fisher shot down Ofw Heinrich Wolpers and his crew in Do 217E-4 U5+IH off Spurn Head, and on 27/28 July Fw Richard Stumpf of I/KG2, and Lt Hans-Joachim Mohring of 3./KG2, were downed by 151 Squadron Mosquitoes. On 29/30 July, when the Luftwaffe bombed Birmingham, Do 217E-4 U5+GV, flown by Ofw Artur Hartwig of II/KG2, fell to Australian pilot, F/O A. I. McRitchie, and crashed into the sea.

On 22/23 August 157 Squadron scored its first actual confirmed 'kill' when the CO, 29-year-old W/C Gordon Slade with P/O P. V. Truscott, destroyed Do 217E-4 U5+LP of 6./KG2, flown by 29-year-old ex-Lufthansa pilot Oblt Hans Walter Wolff, Deputy Staffelkapitan, 20 miles from Castle Camps.

In September 151 Squadron added two more Dornier Do 217E-4s to its 'kill' total. F8+AP, on loan to 3./KG2 and piloted by Fw Alfred Witting, was shot down by Ian McRitchie, the Australian, on 8/9 September when the Luftwaffe attacked Bedford; and during a raid on King's Lynn on 17 September, F/L H. E. Bodien DFC blasted U5+UR of 7./KG2 piloted by Fw Franz Elias. It crashed at Fring and all four crew were taken prisoner. On 30 September 157 scored its first day combat victory; a Ju 88A-4 downed by W/C R. F. H. Clerke, off

Mosquito NF.II prototype W4052 on a test flight with early nose-mounted airborne radar. The Mosquito night fighter was progressively improved, mainly by the introduction of more efficient AI radar. (via Philip Birtles)

Mosquito NF.II DD750 in flight. One such Mosquito was flown on 17 September 1944 by F/L H. E. Bodien DFC when he destroyed U5+UR of 7./KG2, piloted by Fw Franz Elias, which crashed at Fring. (via Philip Birtles)

Holland. It had been a particularly bad month for KG2, which on 19 August 1942, during the Dieppe operation, lost 16 Do 217s and had seven damaged. By October 157 Squadron had added three more enemy victories.

On 15/16 January 1943 151 Squadron scored the first Mosquito 'kill' of the New Year, when Sgt E. A. Knight with Sgt W. I. L. Roberts, shot down Do 217E-4 U5+KR of 7./KG2 during a raid on Lincoln. The Canadian Mosquito pilot aimed his first burst from quarter astern and hit the enemy's port engine. The pilot, Lt Günther Wolf, dived and carried out evasive action. Uffz Kurt Smelitschkj, the dorsal gunner, returned fire. Knight blasted the Dornier again and there was no more firing. His third burst caused pieces of the German bomber to fly off and it crashed at Boothby Graffoe, near Lincoln, killing all aboard.

On 17/18 January over France a Mosquito Intruder destroyed a Ju 88A-14 of I/KG6 (an experienced Pathfinder unit). W/C C. M. Wight-Boycott, in a Beaufighter, shot down two Ju 88s and a Do 217 and damaged another. (In October 1943 Wight-Boycott DSO moved to command 25 Squadron at Church Fenton, equipped with the Mosquito NF.II.) On 22 January a 410 (RCAF) Squadron Mosquito claimed a 'probable' Do 217E and then there was a lull in the Mosquito 'kills' until 18/19 March, when Fliegerkorps IX set out to attack Norwich. Between 22:55–23:30 hrs, 20 crews aimed 18 tonnes of high explosive and 19.2 tonnes of incendiaries on the part of the city that ran north and north-west of the large buildings in the city centre. In all, 3.3 tonnes actually fell on the streets, houses and factories. Some 13 junior crews, who were on the raid to gain combat

This ground test firing fusillade of four Browning machine guns and four Hispano cannon graphically illustrates the effect the Mosquito's devastating fire power had on German intruders over Britain in 1943/44. (via Jerry Scutts)

experience, attacked harbour installations at Great Yarmouth.

Mosquito and Beaufighter night fighters had already taken off to intercept the bombers heading for Norwich. F/O G. Deakin with P/O de Costa of 157 Squadron took off from Bradwell Bay at 22:00 hrs in their Mosquito NF.II and were vectored out to sea by GCI at Trimley Heath. S/L Kidd, the controller, directed the Mosquito crew towards an enemy aircraft approaching Orfordness. They got an AI contact with a Ju 88 at 9,000 ft range. (Deakin eventually obtained a visual sighting at 2,500 ft and recognized his prey.) The Ju 88 was climbing so he opened up the throttles and climbed steeply behind him before opening fire with a long burst of four cannon and two Browning machine guns at 600 ft dead astern. The Mosquito pilot continued firing while the Ju 88 'corkscrewed' in vain. Deakin carried on firing into the doomed bomber until all his ammunition was exhausted. The enemy raider flew straight and level, then disappeared, falling into the sea about four miles off Southwold.

A Coltishall-based 68 Squadron Beaufighter flown by F/O P. F. Allen DFC with F/O G. E. Bennett, destroyed a Do 217E, a 6./KG2 machine flown by Hptm Hans Hansen. In the meantime a Mosquito NF.II of 410 (RCAF) Squadron flown by F/O D. Williams with his navigator P/O P. Dalton, had taken off from Coleby Grange at 22:45 hrs and was directed towards 'trade' in the King's Lynn area. F/L Tuttle at Orby Control directed the two Canadians towards a 'bogey' three miles distant flying at 240 mph. Williams increased speed to 260 mph and Dalton picked up the contact at two miles range. Suddenly, another contact appeared at 1,000 yd, below and slightly to port. Williams put the nose down and at 8,000 ft made out the unmistakable form of a Do 217, flying along at 2,000 ft dead ahead. U5+AH (Werk No 5523) belonged to I/KG2 and was being flown by Uffz Horst Toifel.

The fear and shock aboard the Dornier at that instant can only be imagined. Toifel must have seen his pursuer because he immediately carried out a half-roll and tried to dive before his gunner, Uffz Heinrich Peter, the radio operator, Ludwig Petzold, or the observer, Obgefr Georg

Officers and aircrew of 418 (RCAF) Squadron, Fighter Command, photographed at Hunsdon, Hertfordshire in November 1944. The Mosquito is FB.VI J-Johnny, with 23 confirmed ''kills'. (Jerry Scutts).

Riedel, could even think about opening fire. Toifel was so preoccupied with trying to lose the Mosquito that he had no time to sight and fire his defensive armament. Williams followed the Dornier down and held his fire as he did so. At 1,800 ft the Mosquito pilot pulled out and shortly afterwards a huge ball of crimson fire could be seen directly below, near Terrington St Clements. Williams could only think that the Dornier did not recover from its dive and therefore crashed.

On 28/29 March 1943 Fliegerkorps IX returned to raid Norwich again. Between 22:00–22:19 hrs 18 German raiders dropped high explosive and incendiaries over Norfolk and Suffolk. Among the night fighters scrambled from airfields in eastern England was a Mosquito NF.II of 157 Squadron flown by F/O J. R. Beckett, who took off from Bradwell Bay at 19:40 hrs. There was no moon and only fair visibility. At first their identification of 4./KG2 Dornier Do 217E-4 U5+NM (Werk No 4375), flown by Fw Paul Huth, was hampered by searchlights and anti-aircraft bursts. A brilliant reddish orange emitted from the Dornier's exhaust system helped identification. Several times Beckett's Mosquito was illuminated by the searchlights and hit by anti-aircraft fire a few times, but he closed in to firing range. Uffz Werner Hans Burschel, the dorsal gunner, peered through his Revi gunsight and immediately opened fire with his MG 131, but the 13-mm rounds passed harmlessly high and to port. Beckett returned fire with two, two-second bursts. He saw strikes and flashes on top of the fuselage of the Dornier before it dived suddenly into cloud a few hundred feet below. Later, they were informed that it had crashed into the sea near Horsey, just north of Yarmouth, at 22:05 hrs. Huth, Burschel, Oblt Gottfried Thorley, the observer, and Uffz Konrad Schuller, the radio operator, were all killed. The victory was shared with a 68 Squadron Beaufighter piloted by F/O Vopalecky with F/Sgt Husar; both Czech.

On 14/15 April 1943, during a raid on Chelmsford, S/L W. P. Green and F/Sgt A. R. 'Grimmy' Grimstone of 85 Squadron destroyed Do 217E-4 F8+AM of 4./KG40, while off Clacton, F/L Geoff Howitt with F/O George

'Red' Irving, destroyed Do 217E-4 U5+DP of 6./KG2 flown by Uffz Franz Tannenberger. F/L James Gilles Benson DFC, with his navigator Lewis Brandon DSO DFC, of 157 Squadron, intercepted Dornier 217E-4 U5+KP flown by Uffz Walter Schmurr south-west of Colchester. 'Ben' Benson gave the 6./KG2 machine a three-second burst at 200 yd with his four cannon from astern and above, but saw no results. He then fired a seven-second burst and saw strikes, first on the port engine and mainplane, which immediately burst into flames. These spread down the port side of the fuselage until the whole aircraft, including the tail, was ablaze. There was no return fire; Uffz Franz Witte, the radio operator-gunner, was dead. The Dornier crashed at Layer Breton Heath, five miles south-west of Colchester. Schmurr, Lt Karl-Heinrich Hertam, the observer, and Uffz Martin Schwarz, the gunner, baled out. Witte's body was found in the wreckage.

On 16/17 April 1947, Fw 190A-4/U8s of Schnelles Kampfgeschwader (SKG) 10 based in France took part in attacks on London. The fast fighter-bombers, each carrying a 250-kg or 500-kg bomb on its centreline, had first been employed in March against Eastbourne, Hastings and Ashford. To be better sited to meet the threat 85 Squadron had, in May, moved from Hunsdon to West Malling, and 157 moved from Bradwell to take their place.

The mainstay of the Luftwaffe's raids on England at this time remained the Ju 88 and Do 217. On 24/25 April F/O J. P. M. Lintott and Sgt G. G. Gilling-Lax of 85 Squadron shot down Ju 88A-14 3E+HS of 8./KG6 and it disintegrated in the air, and the wreckage fell in Bromley, Kent. On the night of 4/5 May 1943 the bulbous glass-nosed Dornier Do 217K-1s of 6./KG2 taxied out at Eindhoven. Onboard one of them, Ofw Heinrich Meyer and his three crew prepared to take off and join the circuit. Their bomb bay normally held either four 500-kg high explosive bombs or ABB500 incendiaries, and they were destined for Norwich. For the 4/5 May raid, III/KG2 at Eindhoven had only recently returned from a sojourn to Carcassonne when the French Fleet was on the point of defecting to the Allies. KG2 and II/KG40 would be joined on the Norwich raid by Ju 88As of I and III/KG6 based in Belgium.

Six Mosquito night intruders were abroad that night and over Holland shortly after KG2 took off. Near Hilversum, Meyer's Dornier was written off when it crashed. It was the start of a bad night for the famed 'Holzhammer' unit. The remaining 42 Dorniers of KG2 and III/KG40, and 36 Ju 88s of KG6, including one aircraft that was to monitor the operation from Cromer, evaded their hunters and flew on low over the North Sea towards the Norfolk coast. Four of the Ju 88s had, at the same time, flown south to create a diversionary attack on the south coast of England.

Over the North Sea the oncoming German bombers noticed about 40 RAF bombers at the same height, these being among 596 RAF bombers that had attacked Dortmund. The Do 217s and Ju 88s approached eastern England hoping that the CHL stations would interpret their blips on the radar screens as 'friendly' bombers. For a crucial period of time it seemed to have worked because the German bombers carried on unmolested and then turned on a heading for Norwich, with their navigation lights on to further fool the defenders. Obst Dietrich Peltz, 'Attack Leader England', intended to deliver upon Norwich its heaviest raid of the war. That it did not happen was due to a fault in the target illumination and guidance system. The showers of flares were released well enough; in fact John Searby, who was in one of the RAF bombers returning from Dortmund, diverted to look at the marker flares and was so impressed he 'wished we had some to equal them'. However, the parachute flares were dropped in the north-west of Norfolk, and the majority of the phosphorous and mixed incendiaries fell harmlessly in fields or did little damage.

Then the defences were alerted. Aboard Do 217K-1 U5+AA (Werk No 4415), Lt Ernst Andres sat in his contoured pilot's seat in close confinement with his crew: Uffz August Drechsler, the radio operator; Obgefr Wilhelm Schlagbaum, the observer; and Flg Werner Becker, the gunner, who sat facing rearwards behind them in his dorsal turret. All four crew

were keen to impress, for flying as an observer for the operation was 31-year-old Maj Walter Bradel, Kommodore of KG2. Bradel, who had succeeded Obrst von Koppelow three months earlier, was probably flying on the raid to help restore shattered morale after heavy losses in his gruppe.

Popular with his crews, Bradel was a former cavalry officer who had flown in the Spanish Civil War, first as a Staffelkapitan, later as a Grupperkommandeur and, finally, as a Geschwaderkommodore in the Condor Legion. He held the Spanish War Medal and the Spanish Gold Cross with Swords. In Norway Bradel was employed as leader of a transport staffel, bringing up supplies and equipment to the mountain troops near Narvik. He then took part as a bomber pilot in operations against England, and later in the Balkan campaign (he was said to have been the first to land and take possession of Athens airfield) and the operations against Crete. In the course of the latter he claimed to have sunk a British destroyer with bombs. On the Eastern Front his chief exploit seems to have been a low-level attack on 500 Soviet tanks in the battle for Grodno. On 17 September 1941 he was awarded the Ritterkreuz (Knight's Cross).

F/O Brian 'Scruffy' Williams with his navigator, P/O Dougie Moore, in 605 Squadron, were complete opposites, but equally dedicated to their task. They patrolled over the Dutch airfields to await the raiders' return. 605 and 418 (RCAF) Squadrons were the first Mosquito night *Intruder* squadrons sent to attack Luftwaffe airfields on the continent. The former had taken over 23 Squadron's Bostons and Havocs and had begun *Intruder* operations over French airfields in July 1942. In February 1943 605 began equipping with the Mosquito, and by May 1943, when 418 received its first Mosquito, the County of Warwick squadron was making its presence felt.

Moore was on his first tour but the 21-year-old pilot had flown over 30 ops on Bostons in 418. Williams was an exceptional pilot. At 51 OTU, the CO, none other than Guy Gibson, had marked his Course Assessment 'Above Average', but had added: 'May get overconfident'. Late in 1942 Williams was sent to an Air

F/O Brian Williams of 605 Squadron, pilot of a very successful Intruder *sortie over Holland on the night of 4/5 May 1943. (Brian Williams)*

Schlander of 2/KG2 is also listed as being shot down near Eindhoven that night.] Then I saw a second one in the same circuit. It was a Do 217 and it also had its green and red navigation lights showing. I went in and made a beam attack. I fired my cannon and saw numerous strikes, but I didn't see it hit the deck so I later claimed a 'damaged'. I saw two more crossing in front of us but I didn't go after them because we had no chance of catching them, so I finished the patrol and flew home to base.

While I was on home leave I received a 'phone call from the CO, W/C C. D. Tomalin. He had rung to tell me that the Do 217 I had claimed as 'damaged' had crashed. Apparently, it had caused a furore in the German newspapers which said that the

W/C C. D. Tomalin, CO 605 Squadron (whose son Andy was OC Battle of Britain Flight at Coningsby until October 1994), who rang to tell Brian Williams that the Do 217 he had claimed as 'damaged' had crashed. (via Philip Birtles)

Crew Refresher Course at Brighton, a euphemism for a 'bad boys school'. He was perplexed, and took his parachute and 'Mae West' with him. Instead, early morning PT on the beach, drill all day and frequent haircuts awaited him. One of his fellow defaulters, a Pole, had been caught with a girl in his bed after he had left his shoes – and those of his lady friend – outside his door for his batman! After three weeks the 'bad boys' were returned to their units – *if* they had behaved. Williams stayed for 10 weeks! Then he was posted, to 605 Squadron at Castle Camps, where he flew his first Mosquito op on 10 March.

Williams and Moore had taken off from Castle Camps about an hour and a half after the raid on Norwich and were stooging around Eindhoven when they chanced upon the returning Dorniers. The first aircraft could be seen circling the airfield with its red and green navigation lights on. Brian Williams recalls:

It was bloody dark. There was no moon. I saw a Do 217. I fired but saw no strikes. Lost it! I'd probably frightened him to death! [The crew of Lt Alfons

Dornier was the one carrying Maj Bradel. He was killed in the crash [at Landsmere, near Amsterdam] and Lt Andres was seriously injured.

Bradel probably died of injuries he sustained because he had not been strapped in. Flg Werner Becker was also killed, although he may have died in the Mosquito attack, and the rest of the crew were injured. All recovered, Andres being promoted to Oblt and receiving the Ritterkreuz on 20 April 1944. He was killed with 5./NJG4 on 11 February 1945.

Six more German aircraft were shot down by Mosquito *Intruders* before May was out. Night fighter Mosquitoes of 157 Squadron shot down two Do 217E-4s of KG2 piloted by Lt Stefan Szamek and Lt Gerd Strufe, on 13/14 May. A Do 217E-4 of II/KG2 was intercepted by a Mosquito NF.II of 157 Squadron from Hunsdon, flown by Sgt R. L. Watts with Sgt J. Whewell, and shot down after an exchange of fire. A fire started in the Dornier's starboard engine and it crashed about 10 miles north-east of Colchester at 02:07 hrs. Near Norwich, a Do 217K-1 of 4./KG2 flown by Uffz Erhard Corty was claimed at about 02:50 hrs.

On the 13th, 85 Squadron moved from Hunsdon to West Malling aerodrome near the main London–Maidstone road, deep in the heart of the orchards and hop fields of Kent, which was occupied by Typhoons of 3 Squadron. The move coincided with some terrific action, for during May 85 Squadron claimed eight aircraft.

On the night of 16/17 May the Fw 190A-4/U8 fighter-bombers of I/SKG10 came streaking in over the Straits of Dover. Much to the chagrin of 85 Squadron, the Typhoons only were scrambled to meet them. The Mosquito crews waited almost an hour before they too were pitched into the fight after it was realized that the Typhoons, which did not have AI, were floundering. S/L Peter Green with F/Sgt A. R. 'Grimmy' Grimstone got off first and picked up an Fw 190 contact at three miles. The I/SKG10 machine had dropped his centreline bomb and was on his way back to France. He never made it. Green shot him down into the sea off Dover. Geoff Howitt and 'Red' Irving shot down the second Fw 190 off Hastings.

F/L Bernard Thwaites, a quiet, pale young fighter pilot, and P/O Will Clemo, his older, former shoolmaster navigator, chased an Fw 190 all the way to the French coast before being recalled to West Malling. He and Clemo kept a close eye on the horizon as they headed back to base. In mid-Channel Clemo picked up a free-lance contact crossing in front. Thwaites shot it down from 50 yd astern. Debris hit the Mosquito but he was still able to score three hits on another Fw 190, knocking a large piece off it, to claim it as a 'probable'. F/O J. D. Shaw and P/O A. C. Lowton braved their own searchlights and brought down a fifth Fw 190 near Gravesend, returning to base with their windscreen coated in soot and their rudder badly damaged.

Back at West Malling, to the accompaniment of 'Yip I Addy 85', F/L Tim Molony, the adjutant, ceremoniously presented the jackpot prize of bottles of whisky, champagne and gin and £5 in cash to Peter Green and 'Grimmy' Grimstone for being the first Mosquito crew to down an Fw 190 over Britain. S/L Bradshaw-Jones, senior controller at Hunsdon, gave a silver Mosquito. Congratulatory signals were received from the sector commander, G/C 'Sailor' Malan and AVM H. W. L. 'Dingbat' Saunders at Group.

There was soon more to celebrate. On the night of the 19/20 May F/O J. P. M. Lintott and his navigator, Sgt G. G. Gilling-Lax, stalked an Fw 190A of 2./SKG10. Gilling-Lax had been a housemaster at Stowe. He had greying hair which topped a long, scholarly face, and he stooped slightly in a rather dignified manner. His voice was quiet and carefully and evenly modulated.* Peering into his scope he guided Lintott onto the tail of the Fw 190, and his pilot shot it down. Their victory was celebrated at West Malling where a dance was in progress, and the remains of the Fw 190A were auctioned off for £105 in aid of the 'Wings for Victory' appeal! On 21/22 May an Fw 190A was shot down into the sea 25 miles north-west of Hardelot by S/L Edward Crew DFC* with F/O Freddie French.

To complete a memorable month, on 29/30 May Lintott and Gilling-Lax shot down the first

Night Fighter by C. F. Rawnsley & Robert Wright. Elmfield Press

Mosquito NF.XV DZ385 in flight. Originally developed from the B.IV airframe to combat high-flying Ju 86s over England, the NF.XV was used during March–August 1943 on high-altitude sorties by 'C' Flight, 85 Squadron at Hunsdon. (via Philip Birtles)

Ju 88S-1 to fall over England. Only 50 of these very fast bombers were built. Most examples, which first entered service with I/KG66 at Chartres, were rebuilt versions of the A-4 with power-boosted BMW 801G-2 engines fitted with the GM-1 nitrous oxide injection system. Stripped of its ventral gondola and most of its armour, and reduced to just one MG131 machine gun, the Ju 88S-1 was difficult to catch. Lintott had to climb to 29,000 ft in stages before he finally saw 3Z+SZ of I/KG66, his victim. A single hit in one of the three high-pressure nitrous oxide storage tanks in the rear bomb bay was enough to blow the aircraft to smithereens. It crashed at Isfield, Sussex.

On 13/14 June W/C John Cunningham, CO 85 Squadron, who had shot down 16 enemy aircraft while flying Beaufighters, pursued Fw 190A-5 CO+LT belonging to 3./SKG10 over his own airfield and shot it down. C. F. Rawnsley, his navigator, wrote:

It was an Fw 190 all right. The single exhaust flickered below the fuselage; the short, straight wings still had the drop tanks hanging from the tips; the big, smooth bomb was still clutched fiercely to its belly...John very briefly touched the trigger, and the guns gave one short bark. The enemy aircraft reared

Night Fighter by C. F. Rawnsley & Robert Wright. Elmfield Press

straight up on its nose, flicking over and plunging vertically downwards. It all happened with an incredible speed. Standing up and pressing my face to the window, I watched the blue exhaust flame dwindle as the aircraft hurtled earthwards.*

The Fw 190, flown by Lt Ullrich, crashed at Nettlefold Farm, Borough Green near Wrotham, but incredibly, the pilot had been catapulted through the canopy in the death dive of the aircraft and was taken prisoner. Cunningham's seventeenth victory was his first on the Mosquito. On 21/22 June F/L Bill Maguire and F/O W. D. Jones of 85 Squadron bagged Fw 190 GP+LA of 2./SKG10 in the river Medway. On 9 July Lintott obtained his fourth victory when, with Gilling-Lax, he shot down Do 217K-1 U5+FP, piloted by Oblt Hermann Zink of 6./KG2. Zink and his crew crashed at Detling and were all dead. The GCI controller who had put Lintott onto the raider saw two blips on his CRT merge and stay together for seven minutes; then they had faded. Two miles from where the Dornier fell the Mosquito crew were also found dead in the wreckage of their aircraft.

Two months earlier, F/L Edward Nigel Bunting, a 27-year-old pilot and experienced night fighter from St John's, Worcester, had

'B' Flight, 85 Squadron at Hunsdon in 1943. F/L Edward Nigel Bunting, who had been one of the officers who operationally tested the high-altitude Mosquito NF.XV at the station and who reached a record altitude of 44,600 ft on 30 March 1943, is standing fourth from left. On 13/14 July 1943 Bunting, with his navigator Freddie French, shot down Me 410A-1 U5+KG, flown by Fw Franz Zwißler and Ofw Leo Raida of 16./KG2, into the sea off Felixstowe. It was the first Me 410 to be shot down over Britain. (Andrew Long)

been one of the officers in 85 Squadron who operationally tested the high-altitude Mosquito NF.XV at Hunsdon. Bunting attained a record altitude of 44,600 ft on 30 March 1943, but the project was abandoned after the demise of German high-altitude raiding. On 13/14 July 1943, when KG2 headed for Cambridge, Bunting and Freddie French took off from the Somerfield wire mesh runway at West Malling at 23:00 hrs in their NF.XII and patrolled the Straits of Dover in search of enemy activity. F/O Parr at Sandwich GCI station gave Bunting a vector towards a 'customer' some 35 miles away. The Mosquito soon narrowed the gap to three miles and Bunting and French could see their prey well below them. French picked up another contact and Bunting pulled away, concerned that the lower aircraft might be a decoy.

French guided Bunting onto the second aircraft and at 7,000 ft range they could see his exhausts. Bunting gave chase for 15 minutes, opening and closing his radiator flaps to prevent overheating. Eventually, a visual was obtained against the light northern sky at a range of 1,800 ft. The Mosquito crew, rightly, believed it to be an Me 410 Hornisse (Hornet). Me 410A-1 U5+KG was being flown by Fw Franz Zwißler and Ofw Leo Raida of 16./KG2. Bunting closed to within 200 yd, but the Mosquito got caught in the Germans' slipstream and he could not aim his guns. He dived below and closed in again before firing two short bursts. The Me 410 burst into flames at once and fell into the sea five miles off Felixstowe. It was the first Me 410 to be shot down over Britain.

Also on 13/14 July, a 410 (RCAF) Squadron Mosquito shot down Uffz Willy Spielmanns' Do 217M-1, U5+EL of 3./KG2, into the sea off the Humber Estuary; and F/O Smart of 605 Squadron, flying an *Intruder* over Holland, shot down Do 217M-1 U5+CK of 2./KG2 which that night had bombed Hull. Uffz Hauck and his crew crashed in the vicinity of Eindhoven. Altogether, KG2 lost four Dorniers that night.

On 15/16 July Bernard Thwaites shot down Me 410 U5+CJ of V/KG2, flown by Hptm Friederich-Wilhelm Methner and Uffz Hubert Grube and heading for London, into the sea off Dunkirk. F/O Knowles of 605 Squadron shot down Do 217M-1 U5+KL, flown by Lt Manfred Lieddert of 3./KG2, on 25/26 July, when the target was again Hull. W/C Park of 256 Squadron rounded off the month by shooting down Oblt Helmut Biermann and Uffz Willi Kroger in their Me 410A-1 U5+BJ on 29/30 July, when the target was Brighton. They fell into the sea 20 miles south of Beachy Head.

One of the heaviest losses to befall KG2 in 1943 was on the night of 15/16 August, when it lost seven aircraft – six claimed by Mosquitoes – in a raid on Portsmouth. W/C Park shot Uffz Karl Morgenstern and Uffz Franz Bündgens' Do 217M-1s into the sea off Worthing. Park's third 'kill' of the night occurred when he shot down Uffz Walter Kayser's Do 217M-1. F/S Brearley, also of 256 Squadron, shot down two Do 217Ms over France; Fw Theodor Esslinger fell near Evreux and Lt Franz Bosbach crashed near St André. P/O Rayne Dennis Schultz of 410 (RCAF) Squadron blasted Do 217M-1 U5+GT of 9./KG2 and sent his namesake, Uffz Josef Schultes and his crew to their doom.

On 22/23 August Geoff Howitt of 85 Squadron, now S/L DFC, with P/O J. C. O. Medworth, took off from West Malling at 23:30 hrs in their Mosquito NF.XII and went on patrol. Off Harwich they zeroed in on Fw Walter Hartmann and Obgefr Michael Meurer's Me 410A-1, U5+AF of 15./KG2. Howitt got a visual on the Messerschmitt's bright yellow exhaust emissions and closed in for the kill. It was difficult to get a sight of the sillhouette and at first Howitt thought his prey was a '210. Almost at once a stray searchlight beam illuminated the aircraft and he could quite easily see that it was a '410. With the German crosses easily visible, Howitt gave the Messerschmitt a short burst, and it immediately burst into flames with a brilliant flash. Showers of burning pieces flew past the Mosquito in all directions. U5+AF fell away, its entire starboard wing on fire, and crashed at Chemondiston. Meurer baled out and came down at Stratton Hall, while Hartman's body

was later found in a field, his parachute unopened.

On the night of 24/25 August a Mosquito NF.XII flown by Capt Johan Räd and radio operator Capt Leif Lövestad of 85 Squadron, took off to look for 'trade'. Räd had been an electrical engineering student and a pilot in the Norwegian Air Force Reserve when the Germans had invaded his country. He and fellow engineering student, Per Bugge, went into the Underground movement in Trondheim before setting sail six months later with 11 others for Britain. After nine days meandering around the North Sea and Atlantic Ocean, they had finally landed in Scotland. Lövestad had fought as an observer in the Norwegian Air Force against the Luftwaffe until they had no aircraft left, and had then gone underground, mapping and sketching the airfields the Germans were building, and taking documents out to the coast for friends to smuggle across to England. In August 1941 Lövestad and 29 others crossed to Britain in a dilapidated old boat and landed at Scapa Flow. Lövestad and Räd were joined at West Malling by three fellow countrymen: Claus Björn, Bugge's argumentative radio operator, who had reached England via Sweden, Russia, Japan and the USA, Lt P. Thoren and Lt Tarald Weisteen.

Räd and Lövestad searched the night sky for a 'kill'. Two Me 410s were lost this night, one of which was U5+EG, an Me 410A-1 of 16./KG2, flown by Fw Werner Benner with Uffz Hermann Reimers. Lövestad worked the AI.VIII set and Räd fired four bursts into the '410, which exploded in a ball of fire. Blazing pieces broke off. Two explosions followed and a parachutist was spotted baling out. The victory was officially shared with W/C R. E. X. Mack DFC of 29 Squadron, which claimed two more victories that night; their first Mosquito victories since converting from Beaufighters.

On 6 and 8 September, 85 Squadron destroyed a total of five Fw 190A-5s. On 15/16 September F/O Jarris of 29 Squadron shot down Ofw Horst Müller and Uffz Wolfgang Dose in Me 410A-1 U5+AF of 15./KG2, off Beachy Head during a raid on Cambridge. A 9./KG2 Do 217M-1, flown by Ofw Erich Mosler, was also shot down by F/L Watts of 488 (RNZAF) Squadron into the sea south-east of Ramsgate. F/O Hedgecoe and P/O Witham of 85 Squadron destroyed Ju 88A-14 3E+FP of 6./KG6. The Mosquito was crippled by return fire, and the crew baled out, their aircraft crashing at Tenterden, Kent. F/L Bunting destroyed a Ju 88A-14 of II/KG6.

In October the Norwegians of 85 Squadron figured in two more victories. On 2/3 October P/O Tarald Weisteen, a small, dark and slightly-built pre-war fighter pilot who had flown Gloster Gladiators before escaping to England with Freddie French, destroyed two Do 217Ks during a raid on the Humber Estuary.

On 7/8 October, when the Luftwaffe raided London and Norwich, Leif Lövestad was flying with F/L Bill Maguire, whose usual radio operator, F/O W. D. Jones, was away on a Navigator Leaders' Course. Maguire, who sported a bushy moustache, was an ex-instructor and a fine pilot who before the war had been a milliner. GCI control warned Maguire and Lövestad that two hostile aircraft were flying in line astern and a mile apart when they caught sight of an enemy aircraft in the moonlight showing reddish-yellow wing-tip lights and a white tail light below its starboard quarter. At 2,000 ft distance Fw Georg Slodczyk of 16./KG2 put his Me 410A into a tight turn. In the back seat, Uffz Fritz Westrich must have known there was a Mosquito on their tail. For several minutes Slodczyk and Maguire weaved and manoeuvred violently. Maguire turned tighter each time and was able to identify their prey. He gave the '410 a short burst using deflection and flashes appeared all along the German aircraft's fuselage and wing. Slodczyk desperately pushed his nose down and dived at full speed for the cover of cloud below. Maguire dived after him and pumped another burst into the '410 from 300 yd, just as Slodczyk disappeared into the cloud.

(Westrich's body was picked up off Dungeness on 13 October and buried at sea.)

Below, S/L Bernard Thwaites with Will Clemo, who shot down an Me 410A flown by Fw Wilhelm Sohn and Uffz Günther Keiser of 14./KG2, (which crashed at Ghent) saw Slodczyk and Westrich descend in flames into the sea and were able to confirm Maguire's 'kill'. On 15/16 October Maguire with F/O W. D. Jones, now returned from his Navigator Leaders' Course, shot down Ju 188 3E+RH of 1./KG6, which went into the sea off Clacton, and Ju 188 3E+BL, also of 1./KG6, which crashed at Hemley, Suffolk, to become the first Ju 188 down on land in the UK.

On 8/9 October 85 Squadron claimed their first Ju 88S-1 when 10 intruders flew in from Holland. 3E+US of 8./KG6 was shot down off Foulness by F/O S. V. Holloway and W/O Stanton. F/L Edward Bunting shot down Ju 88S-1 3E+NR of 7./KG6 into the sea 10 miles south of Dover at 20:20 hrs; Fw W. Kaltwasser, Obgefr J. Jakobsen and Uffz J. Bartmuss were all killed. Bunting and F/L C. P. Reed claimed Me 410 U5+LF of 15./KG2 on the night of 17/18 October. Another notable night was that of 10/11 December 1943, when the Luftwaffe attacked Chelmsford. The loss of three of the four Do 217Ms of KG2 on the raid was attributed to F/O Schultz of 410 (RCAF) Squadron.

By 20/21 February 1944 Mosquito night fighters had, since the start of 1943, claimed to have shot down just over 100 Luftwaffe raiders. As the Luftwaffe became short of aircraft, new types, like the Heinkel He 177 Greif (Griffon), were employed. A handful of these bombers had been used during 1942 and some were used on the night of 21/22 January 1944 when 92 enemy bombers headed for London in the first of a series of revenge raids on Britain code-named Operation *Steinbock*.

Chapter Nine

Capricorn Rising

Unteroffizier Ernst Werner lay crouched behind his MG 131 machine gun in the nose of the grey-blue Heinkel He 177A-3 Greif, as it sped noisily and inexorably toward the enemy coast. Soon the dull black undersurfaces of the bomber, converted for night operations against England, began to merge with an invisible sky. A long gondola below the nose, added originally to house the FuG 203 control unit for wing-mounted Hs 293 anti-ship missiles, could station a powerful 75-mm cannon, but this had been replaced by a machine gun to save weight. From the glass nose the 21-year-old bordschutze (gunner) could see the shimmering waters of the English Channel slip by like a blur. His flugzeugfuhrer (pilot), Ofw Wolfgang Ruppe, a Berliner, was, at almost 27 years of age, the oldest of the six-man crew. Uffz Freidrich Beck, the bordfunker (radio operator), had celebrated his twenty-third birthday less than a week before. Fellow Uffz, Georg Lobenz, the kampf beobachter (observer), had just turned 22. Bordschutzen Obgefr Georg Markgraf and Obgefr Bordwart (ground crew), and heckschutz (tail gunner) Obgefr Emil Imm, made up the remaining positions.

A white 'Q' on a black shield painted on the nose of the He 177 served notice that the aircraft belonged to 3./KG100 based at Châteaudun, 40 miles south-south-west of Paris. The third staffel of I/KG100 had arrived at the airfield on 18 December 1943 and had been joined the following day by the first staffel of I/KG40, which had converted to the He 177 from the Focke-Wulf Fw 200 Kondor at Fassberg. Both staffeln had

been placed under the command of Generalmajor Peltz, Angriffsführer (Attack Leader) England, who had assembled a small fleet of all types of bombers and fighter-bombers for dive-bombing over England as retaliation for RAF heavy bomber raids on German towns and cities

Ever since its inception in 1938 the He 177 had been plagued with problems. Six of the eight prototypes had dived into the ground, and 25 of the pre-production models crashed on take-off or as a result of in-flight engine fires. An original specification which insisted that the heavy bomber and ship-killer also be capable of dive-bombing, was partly to blame for its protracted development. Now, at last, on the night of 21 January 1944, the Heinkel was finally being used in the dive-bombing role. After taking off, the He 177 crews normally climbed as high as possible while still over German-controlled airspace on the continent, before penetrating the British defences in a shallow dive at around 400 mph. Even the Mosquito was hard-pressed to deal with these tactics. After making their attack, the He 177s would return home at low-level.

Pathfinders led the bombers, including 15 He 177A-3s of I/KG100, to London, and *Düppel* (German *Window*) was scattered by the attacking force in an effort to confuse the radar defences. The first He 177 to be shot down over the British Isles, He 177A-5 Werk No 15747 of I/KG40, fell to the guns of a Mosquito flown by F/O H. K. Kemp and F/Sgt J. R. Maidment of 151 Squadron from Colerne, crashing at Whitmore Vale, near Hindhead, Surrey. Only the tail

Heinkel He 177A-5 Greif of II/KG40 at Bordeaux-Merigra. On 19 December 1943, 1. Staffel of I/KG40, which had converted to the He 177 from the Fw 200 Kondor at Fassberg, joined 3. Staffel of I/KG100 at Châteaudun, also equipped with the He 177, for Steinbock operations against England. (ARP)

assembly about three feet forward of the fin survived relatively undamaged. F/O Nowell and F/Sgt Randall of 85 Squadron claimed an He 177 of 2./KG40. Altogether, the first *Steinbock* raid cost the Luftwaffe 21 aircraft.

Units were rested until the night of 28/29 January, when 16 Me 410s and 10 Fw 190 fighter-bombers raided East Anglia, Kent and Sussex again. One Me 410 was destroyed by a Mosquito but one of the defending fighters was lost in action. The following night the Luftwaffe force also included He 177s of 3./KG100 and I/KG40. Some 130 of the 285 enemy aircraft tracks penetrated inland, 30 reaching London. Bombs were dropped in a wide swathe across Hampshire, the Thames Estuary and Suffolk. A Mosquito of 410 (RCAF) Squadron, flown by Lt R. P. Cross (RNVR) and Sub/Lt L. A. Wilde (RNVR) and equipped with AI.VIII radar, was just gaining height after taking off from Castle Camps at 20:30 hrs when they received a vector from F/L Parr at GCI Control at Trimley Heath. A 'bogey' had been picked up on radar, and Parr told Cross to climb to 15,000 ft. Wilde picked up the 'ban-

dit' (a Ju 88) at 20:39 hrs, three miles distant (the AI.VIII radar set had a range of 6½ miles straight ahead), flying west. Cross closed in behind the unsuspecting raider. A 5-min chase ensued and finished with Cross lifting his nose up and blasting the Junkers with two short bursts of 20-mm cannon fire. Cross and Wilde did not see any hits on the Ju 88 when firing. A Ju 88A of 3./KG54, which crashed at Barham, Suffolk, about this time, fell to a 68 Squadron Beaufighter.

On the night of 3/4 February 240 enemy aircraft operated in two phases over London and south-eastern England. 95 went inland, 17 reached London, and 14 were lost. They were met by six squadrons of Mosquitoes. 410 (RCAF) Squadron got six Mosquito NF.XIIIs off from Castle Camps. Canadians F/O E. S. Fox and F/O C. D. Sibbett took off at 04:00 hrs and were vectored by Sgt Burton at GCI Trimley, who gave them a 'bandit' crossing starboard to port. Sibbett worked his AI.VIII radar set until he obtained a contact 3½ miles distant at 18,000 ft. Fox turned to port and closed to 2,000 ft. The German intruder was dropping *Düppel* and Sibbett lost contact

Dornier Do 217K-1 of Lufflotte 2 in flight. On 3/4 February 1944, when about 60 German intruders pene-trated south-east England and London, three Do 217s fell to Mosquito crews. (via ARP)

temporarily as his screen became cluttered with pulses. He radioed Control but before they could respond, contact was regained and Fox set off in pursuit.

The Mosquito pilot closed to 200 ft and the German, a Do 217, immediately began violent evasive action to shake off his pursuer. Fox gave the Dornier a one-second burst but the shells missed as he peeled off to starboard. Fox turned right, then left, and regained contact again. He stalked the enemy bomber for 10 min and maintained visual contact despite continued violent evasive action on the part of the German pilot. The Canadian closed to 200 ft and gave him a two-second burst. A large piece flew off the enemy aircraft and it exploded. Fox orbited and watched the flaming wreckage hurtle down into the sea. It impacted and exploded with such force that the tops of the clouds were illuminated over a wide area. (The only Do 217M-1 lost this night came from 8./KG2 – U5 + JR – but crews of 85, 410 and 488 Squadrons each claimed one!)

Fellow Canadians F/O W. G. Dinsdale and his observer, F/Sgt J. E. Dunn, also of 410 (RCAF) Squadron, picked up a radar contact and closed to 2,000 ft, slightly below the 'bandit' which was flying at 15,000 ft at about 220 mph near Stapleford Tawney. Dinsdale drew to the left to prevent overshooting his prey. It was a Ju 88 flying straight and level, seemingly oblivious to the Mosquito's presence. However, just as Dinsdale turned into an attacking position, the Ju 88 peeled off violently to port and headed directly for them! It flew dangerously close underneath and its fin or tailplane clipped the Mosquito's starboard pro-

peller as it passed. Dinsdale temporarily lost control, regained it again, and dived the aircraft to the left. Despite Dunn getting several more contacts, the enemy aircraft disappeared before the Canadians could attack again. They could only claim a 'damaged'.

A Mosquito NF.XIII, flown by F/O H. B. Thomas and W/O C. B. Hamilton of 85 Squadron at Biggin Hill, was climbing to 20,000 ft when they received a vector from the Sandwich controller to intercept two contacts. One turned out to be a friendly fighter and the hunt was called off. Then another contact was obtained and the hunt was on again. This time it was a German bomber. At 1,500 ft distance the 'bandit' was made out to be a Do 217. Thomas closed from 300 to 100 yd before opening fire. In three very short bursts, each lasting just 2½ seconds, 120 20-mm rounds were pumped into the hapless Dornier. Thomas observed strikes, and with the third burst the Dornier exploded and the starboard engine erupted in flames. Thomas broke off, his windscreen covered in oil, and watched the German aircraft fall away, well alight. It, too, hit the sea and lit up the clouds with an orange glow. Thomas and Hamilton returned to Biggin and were told to orbit the station as 'hostiles' had been reported overhead, but flying debris from the Dornier had penetrated the Mosquito's port engine and five miles west of the base Thomas feathered the propeller and landed.

The fourth 'kill' of the night went to Dutchman F/Sgt C. J. Vlotman and his navigator, Sgt J. L. Wood, of 488 (RNZAF) Squadron at Bradwell Bay. On his AI.VIII, Wood picked up a

Do 217 gently weaving at 17,000 ft, 2½ miles distant. Vlotman was directed by ground control until he was able to make contact at about 1,000 yd. The Dutchman closed to 300 yd dead astern and let fly with his four 20-mm cannon. His port inner stopped, fouled by loose rounds, but the shells had done their work. The Dornier peeled off to port, its left side and engine aflame. Vlotman followed the stricken fighter-bomber down and gave it two more short bursts to make the 'kill' certain. It spun violently down, shedding pieces of debris. The enemy cockpit was well alight and no crew were seen to bale out as it went down over the North Sea, 40 miles off Foulness Point, Essex.

The fourth major *Steinbock* attack took place on the night of 13/14 February, and Mosquitoes were again triumphant. S/L Somerville of 410 Squadron destroyed Ju 88S-1 Z6+HH of Maj Helmut Schmidt's I/KG66 pathfinder unit, and it fell at 21.10 hrs at Havering-Atte-Bower, Essex. It was hit by AA gunfire. F/O Schultz bagged a Ju 188, as did a 96 Squadron pilot and F/L

Edward Bunting, now of 488 (RNZAF) Squadron. A total of eight enemy aircraft failed to return. Five Ju88s from KG6 went into the sea, and a Ju 188 crashed in France on return. Altogether, the *Capricorn* raiders attacked targets in Britain on eight nights in February, including a devastating raid on London on the 18th whose success owed much to the Ju 88 pathfinders of KG6 and KG66. Fortunately for British civilians, the intended wholesale use of V1 flying bombs had not materialized, and Luftwaffe morale was further sapped by the poor performance of the He 177.

On the night of 20/21 February, 95 German raiders crossed the English coast between Hythe and Harwich, heading for London. Mosquitoes of 25 Squadron, which had arrived at RAF Coltishall near Norwich on 5 February, were alerted. At 21:10 hrs P/O J. R. Brockbank and his navigator-radio operator, P/O D. McCausland, took off in their Mosquito NF.XVII, code-named *Grampus 16*. F/L Joe Singleton and his observer, F/O W. G. 'Geoff' Haslam, also took off at about

In February 1944 125 Squadron at Valley began replacing its Beaufighters with the Mosquito NF.XVII. On 11 February pilot Bill Gill and his navigator, Des Hatchins, were in the circuit at Valley when a Botha trailing a drogue cable sliced six feet off the starboard wing of their Mosquito. Gill put down safely and three days later the repaired Mosquito was flying again. In April–May 1944, 125 squadron claimed 10 victories while engaged in the night defence of Great Britain. (AVM Bill Gill)

the same time. Both aircraft were equipped with AI.X radar, and a Mosquito NF.XVII had yet to shoot down an enemy aircraft at night. As soon as they cleared the circuit both aircraft were handed over to GCI at Neatishead, from where the controllers gave them their instructions. *Grampus 16* was told to climb to 17,000 ft while Singleton (*Grampus 20)* was ordered to climb to *Angels 18* (18,000 ft). At 21:43 hrs he was passed on to the Chain Home Low (Radar) Station at Happisburgh who gave him new vectors after they had picked up a 'bogey' going eastwards at *Angels 10.*

Meanwhile, at 21:37 hrs, Brockbank and McCausland obtained a contact, at seven miles range, on an aircraft crossing from left to right. Brockbank throttled to 2,650 revs at +4 boost and gained gradually on the target. His prey was Ju 188E-1 U5+LN flown by Lt Ewald Bohe of 5/KG2. Bohe weaved gently at first and then made more violent manoeuvres in an effort to shake off the Mosquito. Brockbank closed in several times to 1,000 ft, but he could not get a visual on the target and was forced to break off each time. McCausland lost contact but Neatishead restored it after a further vector. At this point a single searchlight pierced the gaps in the cloud and illuminated the fighter. Bohe 'corskscrewed' violently and tried to outdistance his pursuer, but Brockbank stuck doggedly to his task, chasing the German for 25 min, gradually closing the gap. At 600 ft he could make out the

enemy's exhaust glows. The Ju 188E crossed gently from port to starboard, and as it was crossing back Brockbank fired two short bursts. Tenaciously, he closed to 75 ft and poured more rounds into the hapless German. It caught fire, flew straight and level for a few seconds and, blazing furiously, commenced a deep death dive through the clouds to crash at Park Farm, Wickham St. Paul, Essex. Both the artificial horizon and direction indicator aboard the Mosquito were put out of action after the cannon were fired, so *Grampus 16* headed back to Coltishall where the time of the 'kill', 22:03 hrs, was logged; the first 'kill' attributed to a Mosquito NF.XVII.

Singleton, meanwhile, had pursued his enemy aircraft at 9,000 ft over the sea to 50 miles east of Lowestoft. Haslam used night binoculars to make a positive identification of the enemy aircraft. (It was Do 217K-1 U5+AR of 7./KG2). At 22:36 hrs Singleton despatched Oblt Wolfgang Brendel and his crew into the sea with a two-second burst from dead astern. Brendel, Fw Bruno Preker, Ofw Bruno Schneider and Uffz Heinz Grudßus, were all posted as 'Missing'. Then Singleton and Haslam picked up the chase again and pursued Uffz Walter Schmidt's KG2 Do 217M-1 to within 20 miles of the Dutch coast before they had to return to Coltishall, low on petrol. All in all, a successful night for the Battle of Britain station, and the first 'kill' to be attributed to a Mosquito Mk XVII.

An He 177 at Châteaudun, 40 miles south-south-west of Paris, and similar to the 3./KG100 He 177A-3 based at Châteaudun and flown by flugzeugführer Ofw Wolfgang Ruppe and his crew on the fateful night of 22/23 February 1944. (via Jean-Louis Roba)

The following night, 22/23 February, He 177s of I/KG100 based at Rheine and 3./KG100 from Châteaudun, were included in the all-out assault on England. Wolfgang Ruppe's 3./KG100 bomber was among those nearing landfall over Suffolk. Very shortly, the young crew, average age just over 22 years, would have an opportunity to drop their bombs on an English town or city. Operation *Steinbock* had been masterminded as retribution for the Allied bombing of German cities, and each raid carried out by the Kampfgeschwaders normally bore emotive codenames like *Munich* and *Hamburg* to remind the Luftwaffe crews that they were embarked on revenge raids for the round-the-clock bombing of centres of German population. Ernst Werner's home town was Saarbrucken. Georg Lobenz, the observer, came from Moosbach. Freidrich Beck, sitting at his radio set, was from Würzburg; while Georg Markgraf and Emil Imm, manning their gun-sighting positions from behind their MG 81, '131 and '151 machine guns and cannon, were from Bahrdorf and Freiburg respectively. Ruppe was from the Charlottenburg district of Berlin. The capital had been bombed repeatedly by RAF Bomber Command and soon it would suffer a new *Luftangriff,* with high explosive dropped by the US 8th and 15th AFs being added to that of RAF Bomber Command.

At around 10,000 ft the cloud was fairly thick, but above it the atmosphere was clear and starry. Everything was going according to plan. Even the powerplants – two coupled, inverted V-12 Daimler-Benz DB610s geared to each four-bladed propeller unit – were functioning well. Ruppe and his crew had not forgotten the endless transmission and cooling problems the engines had caused since the Gruppen had converted to the He 177. In the aircraft's bomb bay nestled four 1,000-kg high explosive bombs and 42 flares (no external bomb carriers were fitted), which, in a deadly harbinger of doom, would rain down on an unsuspecting population and be followed by hundreds of tons of high explosive. In the cockpit a set of four painted bomb levers – one for bomb jettisoning and three for bomb door opening – were in the 'Off' position. Lobenz intended to drop his bombs before the night was over. The only way Ruppe and his men would be stopped now was if they were shot down by flak or caught by one of the deadly 'Moskitos'.

Mosquito night fighter teams like F/L Bill Baillie and his navigator-radio operator, F/O Simpson, were always on the lookout for 'bogies' in their part of the sky. They had taken off from Coltishall at 21:25 hrs and had not been on patrol long when F/O Humphries, one of the controllers at the radar station at Happisburgh, told them that there was the possibility of 'trade' south-west, travelling west about 20 miles away. They were vectored to within three miles of the contact when the radar station said they could not give much more help. At three minutes after midnight Simpson picked up two blips on his AI.X cathode ray screen at two miles range, 10–15° above at 17,000 ft. Baillie set off in hot pursuit and within minutes had narrowed the range to just 2,000 ft. He could see the exhausts and resins of the rear aircraft. At this point the rear blip veered away to the left and the other went slightly to the right as the enemy aircraft carried out mild evasive action. Had they picked up the Mosquito's presence? Baillie and Simpson peered ahead through the narrow windscreen of their fighter. Immediately they looked away, dazzled momentarily by groping searchlight beams which bathed the Mosquito in bright light before they were eventually extinguished.

Their night vision restored, Baillie and Simpson strained in the direction of where their quarry should be. Baillie narrowed the gap, closing to 400 yd from the blip. And there it was! At 14,000 ft they made out a rough outline against the night sky; a large black silhouette of fuselage and engines ploughing along, intent on death and destruction. It motored on as if it owned the sky. Even the exhausts emitted no flames. They were at one with the black expanse and dark grey cloud shapes. Baillie stared intently. 'It's a Dornier Do 217,' he reported, and closed to just 200 ft astern. Surely Emil Imm, holding his MG 151 20-mm cannon tightly in his gloved hands in his cramped tail turret, could not fail to spot their adversary? It was just 23 minutes after midnight. Baillie opened up. Any later and he would have overshot. A fusillade of 60 HEI rounds and 62 semi-armour-piercing incendiaries blasted into the enormous shape in front of him. Baillie broke sharply away to the right in a stomach-wrenching turn as pieces of flying debris ripped into the soft fabric of his wings and fuselage. He was that close. None of the gunners, not even Emil Imm, who was closest, had time to fire their weapons. Ironically, in what to Imm might have appeared a parting shot or a salute to a fallen foe, Baillie's cannon inadvertently fired again in the momentum of the broken-off attack.

The front fuselage section of the He 177, with the black shield motif that had failed to do its magic, disintegrated in the air and fell to earth, its umbilical link with Imm in the tail severed completely. The doomed souls of He 177A-3 5J+QL fell to their deaths trapped like drowning men aboard a sinking ship. Like a ruthless assassin intent on their destruction, unseen *g* forces exerted superhuman strength, pinning them in their seats, holding them, crushing them, until the impact finally released the hold it had exerted briefly but significantly over the young Germans. The wreckage fell in the vicinity of Wolsey House Farm, Yoxford and lay scattered over an area about a quarter of a mile across. Trapped and frightened beyond belief, Emil Imm floated down in his 'flying bomb' – a turret with an empennage – and waited helplessly for the merciful impact.

It was 09:45 on the morning of Wednesday, 23 February when Kenneth Kiddle and John Chapman, farm labourers laying drainpipes, discovered the tail of the He 177 1¼ miles from the rest of the wreckage, in a field at Park Gate Farm, Kelsale. Kiddle had been at work several hours when he happened to look through a hedge and spot the tail with a swastika on it. Ten hours had passed since the German bomber's demise. Unbelievably, Imm was alive; stiff with cold, semi-conscious and badly shocked – but alive! Kiddle revived the young German airman with tea from his flask. Imm murmured 'Coffee'. Police Constable Sidney Meadows arrived at the scene to find the rear gunner semi-conscious in his seat. With the help of the two labourers he extricated Imm from the tail, rendered what aid they could, and sent for assistance. An RAF officer said later: 'He made a perfect landing. The tail unit must have acted like a glider. There were no marks whatever on the shield.'

The bomber with the black shield and the white 'Q' containing the remains of Ruppe and his four other comrades, was crumpled and broken like the black shield of Bosworth Field, where, too, the dead and dying had lain after battle. Meadows reported:

The cockpit containing four men landed in a ditch about 100 yd north-west of the main part of the plane. Both these parts of the machine were blazing furiously and there was a large quantity of ammunition and incendiaries exploding in the cockpit. There was absolutely no hope of extricating these four men who were pinned inside the framework of the cockpit. No one could approach them for exploding ammunition and blazing wreckage. In my opinion these men were killed when the cockpit struck the ground as, by the position of the bodies, they had made no attempt to escape.

Later that day PC Twite of Kelsale arrived and later, PC Allum of Westleton. A search was made and about 11 a.m., another member of the crew [Uffz Ernst Werner] was found dead in a field at Wolsey Farm, about 400 yd south of the main part of the plane. In the afternoon the remains of the four men were recovered from the burnt-out wreckage of the cockpit. The heads of all four bodies were burnt off; also the greater part of the arms. One body was minus a leg. The missing limbs were burnt to ashes. The bodies were unidentifiable.

Emil Imm, the heck-schutz, was taken to a Temporary Clearance Station at Saxmundham and then moved to Colchester Military Hospital. He lived to see his 22nd birthday, on 26 March, and was reported later to be in 'an English POW camp'. Operation *Steinbock* itself would finish a few weeks later, on 29 May. Meanwhile, a communal grave was dug at Yoxford Cemetery and on Friday, 25 February the coffins containing the bodies were conveyed from Wolsey Farm by two RAF tenders from RAF Darsham for the funeral. Officers and men from Darsham acted as bearers. After the coffins had been lowered into the grave the officers stepped up and saluted. The bodies in four of the coffins were unknown. The only flier to have been positively identified was Uffz Ernst Werner; Birthplace: Saarbrucken, 20 January 1923.

He had been born under the sign of Capricorn.

Chapter Ten

The 'Baby Blitz'

Oberfeldwebel Ruppe's He 177 was one of 150 Luftwaffe bombers which crossed East Anglia on the night of 22/23 February 1944. By and large they got through. Only two Me 410s were lost. One fell to Caldwell and Rawling of 96 Squadron at Framfield, Sussex; the other to AA fire at Radnage, Buckinghamshire. S/L C. A. S. Anderson with his observer, F/Sgt G. P. I. Bodard, of 410 (RCAF) Squadron, were on interception patrol at 20,000 ft in their Mosquito NF.XIII from Castle Camps when they were vectored north by Trimley GCI, who told them to climb to 23,000 ft to investigate a 'bogey' near Earls Colne. Trimley told the two Canadians to descend to 18,000 ft and it was at this point that Anderson and Bodard made contact. A German raider was flying along two miles in the distance, well below the height of the approaching Mosquito. The Trimley controller had done his job well.

Anderson closed but before he could line up his guns he had overshot the bomber. He orbited and Bodard picked up the 'bogey' on his screen again, range 1/2-mile, and still below. The same thing happened again! Anderson orbited a second time and Bodard made contact, range 3/4-mile. Anderson closed slowly this time, to 500 ft, and obtained a visual. The twin-engined enemy machine began carrying out a wild evasive action and visual contact was lost several times until Bodard managed to hold the contact and Anderson could close to 50 ft. It was a Ju 88A-4 of 9./KG6, one which had taken off from Melsbroek to bomb London.

Astern and below, Anderson lined up to fire.

Just as he was about to launch a fusillade of 20-mm cannon and HEI rounds, the Ju 88 pilot peeled off violently to the left and spoiled his aim. However, Anderson managed to get in a short burst from 150 ft and he was pleased to see some of the rounds find their mark on the fuselage and starboard engine, which caught fire. The Junkers levelled out and Anderson attacked again, this time from 75 yd. The stricken bomber was hit further and the German crew, impotent it seemed, must have known they were doomed. The pilot refused to give up the struggle, however, and turned to the right as Anderson pumped more shells into the target. Small explosions danced on the Junkers' fuselage and, finally, it burst into flames. It spun away into the night and broke up before plunging into the North Sea.

Bodard returned to Trimley GCI control. F/L Carr calmly informed the Mosquito crew to go to 17,000 ft; he had picked up another 'bogey' over Essex. Range, three miles. Anderson closed in while climbing, but the enemy aircraft was too high and he undershot. Bodard lost contact and asked Trimley for help. Carr gave them a vector of 270° and Anderson closed on the enemy to 500 ft. A visual was obtained but this 'kill' was not going to be any easier than the previous one and the enemy pilot immediately carried out evasive action. Contact was maintained, however, and Anderson closed to 150 ft, keeping underneath and to one side, just to be on the safe side. The two Canadians made the bomber out to be a Ju 188E-1. Immediately, the German bomber dived to the left. Anderson gave a short burst from 50 yd and the rounds struck home on

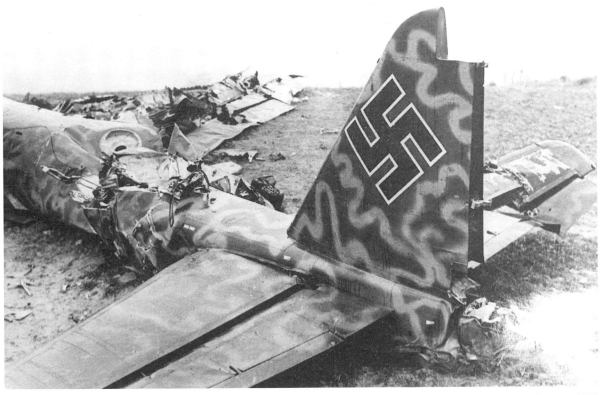

On the night of 24/25 February 1944, this Ju 88A-4 of 8./KG6 was downed by F/L R. C. Pargeter and F/L R. L. Fell of 29 Squadron at Withyham; one of six 'kills' claimed by the squadron that night. (ARP)

the side of the Junkers' fuselage and wings. The wounded animal took further violent evasive action and lost height, but the Mosquito crew would not be shaken from their stride. Anderson pumped more bursts into the Junkers and a fusillade which struck the cockpit area seemed to signal the end of the German bomber. It dived steeply, levelled out momentarily and finally spun in, out of control. Anderson followed it down and pulled out at 6,000 ft when he recognized that the Junkers was finished.

With characteristic understatement, Britons by now called the Operation *Steinbock* raids the 'Baby Blitz'. Mosquito night fighter crews encountered all manner of German bomber and fighter types, including Do 217s, Me 410s, and even the occasional Fw 190 and He 177. On 23/24 February three enemy aircraft were lost and a Do 217 fell to AA fire. The following night Mosquito crews claimed three 'probables' and eight enemy aircraft shot down. One was a Ju 88A-4 of 8./KG6 downed by F/Lt R. C. Pargeter

and F/Lt R. L. Fell of 29 Squadron (which claimed six this night) at Withyham, Sussex. A 3./KG100 *Greif* was shot down by F/L P. F. L. Hall and F/O R. D. Marriott of 488 Squadron and it fell at Lamberhurst, Kent. *Steinbock* raids continued over East Anglia and London throughout the remainder of February and into March. The 'Baby Blitz' showed no sign of easing up and 70 aircraft attempted to bomb London on 1 March. Only 10 managed to evade the defences and reach the capital, however.

On the night of 14/15 March, 140 German raiders crossed the coast of eastern England in four waves. Two-thirds of the force crossed between Cromer in Norfolk and Shoeburyness, Essex, while a smaller wave crossed over Sussex. Some of the bomber force used skill and daring to infiltrate British airspace under cover of returning Mosquitoes, and *Düppel* was dropped to complete their disguised approach. Most of the invading bombers crossed the coast between Great Yarmouth and Southwold at heights rang-

F/L Joe Singleton DFC (left) and F/O Geoff Haslam of 25 Squadron who shot down a Do 217 on the night of 20/21 February 1944, and added further victories on 19/20 March. (W/C J. Singleton)

ing from 14,000–24,000 ft, before turning south for London and its environs. The incursions were met in some strength by a determined force of Mosquitoes. Seven of 410 (RCAF) Squadron at Castle Camps were scrambled to intercept. Lt Harrington (USAAF) and Sgt D. G. Tongue destroyed Ju 88A-14 B3+CK from 2./KG54. It fell at Hildenborough, Kent, and S/L Green got a Ju 88. Ju 188E-1 U5+BM, flown by Lt Horst Becker of 4./KG6, fell to the guns of F/L Edward Bunting of 488 (RNZAF) Squadron. It broke up

in the air and crashed in flames at White House Farm, Great Leighs, near Chelmsford. Becker, Uffz G. Bartolain, Uffz A. Lange, Uffz G. Goecking and Ofw H. Litschke, were killed.

Meanwhile, Joe Singleton and his observer, F/O Geoff Haslam, of 25 Squadron had taken off from Coltishall at 21:05 hrs for a *Bullseye* exercise (when training aircraft from the bomber OTUs were engaged by the sector searchlights and subjected to dummy attacks by night fighters). Singleton had just returned to the squadron after instructing, being promoted to F/L and receiving the DFC. Sector Control passed them on to Neatishead GCI. At 18,000 ft Singleton asked his controller if there was any 'trade'? There were 'possibilities', came the reply, and a few minutes later, on a vector of 140°, Singleton and Haslam obtained a head-on contact at 4½ miles. Singleton went in pursuit, guided by Haslam. Haslam was able to make contact and hold it. The enemy plane was at about 16,000 ft, flying along at approximately 240 mph. The two men observed that it was taking the normal 'corkscrew' evasive action. Singleton closed to 1,000 ft. Haslam raised his night binoculars to his eyes. 'It's a Ju 88!' he said.

At this the Mosquito went in closer until Singleton was within 75 yd of his quarry. A three second burst of 20-mm cannon – less than 120 rounds – produced a big explosion. Fire erupted on the left-hand side of the Junkers' fuselage, and Haslam and Singleton could quite clearly see the black crosses on the underside of the port wing as the stricken bomber toppled over and fell, burning fiercely. The leading-edge of the Mosquito's starboard mainplane took some of the flying debris from the doomed '88 as it disappeared into 8/10ths cloud at 5,000 ft. Almost immediately, the clouds were illuminated by the blaze from the Junkers, which crashed into the North Sea five miles east of Southwold. (The Ju 88 was from KG30, which lost a second aircraft this night.)

On 19/20 March, Singleton and Haslam were among the aircrews at readiness in 25 Squadron at Coltishall who were alerted to intercept a force of about 90 bombers over the North Sea, heading for Hull.

Singleton and Haslam had taken off from Coltishall at 20:55 hrs in Mosquito NF.XVII

HK255. Neatishead radar told them to 'hurry and climb to 16,000ft' as a contact had been made. At about 8,000 ft the CHL station at Happisburgh gave them a vector towards 12 'bandits' crossing up ahead of them. At 16,000 ft Haslam established contact on his American-made AI.X radar at 8½ miles range (the AI.X set had a range of 8–10 miles in an arc at most altitudes). Singleton wrote later:

We turned to port and followed, closed the range and obtained visual 10° above at 1,600 ft. We identified it as a Junkers and closed to about 100 yd. I gave him a 2½-second burst from dead astern. It exploded. As we were still closing we had to pull up steeply to avoid collision; debris from the enemy aircraft spattered our aircraft. We orbited and watched the enemy aircraft go down in a steep dive to port in flames. When it had dropped to about 5,000 ft it broke up completely, and several burning pieces hit the sea, and cast a glow over a wide area.

Their first victory of the night had gone down at 21:20 hrs, 56 miles NNE Cromer. After fixing the position with Neatishead, Singleton and Haslam were given a vector by Happisburgh. Haslam got a contact at 4½ miles range, crossing slowly from right to left. Singleton closed in behind and slightly below the intruder and obtained a visual at about 1,500 ft. The unsuspecting machine (Ju 88) was not making any evasive manoeuvres. At 21:27 hrs, Singleton took careful aim from 100 yd dead astern and fired a 2½-second burst. The centre of the Ju 88's fuselage exploded and the aircraft went down almost vertically before it fell into The Wash, where it continued to burn fiercely on the surface for a few seconds. Singleton orbited the scene and obtained a fix of the position from Neatishead, 65 miles NNE Cromer.

Almost immediately, Haslam obtained a third contact, at four miles range. He watched it crossing hard right to left on the scope of his AI.X and directed Singleton accordingly. The pilot made a hard turn left and followed the blip at 230 IAS and at a height of 16,000 ft. This Ju 88 put up a fight. It carried out a series of quite violent evasive manoeuvres and changed height several times as the Mosquito closed to 1,500 ft. At 21:33 hrs Singleton fired a 2½-second burst at 125 yd dead astern. The German's starboard engine emitted a myriad of sparks which danced along the nacelle until it erupted in flames. The Ju 88 pilot fought frantically, but uselessly, with the controls as his aircraft dived like a shot pheasant. Singleton delivered the *coup de grâce*

One down, two to go! An artist's depiction of the first of the three Ju 88 victories, all in the space of just 13 minutes, scored by F/L Singleton DFC and F/O Haslam on the night of 19/20 March 1944. (via W/C J. Singleton)

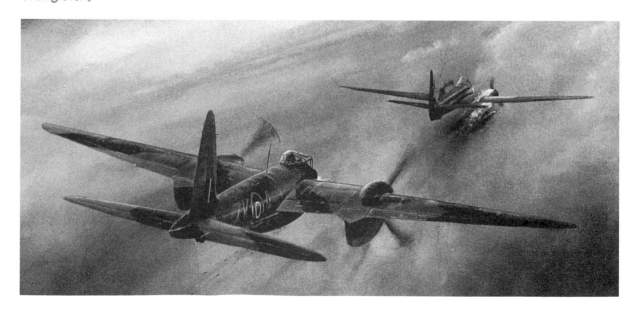

1. F/Sgt Glossop
2. F/Sgt Christian
3. F/Sgt Tait
4. P/O Travers
5. F/Sgt Greenwell
6. F/Sgt Pickles
7. F/Lt Grieves DFC
8. F/O Henderson
9. F/Sgt Hitchcock
10. Sgt Noble
11. F/O Young
12. P/O Wilson
13. F/Lt Irwin
14. F/Lt Singleton DFC
15. F/O Gibbs
16. Sub/Lt Smith
17. F/O Robins DFC
18. F/O Harwood
19. F/O Gray
20. Lt Green
21. Sub/Lt Franck
22. S/L Mitchell
23. F/O Brockbank
25. F/O McCausland
26. F/O Cox
27. Wg/Cdr Wight-
     Boycott DSO
28. F/O Butt
29. F/O Haslam
30. S/L Baker
31. P/O Franklin
32. F/L Carr
33. P/O (?)
34. F/Sgt Patterson
35. W/O Barnard
36. F/Sgt Hutchings
37. F/O Carne
38. Lt Toynbee
39. W/O Cragg
40. F/L Baillie
41. P/O Simpson
42. F/O Linthune
43. F/Lt Saunders DFC
44. F/O Hamilton
45. Lt Teuton
46. F/O Saunderson
47. P/O Carter (?)
48. F/O Cumbers DFM
49. P/O George
50. Sub/Lt Adams
51. F/O Melville
52. F/Sgt (?)
53. 'Popski'

25 Squadron pilots and navigators. (W/C J. Singleton)

with a 3-second burst at 500-600 yd range and the aircraft disintegrated into a blazing inferno. Burning debris flew off in all directions as it plummeted into the sea, 63 miles NNE Cromer at 21:33 hrs. The water engulfed the flaming bomber and eventually snuffed out its flames and the lives of the crew – if they were not already dead.

Singleton levelled out, but both engines were running very roughly. The needle on the port radiator dial quivered on 140º, while the starboard indicated 120º. Singleton immediately throttled back, opened his radiator flaps and succeeded in cooling the engines slightly. Happisburgh were informed by radio that the 'Mossie' had engine trouble, and they responded quickly by giving the ailing night fighter a vector and telling the crew to go over to GCI at Neatishead. They crossed the coast at 5,000 ft. By now the port engine was very hot and was emitting a succession of sparks, so Singleton feathered the prop. He flew on towards Coltishall with both engines throttled as far back as was practical without losing too much height. The radiator temperatures were by now reading 130–140º and he told Haslam to get ready to bale out.

Singleton called Coltishall and asked for the aerodrome lighting to be switched on so he could see the base from the coast and make a direct approach. Both engines were still running, but very roughly, and the aircraft was gradually losing height. Singleton had decided to land with wheels and flaps up. At about 1,000 ft, the starboard engine seized and burst into flames. Haslam operated the starboard engine fire extinguisher while Singleton switched on the port landing light. He tried to get more power from the port engine, but this also seized. At 140 mph Singleton levelled out and suddenly felt the aircraft hit the ground. Haslam opened the top hatch and jumped out; Singleton followed a few seconds behind him. They ran about 25 yd from the wrecked Mosquito, which had come down at Sco Ruston, half a mile from Coltishall, and sat down.

Singleton saw that the engines were burning at the cylinder heads and went back and climbed into the cockpit to switch off petrol and other switches and look for the fire extinguisher. He could not find it, so he clambered down and threw clodfulls of earth onto the engines and had extinguished the flames in the starboard Merlin by the time the fire tender and ambulance arrived. Singleton and Haslam were treated for slight head injuries. On examination, it was found that the engine trouble was caused by both glycol tanks, which had been holed by flying debris from the Ju 88. Singleton and Haslam's three Ju 88 victories (probably all from II/KG30), which they destroyed in the space of an incredible 13 minutes, and the loss of six other aircraft, could have done little for the morale of the Luftwaffe raiders. They aborted the raid and no bombs fell on Hull! One of two Do 217s of 2./KG2 destroyed was shot down by a Mosquito of 264 Squadron and crashed at Legbourne, Lincolnshire, at 22.04 hours. An He 177A-3 of 2./KG100 was destroyed by a Mosquito of 25 Squadron and crashed into the sea off Skegness at 21.46 hours. Two other Ju 88s, one from

On 21/22 March 1944 F/O S. B. Huppert and P/O J. S. Christie of 410 (RCAF) Squadron, in Mosquito HK456, shot down a Ju 88A-4 of 4./KG30 at Latchingdon, Essex. On 3 July 1944, Huppert, in MM570, destroyed a Ju 188 and an Me 410, before being shot down by defensive fire from the Hornisse. (ARP)

This was taken in the Mess at RAF Coltishall around midnight on 19 March 1944, following Singleton and Haslam's crash half a mile from the Station at the end of their successful operation when they destroyed three Ju 88s in quick succession. From left, F/O Franklin, F/O Grey, F/L Singleton DFC, ?, Harwood, and F/O Haslam.

II/KG54, and a Ju 188 of 2./KG66, crashed into the sea near the Humber Lightship. Next day, C-in-C Fighter Command, AM Sir Roderick Hill visited Coltishall and Singleton was awarded the DSO. He finished the war with seven aircraft 'kills'.

On 21/22 March 25 Squadron Mosquitoes were on patrol again as raiders attempted another strike on London. Some 95 aircraft crossed the Suffolk coastline and headed towards an area south-east of Cambridge where they were to make their turn south and head for the capital. Part of the force acted as a diversion, approaching between Great Yarmouth and Felixstowe. Two Ju 88s, flying at 23,000 ft, were intercepted by F/L R. L. Davies and his navigator, F/O B. Bent, aloft in their Mosquito NF.XVII from Coltishall. Davies shot down the first '88 into the sea 35 miles south-east of Lowestoft. Two of the crew parachuted out before the aircraft disintegrated and disappeared into cloud at about 7,000 ft. The second Ju 88 gave its presence away by firing a Chandelier flare and was promptly

despatched into the sea 25 miles south-east of Southwold. (Two Ju 88s of II/KG54 and a Ju 88 from 7./KG6 were lost this night.) Meanwhile, Fw 190s and Me 410s had taken off from bases in France and were also *en route* to London. 410 (RCAF) and 488 (RNZAF) Squadrons orbited over their patrol sectors until directed by their GCI stations on intercept paths. A 410 (RCAF) Squadron Mosquito flown by F/O S. B. Huppert and P/O J. S. Christie, shot down a Ju 88A-4 of 4./KG30 at Latchingdon, Essex and a 456 (RAAF) Squadron Mosquito destroyed a Ju 88 off the south coast; but there was also plenty of 'trade' over Essex for the marauding Mosquitoes of 488 (RNZAF) Squadron at Bradwell Bay.

F/Sgt C. J. Vlotman and his navigator-radio operator, Sgt Wood, were scrambled at 23:35 hrs under Trimley Control. F/L Parr vectored them towards the incoming raiders over the sea near Herne Bay. At about 500 ft range they spotted a Ju 188, which was the leading aircraft of the attack, dropping *Düppel* in profusion. Vlotman opened fire from dead astern and despatched the

Junkers into the sea. He was next directed to another contact heading in a westerly direction. The controller vectored him to within six miles of the aircraft, a Ju 88 of II/KG54, which was flying at 16,500 ft. Vlotman approached slowly, got to within 500 yd and, although he could not positively identify it, could quite clearly see that the enemy machine was dropping vast quantities of *Düppel*. Vlotman opened fire with his four cannon from 200 yd. The Ju 88 shuddered under the impact of the rounds and fell into the sea near Herne Bay. Fragments of metal and Plexiglas peppered the dome and radiator of the Mosquito and holed the starboard glycol tank. Coolant spilled away into the night, and when the glycol temperature rose to 150° Vlotman knew it was time to feather the starboard engine. He landed

back at Bradwell on one engine, none the worse for wear.

S/L Edward Bunting, now a DFC in 488 (RNZAF) Squadron, with his navigator, F/L C. P. Reed DFC, had also been scrambled from Bradwell. Bunting obtained a contact at 1¾ miles, slightly above, and immediately went below. He throttled right back and closed rapidly to 2,000 ft on a Ju 88A-4 dropping *Düppel*. Searchlights flicked on and a shaft of bright white light latched onto the enemy aircraft and held it. 4D+AT, flown by Ofw Nikolaus Mayer, was a 9./KG30 machine from Varêlbusch. Other beams coned Bunting's Mosquito. As Reed radioed for a 'douse', Mayer wriggled and wrestled like a caged predator in his attempt to escape the groping fingers of light, before finally elud-

S/L Edward Bunting and F/L C. P. Reed DFC of 488 (RNZAF) Squadron, examine the remains of the Ju 188E-1 3E+BK of 2/KG6 flown by Lt. G. Lahl. It came down at Butler's Farm, at Shopland, Essex. In the photo, from left, S/L Bunting DFC is in the hole pointing, F/L C. P. Reed DFC, navigator, F/L J. A. S. Hall (who shot down a Ju 88 at Earls Colne), AM Sir Roderick Hill, AOC ADGB, W/C R. C. Haine, CO 488 Squadron, and F/Sgt J. L. Wood, navigator.

ing the Mosquito crew's attentions.

The Mosquito dived onto the fleeing Junkers, which steadied into a mild, drunken weaving. Bunting fired a burst of machine gun fire into the bomber from 200 yd astern. It caught fire in the left wing root and engine and flames appeared. Encouraged, Bunting again took aim and gave the Ju 88A-4 another burst from 300 yd. Bunting's camera gun recorded the image of the Ju 88 turning over on its back and commencing its flaming death dive over Suffolk. What it could not capture was the resulting crash, a split-second later, at Blacklands Hall, Cavendish, Suffolk, where the bomber's fuel tanks exploded and its engines buried themselves deep into the soil. Fw K. Maser and Fw Karl-Heinz Elmhorst had baled out and were taken prisoner. Mayer and Ofw W. Szyska died in the crash.

At around the same time, F/L J. A. S. Hall with F/O J. P. W. 'Jock' Cairns of 488 (RNZAF)

Squadron, shot down Ju 88A-14 3E+GS of 8./KG6 from Melsbroek, and it fell on Earls Colne airfield where the aircraft and one of its 500-kg high explosive bombs exploded, damaging three B-26 Marauders of the 323rd Bomb Group, US 9th AF.

Meanwhile, Bunting and Reed orbited the scene of their 'kill' and were then *Gauntletted* south-east. Reed reported *Window* and they eventually made contact at 3¾ miles range. Bunting closed fairly fast to 4,000 ft when he was suddenly illuminated by searchlights again. They obtained a 'douse' but the enemy aircraft, Ju 188E-1 3E+BK of 2./KG6, flown by Lt G. Lahl, had begun very violent evasive action. They nearly overshot beneath him although the Mosquito was only doing 130 mph IAS. Lahl peeled off to port; Bunting turned hard left. Reed regained contact on his AI.VIII at about 4,000 ft and followed him on his scope. They pursued

A total of 10 enemy aircraft were claimed destroyed by Mosquito night fighters on the night of 24/25 March. Three were brought down over land, including this Ju 88A-4 of 6./KG6 which was shot down by W/C Hampshire DSO and F/O T. Condon of 456 (RAAF) Squadron at Walberton, Sussex. (ARP)

F/O E. R. Hedgecoe (right) and F/O N. L. Bamford pose in front of their burned and scorched 85 Squadron Mosquito NF.XII after being caught in the explosion when they destroyed a Ju 88 of II/KG54 the previous night, 24/25 March 1944. (via Jerry Scutts)

Lahl through a hard, climbing turn to the right and Bunting took a quick shot at 300 yd, but he could not get on enough deflection and his shots missed. The two adversaries gyrated in tight turns and another steep climb before Bunting got into the favoured astern position. Peering through his gun-sight with its diffuser, he repeatedly pumped short bursts into the '188 from 250 yd. It dived, hit the ground, and exploded near Butlers Farm at Shopland, Essex shortly after 01:10 hrs. Lahl, Uffz J. Fromm, Uffz R. Budrat and Obgefr Schiml, were all killed. Uffz E. Kosch baled out, injured, and was taken prisoner. Bunting added a Bar to his DFC and he had nine enemy aircraft confirmed destroyed, including a Ju 88 on 12/13 June and an Fw 190 on 16/17 June, before he was shot down and killed by flak on 30 July 1944 while chasing a radar contact over France.

Another Ju 188E-1, U5+AN, flown by Uffz Martin Hanf of 5./KG2, was lost on the night of 24/25 March when it was intercepted over the North Sea by a Mosquito NF.XVII flown by F/L

V. P. Luinthune DFC with F/O A. B. Cumbers DFC of 25 Squadron at Coltishall. Strikes, followed by the vivid orange glow of an explosion, signalled the end of the Junkers. Hanf and his four crewmen died in a watery grave 45 miles south-east of Lowestoft. A total of 10 enemy aircraft were claimed destroyed by Mosquitoes that night. Mounting losses – Mosquitoes shot down nine enemy raiders attacking mainly London and Bristol during 23–28 March 1944 – meant that KG2 had to operate a diversity of types despite the fact that Obst Dietrich Peltz, 'Attack Leader England', had wanted KG2 re-equipped with Ju 88s. He disliked the Do 217, which he considered unsuitable for night raids over Britain and more suited for use as a day bomber over the Eastern Front.

On 13/14 April 96 Squadron shot down a German raider, and on the night of 18/19 April, when the last 'Baby Blitz' raid was made on London, a further eight fell to the Mosquitoes. A 4./KG2 Ju 188E-1, U5+DM, flown by Hptm

Helmuth Eichbaum, was shot down off Southwold by F/L R. M. Carr with F/L Saunderson of 25 Squadron at Coltishall; while a 5./KG2 Ju 188E-1, U5+KN, piloted by Fw Helmuth Richter, was shot down by W/C C. M. Miller DFC, CO 85 Squadron at West Malling. F/O S. B. Huppert of 410 (RCAF) Squadron at Hunsdon shot down an He 177 of 3./KG100 flown by Fw Heinz Reis, which fell near Saffron Walden. Two Ju 88s were destroyed by P/O Allen and S/L Green DFC of 96 Squadron, and its new CO, W/C Edward D. Crew DFC*, shot down an Me 410A-1 of 1./KG51 over Brighton. F/L J. A. S. Hall and W/O R. F. D. Bourke of 488 (RNZAF) Squadron each claimed a Ju 88.

From 20-30 April, Mosquitoes claimed 16 enemy raiders as *Steinbock* raids were made on Hull, Bristol, Portsmouth and Plymouth using He 177, Ju 188 and Do 217 aircraft. Nine raiders were shot down by Mosquitoes on 14/15 May when over 100 Luftwaffe raiders attacked Bristol. A Ju 188 and three Ju 88s were destroyed on 22 May when Portsmouth was again the target.

On 28/29 May W/C C. M. Wight-Boycott DSO, CO 25 Squadron at Coltishall, with F/L D. W. Reid, were directed by Neatishead GCI towards a 'bogey' over the North Sea. It was an Me 410 Hornisse, 9K+KP, of KG51, flown by Fw Dietrich and Uffz Schaknies, which was returning from an intruder mission in the Cambridge area. At 02:39 hrs, Dietrich had attacked a Stirling I of 1657 OCU on approach to Shepherd's Grove. The pilot, F/O W. A. C. Yates, and all the crew were killed when it crashed on a dispersal, hitting and badly damaging another Stirling to such an extent that it too had to be written off. Dietrich and Schaknies sped off towards the coast and headed home. They did not make it. Wight-Boycott (who, on 23/24 June would add a Ju 188 destroyed to his score) approached the Me 410 almost at sea level and fired a half-second burst into it from 700 ft. Dietrich and Schaknies fell into the sea 50 miles off Cromer. The wreckage could be seen burning on the water from 20 miles away.

It was the final day of the 'Baby Blitz'.

85 Squadron pilots and navigators at RAF Hunsdon in 1943. Edward Nigel Bunting is sixth from left in the first row. His navigator, F/L C. P. Reed DFC is fifth from left. Bunting added a Bar to his DFC and had nine confirmed 'kills' before he was shot down and killed by flak on 30 July 1944 while chasing a radar contact over France. (Andrew Long)

Chapter Eleven

'Divers' and 'Doodlebugs', Widows and Orphans

It had been intended that V1 flying bombs would rain down on Britain as part of the *Steinbock* offensive, but, fortunately for the civilian population of this island, problems delayed the anticipated 'rocket blitz' until 13 June 1944. On this day 10 V1s were catapult-launched at the capital from sites in north-eastern France. The Vergeltungswaffe 1 (Revenge Weapon No 1), or Fieseler Fi 103 Kirschkern (Cherry Stone), was a small pilotless aircraft with a 1,870-lb high

Geoffrey de Havilland Jr. does up his parachute harness before climbing the ladder into a Mosquito fighter on 2 June 1944, prior to taking part in a film tribute at Hatfield to reconstruct the first flight of the Mosquito at Salisbury Hall, Hertfordshire.

explosive warhead which detonated on impact.

It was on 12 June 1943, when F/L R. A. Lenton in a Mosquito took photos of a rocket lying horizontally on a trailer at Peenemünde, that the attention of RAF intelligence at Medmenham was aroused. On 23 June F/Sgt Peek brought back more photos of rockets on road vehicles for Medmenham so clear that news was relayed immediately to Prime Minister Winston Churchill. In all, six Mosquito pilots of 540 Squadron at Leuchars photographed Peenemünde, and all were dead within six months. In August 1943 Peenemünde was bombed by the RAF but trials continued and by mid-June 1944, V1s were ready to launch against London and southern England.

The first V1 destroyed by a Mosquito was launched on 14/15 June 1944 and fell to F/O Schultz of 605 Squadron from Manston, who was on a freelance sortie over the sea when he was passed by a 'queer aircraft' flying in the opposite direction. Schultz turned and gave chase, going through the 'gate' as he did so, and shot it down. He flew straight into the debris and returned to Manston with little skin left on his Mosquito. Ben Johnson, a Fitter IIE, recalls:

Both engines later had to be changed. Within a matter of about two weeks, every aircraft was u/s as engines were swopped for American Packard-built engines, which took about 15 hours per 'kite'. We were sent some WAAFs to help out, but with the restrictions on what they were allowed to do, it only made for harder work to keep to our targets. Just prior to this, all Rolls-Royce engines had to have the Sun wheels in the reduction gears changed.

Incredible as it now seems, RAF Mosquito interceptor crews were not appraised of the coming V1 threat. F/L R. W. 'Dickie' Leggett, who with

'Dickie' Leggett (left) and his navigator, E. J. 'Midi' Midlane. (Richard Leggett)

125 Squadron at Hurn, May 1944. 'Dickie' Leggett is seated fourth from right. E. J. Midlane, his navigator, is fifth from right, behind the RN officer. The CO, W/C Johnny Topham DSO DFC & Bar, is to his right; 'A' Flight's CO, S/L Bill Gill DSO, is to his left. To his left is S/L Eric Barwell DFC & Bar. The aircraft is Mosquito NF.XVII MJ899. (Richard Leggett)

F/O Egbert J. 'Midi' Midlane was stationed at Hurn, near Bournemouth, explains:

It is absolutely absurd to think that here we were in a front-line squadron [418] and we hadn't been briefed about 'buzz bombs'. On the night of 18/19 June we had just done a normal routine patrol, had landed and were refuelling, when we were intercepted and told to hurry up and get off again to intercept some 'pilotless aircraft'! We were very disbelieving and said some pretty rude things to the IO. We were put on patrol by a GCI station at about 1,500–2,000 ft. It was still dark. After about 45 min of absolute boredom (we were already pretty fed up after the previous two to three-hour patrol where nothing had happened) everything happened at once! The GCI station got a contact. At the same time this device with this great big flame came within 300 ft, going across at 90° to us. We were worried and awake. I turned the aircraft around as best I could and my navigator immediately got a contact on his radar. We were cruising at around 220 mph. I immediately put on full throttle, but of course this 'thing' was doing 400 mph+ and left us looking rather stupid! We took a great interest for another hour or so, but no more came along so we went back and reported what we'd seen. We were furious at not being briefed.

Over the coming weeks Tempests, Spitfires and Mosquitoes chased the 300–420 mph pilotless bombs in the sky. Tempests of the Newchurch Wing destroyed 580 'Doodlebugs', as they were dubbed by the press, or *Divers* as they were code-named, while Spitfire XIVs brought down a further 185. Mosquito NF.XIIIs of 96 Sqdn based at Ford shot down 174, and Mosquitoes of 418 Sqdn, stationed at Holmesly, Hurn and Middle Wallop, destroyed a further 90. Ground batteries in the 'Diver Box' accounted for the rest.

On 25 June 1944 85 and 157 Squadrons in 100 Group were switched to anti-*Diver* patrols. (By the start of 1945 85 Squadron were still using AI.VIII radar sets, but at least their Mosquitoes were made more powerful, with the injection of nitrous oxide (better known as 'laughing gas') with petrol, to give the added power needed to catch the V1s.) They operated against the 'Doodlebugs' until 20 August when both squadrons resumed bomber support duties from Swannington. F/L R. W. Leggett recalls:

The anti-*Diver* patrols were a free-for-all. You had to dive down on these things at an enormous rate of knots – absolutely flat-out – and do the best you could. There was no real control about it. (Our Mk XVII Mosquito didn't have the power of the Mosquitoes with injection.) Because it was a free-for-all, when we got close, to avoid collision with other night fighter chaps going in, we were briefed to switch on our navigation lights. Colliding with another aircraft was

Mosquito PR.XVI NS502 of 544 Squadron wearing black and white D-Day invasion stripes and carrying black slipper tanks. (via Ron Mackay)

embarrassing. However, all the Fw 190s had to do was hover around, knowing some fool would have his nav' lights on. It was a fairly obvious 'cat and mouse' game. Chaps didn't come back from these V1 things; a couple of friends in particular. It is my opinion they rather stupidly put on their nav' lights, lined up, and got one up the backside from an Fw 190. Easy! This was all part of the anti-*Diver* game. I could see the other aircraft coming in with their lights on. Very useful for me to see them, but I wasn't going to put my nav' lights on and I didn't bother to tell them!

By the end of June 1944, 605 Squadron had shot down 36 'Doodlebugs' and in July, a further 29 were destroyed by the squadron. One of its pilots was F/L Brian 'Scruffy' Williams. On 6/7 July 1944 Williams took off with W/O S. E. Hardy at 01:45 hrs to carry out a *Diver* patrol. In all, they saw eight V1s. At 02:05 hrs Williams attacked and destroyed the first of three, eight miles south of Dungeness at 6,000 ft. His second 'Doodlebug' exploded after a burst from 500 yd astern, five miles north-north-west of Le Touquet, and the third exploded 15 miles east of Dungeness. On 18 August Brian Williams sighted a group of eight 'Doodlebugs' crossing the French coast between Le Touquet and Boulogne at 2,000 ft. He attacked and shot down two. He exploded the first with a short burst from dead astern, about four miles off Dungeness, and he destroyed the second with two short bursts from astern and slightly above, about 10 miles north-west of Le Touquet.

By September the Allied advance had overrun launching sites in the Pas de Calais. (Thankfully for the troops hitting the beaches all along the Normandy coastline on D-Day, 6 June, they had no need to fear bombing by the V1s.) However, the Allied advance had not wrong-footed the Luftwaffe, who mounted a new terror blitz from the skies by air-launching 'Doodlebugs' from aircraft over the North Sea. By August 410 V1s had been air-launched against London, Southampton and Gloucester, all of them being fired from Heinkel He 111s of III/KG3 based at Venlo and Gilze Rijen in Holland, after experiments at Peenemünde in 1943 had resulted in several He 111s being modified to H-22 standard to carry a V1 under its wing. Normally, the Heinkels took off at night, flew low over the North Sea to evade

radar and climbed to 1,475 ft before firing their missiles from approximately 50 miles off shore.

In September 1944 the Allied advance forced III/KG3 to abandon its bases in Holland and move to airfields in Germany. Only the radar-equipped Mosquito, and Tempest V night fighter, were able to counter the new threat. On 25 September Mosquitoes downed their first He 111H-22s over the North Sea, the 'kills' being credited to 'Mossies' of 409 and 25 Squadrons. On the night of 28/29 September 25 Squadron at Coltishall had further success. A Mosquito NF.XVII flown by W/C L. J. C. Mitchell, with navigator F/L D. L. Cox operating the fitted AI.X, took off at 00:55 hrs to intercept some anticipated 'trade' over the North Sea.

At 3,500 ft, 40 miles east of Great Yarmouth, they saw a V1 being launched from a Heinkel. Mitchell carried out a diving turn on the enemy machine. At the same time, 'Greyfriars' Control informed them that the Heinkel was also turning to port. Mitchell lost height to 600 ft in a turn and Cox made contact at 2½ miles range. Mitchell closed at 200 ft above the sea and obtained a visual at 1,300 ft. Cox raised his night glasses and confirmed the 'bogey' as an He 111H-22. Mitchell gave it a short burst from 400 ft dead astern. It exploded, flinging debris into the night sky and into the path of the onrushing Mosquito. Mitchell yanked the stick hard right and then turned back to see the German aircraft crash in flames into the sea, where it burned for two to three minutes before sinking beneath the dark waters.

Mitchell and Cox returned to their patrol line and saw another V1 being launched. Losing height, Mitchell sped off after the 'Doodlebug', informing 'Greyfriars' Control of his bearing. They vectored him towards the source of the launch. Cox eventually obtained contact on a converging course. He waited patiently until the range closed to about one mile and then carried out a hard turn to port, so as to close in behind the enemy machine. The Mosquito lost height to 150 ft and pounded over the waves at 220 mph as the Heinkel sailed along at a leisurely 180–190 mph, seemingly oblivious to its imminent demise. At 1,500 ft range the Mosquito crew got their visual confirmation that it was an He 111 and Mitchell let loose with a short burst from 600 ft. Pieces flew off the He 111's right wing and Mitchell added to its misery with another short burst, this time from 400 ft. The port engine burst into flames and the Heinkel crashed in flames into the sea. Mitchell searched for survivors until 06:15 hrs, but his action had been total.

On 5 October a 25 Squadron Mosquito brought down another Heinkel He 111H-22 over the North Sea. 125 (Newfoundland) Squadron bagged another of the V1 launchers on 25 October and on the night of 30/31 October were out again seeking Heinkels over the North Sea. S/L L. W. G. Gill with his navigator, F/L D. A. Haigh, took off from Coltishall at 07:25 hrs in a Mosquito NF.XVII and were vectored by Hopton Control at full speed towards some 'trade' reported to the east. Contact was obtained at 2¹/₂ miles range and Haigh instructed Gill to turn hard right. At 7,000 ft range they obtained a contact again. Gill got a fleeting glimpse of the Heinkel as it passed above them on the opposite vector. He closed rapidly to 4,000 ft and started to get fleeting sightings of the bomber as it passed through broken cloud. By now the Heinkel had released its flying bombs and was turning left and starting to descend slightly. Gill closed range rapidly to 1,000 ft and opened fire with a long burst. Haigh and Gill saw the shells hit home around the right engine and fuselage, and pieces of debris scattered in all directions as the Heinkel dropped like a winged bird. Gill gave it another burst and saw hits strike the tail. Gill was now overshooting so he broke away.

To his chagrin, the Heinkel went down to sea level, straightened out and climbed slowly, frantically seeking cover in the cloud. It was a futile gesture; cloud was no hiding place for a searching AI.X radar and its trained operator. Haigh busily operated his AI set until he regained contact with the fleeing Heinkel at 4,000 ft range. Gill closed in, determined to finish off the Heinkel once and for all. In desperation Fw Warwas, the pilot of the 4./KG53 machine, carried out violent evasive action and climbed slightly, with one of his Jumo 211 engines smoking. Gill mercilessly pumped another long burst into its sides from 1,000 ft range. This time the German aircraft floundered, caught fire, and went

straight down into the sea.

Eleven minutes later Gill and Haigh carried out an attack on another He 111H-22. Although Gill obtained strikes before his ammunition ran out, he and his navigator were unable to confirm if it had crashed into the sea because of the 600-ft cloud base and prevailing scattered heavy rain storms in the area. Gill and Haigh were credited with a 'damaged', to go with their earlier He 111 'kill'.

Despite the losses during October, I/KG53 (III/KG3 redesignated) was joined by II/KG53 and III/KG53 for further air-launching of V1s. On the night of 5/6 November a 68 Squadron Mosquito NF.XIX fitted with AI.X and piloted by F/Sgt Neal, took off from Coltishall to intercept incoming 'trade' over the North Sea. F/Sgt Eastwood, his navigator, obtained a contact at 1¹/₂ miles range, flying at an altitude of 1,000 ft. Cloud was 10/10ths at 2,300 ft but Neal and Eastwood had no difficulty finding the V1 launcher, which was travelling at 150 mph. Neal dropped to 1,000 ft, closing to 2,500 ft range but flying at 160 mph indicated, overshot and returned to patrol. They picked up contact again at two miles and closed to 1,000 ft, then 500 ft. At 1,500 ft altitude they watched the He 111 release its flying bombs. For 20–30 seconds the Heinkel followed in the path of the V1s, before gradually losing height and turning hard to starboard. The two sergeants followed on AI and obtained a visual at about 200 yd range, 900 ft altitude. Neal gave the enemy bomber a two-second burst and the aircraft dived steeply to starboard and crashed into the North Sea. A red glow was visible for 15 miles.

On the night of 10/11 November 125 Squadron at Coltishall despatched a Mosquito at 18:25 hrs to intercept a contact over the North Sea. F/L G. F. Simcock and his navigator, F/O N. E. Hoijne, took off in their NF.XVII, call sign *Goodwill 27,* and headed out across the inhospitable waters, vectored first by Neatishead GCI, then Hopton CHEL. Simcock wrote later:

I saw what proved to be flying bombs being released and asked Hopton if any information available. Control had no information so turned in direction of flying bombs. We obtained a contact on target crossing from starboard to port, going east, but Hopton turned us away from this and then back towards it again. As we were turning back, I saw, slightly behind us, a Heinkel 111 by the light of its flying bomb. Turned towards it and obtained contact at three miles range, our height being 1,000 ft and target's about 1,500. Target did a wide turn to port and slowly lost height to 200 ft, approx ASI 200. Followed on AI through heavy shower and closed in, getting visual at 800 ft. Target was then down to 150 ft, ASI 150. I originally intended to shadow e/a on AI hoping that he would gain height on approaching coast, but as there was more dirty weather ahead, decided to open fire at once rather than risk losing contact. Opened fire with a long burst at 600 ft, closing to 400 ft approx. Target then at 100 ft height. Many strikes were seen on port engine and port wing root and port side of fuselage. There was a large whitish-yellow flash from the port engine and a large piece flew back from it. My observer reported seeing another flash from the port side of the fuselage, but I did not see this. E/a immediately slowed down and went into a steep port bank. I had to break away – ASI then 140 – to avoid collision. Broke to starboard and then turned back to port again and attempted to regain contact. We searched area thoroughly at about 75 ft, scanning up, but no contact obtained. The sea was very rough with 'white horses', and it was extremely dark, so consider it unlikely, as it was not on fire, that I would be able to see it hit the sea. I claim one Heinkel 111 probably destroyed.

On 10/11 November F/Sgt A. Brooking and P/O Finn of 68 Squadron shot a Heinkel He 111H-22 into the sea. On 19 November a 456 (RAAF) Squadron Mosquito NF.XVII flown by F/O D. W. Arnold and his navigator, F/O J. B. Stickley, chased and finally caught up with an He 111 75 miles east of Lowestoft. Arnold fired his cannon from 400 yd. The He 111's ventral gunner returned fire, hitting the Mosquito in the right propeller. Debris embedded itself in the leading-edge of the right wing. As the Heinkel turned away, Arnold fired another burst and the starboard engine caught fire. He fired a third burst. Climbing suddenly to 1,200 ft, the still burning He 111 started to break up before falling over to the right in a stall turn into the sea. The waves almost immediately snuffed out the shower of sparks and doused the flames.

Another 456 (RAAF) Squadron crew, F/O F. S. Stevens and his observer, W. A. H. Kellett, chased their quarry in the early dawn of 25 November. They took off from Ford at 06:25 hrs,

and the two Australians saw four bright flashes on the horizon about 1,000 ft below them. Stevens dived to 1,500 ft and Kellett obtained two contacts at about two miles range. They chose the nearest blip, which appeared to be taking evasive action and was flying east, back to Holland. Stevens dived the Mosquito until he was just 500 ft above the sea, then set off in pursuit. The He 111 settled onto a course for home at 500 ft, changing height every now and again and weaving continuously.

Kellett's C-scope had malfunctioned, so very slowly, Stevens closed the gap between them and the retreating Heinkel until they could see the enemy machine just 800 ft in the distance. All at once the Heinkel turned violently to starboard. Stevens carried out a half-orbit and contact was immediately regained. There was no cloud but it was very dark, and the two Australians had difficulty making out the fleeing bomber. There was no mistaking its return fire though. Twice the Heinkel's gunners opened up from 800 ft, but Stevens bravely closed in still further, to 600 ft, and they were able to identify it positively as an He 111. It was flying at 900 ft. Stevens opened fire with a two-second burst from his cannon and the enemy's left engine immediately burst into flames. He closed to 150 ft, a second two-second burst going right through the fuselage which erupted in flames, illuminating the peculiar dull light grey tail fin with its evil black swastika outlined in white. Stevens broke to starboard. The flaming torch fell, shedding a dozen or so bright green incandescent balls in its fiery wake before it hit the water about 10 miles west of Texel. All the crew were picked up by German ASR.

On 17/18 December P/O K. D. Goodyear and his navigator, P/O J. Borrows, of 125 Squadron at Coltishall damaged an He 111H-22 while flying Mosquito *Goodwill 41*. At 05:50 hrs on 23/24 December Dick Leggett and 'Midi' Midlane, back in Norfolk after their stint at Hurn, took off from Coltishall in their Mosquito NF.XVII, call sign *Goodwill 37*. They knew they would soon find some 'trade' over the North Sea. Leggett explains:

The British 'Y' Service would get information that V1-carrying Heinkels would be taking off, and we'd

Northrop P-61 Black Widows wearing invasion stripes. Aircraft recognition, particularly at night, left a lot to be desired and led to mistaken claims for Ju 88s when in fact the 'kill' was a Mosquito. (Merle Olmsted)

be told that at such and such a time they would be in place. No other op was as tidy as this. We looked at our watches and thought, 'My goodness, they'll be here in another few minutes'; and sure enough, right on the button, it would all happen. It was a question of whether you'd be the lucky one because there were lots of us.

I looked at my clock and knew that at around 02:30 hrs there would be several Heinkels in the usual place. The enemy obviously did not know we were going to meet him. Being in a position to stab him in the back in the dark was a nice way to fight a war. One was mentally tuned to this. We felt sorry for our bomber chaps. We in the night fighter force didn't have to drop bombs on women and children. We had to kill Germans who were trying to do things to our women and children with nasty weapons. It was a very clear and clean way to fight. Sure enough, almost on the dot we saw the flash of a V1 being launched. At the same time ground control said they had contact.

Tally-ho!

There might be 12, 13, 14 of these Heinkels, all doing it at once. It was a timed op. Then they'd turn to port. I don't know why but they always did this. Then they would go down very rapidly and head for home. Our job was to lose height quickly, go below 100 ft, and pick up the Heinkel. The Mk X was a good AI, but there was a lot of sea returns and it depended on the expertize of the navigator. I had a very good one. Sure enough, the Heinkel turned left and at two to three miles we got a contact. It wasn't a good night. There was rain and 'stuff' about. The Germans only came when the weather was bad.

Leggett took off after the Heinkel, using his highly accurate radio altimeter to maintain position and height behind the fleeing German:

We started to close. It was still dark and there was a lot of cloud. You knew perfectly well that on our straight and level course behind him we would get a tremendous wash from his engines. I felt it. Then for some reason, he started to turn away slightly, as if he had an indication that we were behind him. It foxed us a bit. Eventually, it settled down again. I closed in on him. It was in cloud. Guns and sights were harmonized at about 200 yd but we could not get a visual, although we could feel his slipstream. We dropped away and my navigator picked up contact again. Some people might have lowered their undercarriage at this point, but I didn't like to. I had as much flap as I dared and managed perfectly well. We waited and we waited. Off Den Helder I was getting concerned. We'd followed him for fully 55 min. We waited as patiently as one can in this situation and eventually, as the dawn was coming up, I closed in at 300 yd range. [The exhaust emissions at 300 ft altitude belonged to a Heinkel 111H-20 of 7./KG53 Legion Kondor.] I fired my cannon in his slipstream and had to put on a lot of throttle to prevent a stall. I got a number of strikes on it and that was it. The Heinkel went in very quickly. When we broke away the cloud base was only at 200 ft. It was a beautiful morning.

The Heinkel came down in Holland and four of the crew were killed, but one of the two gunners survived.

Of 50 Fi 103s which were air-launched from Heinkel He 111s against Manchester on 24 December 1944, 30 crossed the coast, but only one actually exploded in the city. A 68 Squadron Mosquito NF.XVII, call sign *Ferro 26* and piloted by F/Sgt Bullus with his navigator, F/O Edwards, in charge of the AI.X scope, destroyed one of the Heinkels with three bursts of 20-mm cannon fire over the sea.

On the night of 6 January 1945 a Mosquito of 68 Squadron claimed the last shooting down of a Heinkel He 111H-22. Three days earlier Dick Leggett and 'Midi' Midlane were sent to the Fighter Interception Development Squadron at Ford to take part in Operation *Vapour*. Leggett recalls:

We were pleased to learn that that the 'boffins' were planning a possible answer to the menacing Heinkels and their underslung V1 missiles. Immediately on arrival we met other night fighter friends and were quickly ushered into a briefing room to meet the head 'boffin', Mr E. J. Smith. He then introduced us to the captain and crew of a Coastal Command Wellington which we had noticed on landing, but had no idea of its significance. The Wellington had been equipped as an airborne GCI station, with Mr Smith as radar controller. The Wellington would fly at 50 ft above the surface of the sea and locate 'bogeys', while we Mosquito hounds, flying at 500 ft above the 'Wimpy' at intervals of a mile, would be directed against the V1-carrying Heinkels.

After several *Vapour* practice patrols, on 14 January six of us flew to Manston for the first op patrol off the Dutch coast. Our navigators used a 'mother beacon' and the AI to position behind the Wellington at one-mile intervals. The whole 'shooting match' flew a 50-mile patrol north to south, parallel to the Dutch coast. Intelligence had told us that something was going to happen. Mr Smith put us onto an unidentified aircraft flying west at about 270° at 100 ft. It was an absolute set-up. Within a few minutes 'Midi' obtained a firm contact on his AI.X and took over from Mr Smith. I was ready, excited and thought, 'This will be easy meat.' Speed was synchronized with the target at 120 mph on a course towards Norfolk at a height of 250 ft. With my gun button to 'Fire', we struggled through the severe downwash of slipstream from the target and quickly achieved a visual sighting while closing to about 100 yd. To our utter disappointment, the aircraft was a Warwick! In strong language I announced my frustration to Mr Smith who replied, 'Shoot it down as it must be hostile.' A fierce argument followed as he explained the target was not responding to IFF, so get on with it! We stupidly nudged closer and closer in an attempt to convince ourselves it was an enemy aircraft. We virtually flew in formation with it, reaffirmed there was no V1 missile underslung and that it was a Warwick. I wanted to tell the pilot how lucky he was that I hadn't fired! We were in the wrong position and we missed the Heinkels going out and we missed them coming back! It was the last night they came.

Altogether, about 1,200 V1s were air-launched against Britain, although of these only 638 approached the coast. KG53 ceased operations having lost 77 Heinkels, 16 of them claimed by Mosquitoes.

* * * * *

For four weeks starting on 28 June 1944, 125 Squadron and six Northrop P-61 Black Widows of the Scorton-based 422nd and 425th Night Fighter Squadrons, 9th AF, carried out comparative night fighter trials from Hurn. (A further detachment also operated from Ford, starting on 15 July, against V1s). The two P-61 squadrons, the only ones to operate in Europe during the Second World War, had arrived in England dur-

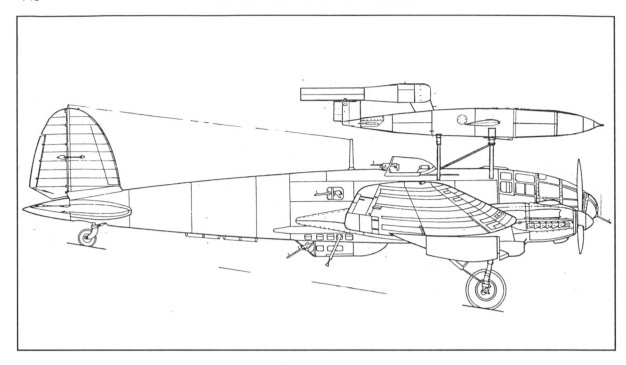

Despite reliable reports of the Heinkel 111/Fi 103 combination sent by agents on the Continent, the Air Ministry at first confused the method of mounting the flying bomb with the 'Mistel' weapon and this drawing was issued on 5 September 1944. Such an arrangement simply would not have been practical with the Fi 103, because of the slow speed of the carrier aircraft. All production versions of the flying bombs could only be carried on the starboard side of the aircraft as the compressed air inlet valve on the bomb was located on the lower port side, being connected to the parent aircraft by a semi-flexible hose. (via Frank Leyland)

ing March–June 1944, being based originally at Charmy Down. F/L R. W. Leggett recalls the arrival of the gloss-black aircraft and their crews, who were commanded by Col Winston W. Kratz of the 481st Night Fighter Operational Training Group:

They were super aircraft and the Americans were great chaps, but we pulled their legs unmercifully because they'd had no luck in shooting down any enemy aircraft. They were unlucky. Personally, I believe it was because they did not have the opportunity, background or feeling for this war. It was not something that could be learned in the classroom. They were not teams like we were in the Mosquito, where a pilot and navigator were an entity.

On 5 July a Mosquito NF.XVII flown by S/L Barwell, of 125 Squadron, flew a combat evaluation demonstration at Hurn against Lt Donald J. Doyle. The P-61 proved faster at 5,000 ft, 10,000

ft, 15,000 ft and 20,000 ft, out-turning the Mosquito at every altitude by a big margin. The P-61 also far surpassed the Mosquito in rate of climb. The Americans concluded: 'We could go faster and slower, up or down. Faster than the pride of the British – a most enjoyable afternoon.'

F/L Leggett, who also flew a mock combat exercise in daylight with the P-61, confirms its speed advantage:

We started at 1,000 ft and had a formal dogfight, getting GCI to set us up about 20 miles apart. We intercepted each other using our AIs. Then we climbed at 5,000-ft intervals to gaps until we reached 30,000 ft. My navigator made notes. Although I outmanoeuvred the Black Widow, it was slightly embarrassing at our 5,000-ft gaps to find it always seemed to be waiting for me. His engines were more powerful. This gave him an extra advantage in the rate of climb, but, surprisingly, not in manoeuvrability.

On 15 July the 422nd NFS flew the first P-61 operation from England, and on the very next night scored the first 'kill' when it downed a V1. On 5 August the 425th NFS shot down a V1 and two days later the 422nd got its first manned aircraft. (The 425th had to wait until Christmas Eve 1944 before it got its first manned aircraft 'kill'.) R. W. Leggett concludes:

We had so many night fighters messing about we often spent the night chasing our chums, especially if the IFF was not turned on. As there were normally about 100 Mosquitoes and 20 Germans, the 'bogey' nearly always turned out to be a Mosquito. Black Widow crews were keen to fire. They were so trigger-happy that it became embarrassing. Much later, I heard one 'kill' on my R/T one night. He fired, then I heard him claiming a '410. 'I've hit it! It's on fire! It's going down in flames!' Then I heard the RAF pilot's voice say, 'He missed by at least six ft! I'm not hit. I'm not going down in flames!'

It was a Mosquito!

Right Dick Leggett, aged 22, at Coltishall in December 1944. (Richard Leggett)

Below Heinkel 111H-16 (5K-HS) of 8./KG3, July, 1944. Air-launching a flying bomb over the English Channel just after sunset – Target Southampton.

Chapter Twelve

Night Intruders

German revenge weapons aimed at southern England had proved such a menace that in June 1944 some *Intruder* Mosquitoes from 100 (Special Duties)* Group in Norfolk, had been detached to West Malling for anti-*Diver* patrols. 100 Group had been formed on 23 November 1943 under the command of Air Commodore (later AVM) E. B. Addison after it became obvious to all that the RAF needed a specialized bomber support force. Nightly, 100 Group despatched Wellington, Halifax, Fortress and Liberator aircraft on radio countermeasures (RCM), and Mosquito operations were extended to include loose escort duties for the Main Force.

Intruder aircraft had already proved their worth on bomber support operations. In June 1943 141 Squadron Beaufighter VIfs fitted with AI.IV *Serrate* (designed to home in on German night fighter radar transmissions) and *Gee*, had been the first unit to be used in this role. In September 141 Squadron converted to the Mosquito NF.II. On 25 November 192 Squadron, equipped with Mosquito B.IV, Halifax and Wellington X aircraft for the electronic intelligence (Elint) role (monitoring German radio and radar), moved to Foulsham from Feltwell. At West Raynham 141 Squadron, equipped with the Beaufighter VI, arrived on 4 December and, on the 10th, 239 Squadron's Mosquitoes joined them. Three days later, Foulsham and Little Snoring were transferred from 3 Group to 100 (SD) Group. 192 Squadron, together with Little Snoring's 169 and 515 Squadrons, equipped mainly with Beaufighters, were absorbed by the new force. 515 had, since

1942, tested the *Mandrel* jamming device on RAF night and US 8th AF daylight bombing raids. On 12 December, 1473 Flight arrived at Foulsham from Little Snoring and in April 1944, the Special Duty Radar Development Unit equipped with Mosquitoes arrived, to become the Bomber Support Development Unit on 1 May. Throughout 1944 and early 1945 192 Squadron crews listened in on enemy radio frequencies and jammed enemy VHF transmissions. They even afforded the RAF control of German fighters.

The first 100 Group operation was flown on the night of 16/17 December 1943, when two Beaufighters and two Mosquitoes of 141 Squadron were despatched in support of the 'heavies' raiding Berlin. In January 141 Squadron shot down three enemy night fighters. On the night of 20 January 1944 169 Squadron flew its first operation in the new command, supporting the Main Force bombers attacking Berlin. On 30/31 January the squadron destroyed a Bf 110 in combat. In February 1944, four more enemy aircraft fell to the guns of the RAF night fighters, but three RAF machines were lost. Despite problems with the Mosquitoes, many of which were war-weary and their engines often proving unreliable, 515 Squadron's Beaufighters and Blenheims were replaced by Mosquito B.IIs, beginning on 29 February, for training on the type. The unit began operations in March, equipped with the Mosquito FB.VI. Some of 605 Squadron's Mosquitoes were operated by 515 on detachment at Bradwell Bay and it was in one of these

* Bomber support from May 1944.

Mosquito RS566 of 515 Squadron at Little Snoring. (via Tom Cushing)

aircraft that the CO, W/C Freddie Lambert with F/L E. Morgan, shot down an He 177 in the first squadron sortie.

In April 1944 the Bomber Support Development Unit (BSDU) was formed at Foulsham for trials and development work on radar and various apparatus carried by aircraft of 100 Group. The BSDU operated a mixture of aircraft, including the Beaufighter, Stirling, Halifax and Mosquito. On the night of 27/28 April, a Mosquito B.IV of 192 Squadron had just touched down at Foulsham when a returning Halifax landed on top of it. Fortunately, none of the crews suffered injury. Also in April, 515 Squadron moved from Bradwell Bay to Little Snoring and flew its first operation from there on 7 April. On 19/20 April German intruders bombed the base and put it out of action. During the month, 169 Squadron shot down four enemy aircraft, including three by P/O W. Miller with P/O F. Bone during a bomber support operation for minelaying in Kiel Bay.

In April–May 1944, three new Mosquito night fighting squadrons joined 100 Group. Mosquito NF.XIIs and NF.XVIIs of 85 Squadron and Mosquito NF.XIXs of 157 Squadron flew in to the recently completed base at Swannington, while 23 Squadron arrived from the Mediterranean to operate from Little Snoring.

The previous incumbents, 169 Squadron and 1692 Flight, moved to Great Massingham. 85 Squadron had been commanded by W/C John Cunningham and 157 had been the first to be equipped with the Mosquito. Now, 85 and 157 Mosquitoes were equipped with the first AI.X radar sets.

On the night of 5/6 June 1944, both squadrons flew their first operations in 100 Group while 21 *Serrate* Mosquitoes were despatched to northern France. 85 Squadron despatched 12 Mosquitoes over the Normandy invasion beaches and four Mosquitoes of 157 (and 10 of 515 Squadron) made *Intruder* raids on Belgian and Dutch airfields. On 11/12 June W/C C. M. Miller DFC, CO 85 Squadron, scored the first *Intruder* 'kill' in Bomber Command when he shot down a Bf 110 at Melun. On 12/13 June F/L James G. Benson of 157 Squadron shot down a Ju 188 at Compiègne. On 25 June some Mosquitoes from 85 and 157 Squadrons were detached to West Malling for anti-*Diver* patrols.

On the night of 5/6 July Mosquito FB.VIs of 23 Squadron flew their first *Intruder* operation with sorties against enemy airfields. A Ju 88 was damaged on 26 July. Later that month, 23 and 515 Squadrons flew daylight escort duty for 'heavies' attacking Bordeaux. In August they continued daylight operations with a series of

Mosquito B.VI HP850 of 157 Squadron which was transferred to 100 Group for bomber support operations in August 1944, by which time the squadron had re-equipped with the NF.XIX. (via Philip Birtles)

Mosquito NF.XIX RS-L of 157 Squadron at its dispersal near St Peter's Church, Haveringland, on whose land part of RAF Swannington airfield was built. Mosquitoes provided 100 Group with a long-range offensive capability throughout 1943–45.

On 30 September 1944 two 515 Squadron Mosquitoes, NS993, flown by F/L Arthur S. Callard and F/Sgt E. Dixon Townsley, and PZ440 flown by S/L Henry Morley and F/Sgt Reg Fidler, set off from Little Snoring for a Day Ranger to Southern Germany. PZ440 lies wrecked in a field at Dübendorf, Switzerland, after taking hits from Swiss AA fire, while NS993 was escorted to Dübendorf by Swiss fighters. All four crew were interned. (Tom Cushing Collection)

Day Rangers (operations to engage air and ground targets within a wide but specified area). The most successful of these was on 29 October 1944 when F/L T. L. L'Amie with F/O J. W. Smith and P/O T. A. Groves DFC with F/Sgt R. B. Dockeray DFM, of 23 Squadron, shot down four and damaged five enemy aircraft.

Meanwhile, on 20 August 85 and 157 Squadrons had resumed bomber support duties from Swannington. In September Mosquitoes of 23 Squadron briefly had escorted RCM Fortresses of 100 Group on *Big Ben* patrols. Previous attempts by the Fortresses to 'jam' V2s had been in vain. On 26 September 23 Squadron flew a *Day Ranger* with two Mosquitoes against Grove aerodrome in Denmark. One of the Mosquitoes was flown by Bud Badley, the other by F/O George Stewart, a Canadian. Canadian airmen on *Intruder* work flew a first tour of 35 sorties, followed by a period usually as instructors at OTUs, or in operational planning at Group HQ; then a second tour of 25 trips would round out their operational obligation and they would be eligible for a posting home. Stewart and his navigator, Paul Beaudet, did their first tour in 11 weeks and were still 'raring to go', so they applied for and were granted a 15-trip extension. They thought that by being very quiet about it, they would be able to sneak in an extra 10 sorties

without anyone noticing. They could then say that they had done their two tours, so they would get back home sooner. But the plan did not work, and as soon as they finished the 15-trip extension to their first tour, they were taken off operations. Stewart recalls:

I'll never forget trying to find Grove aerodrome, just before our attack on the *Freya* radar installation. Before we knew it, we were right in the centre of it at nought ft. The Germans were as surprised as we were. First thing I saw was an erk adjusting camouflage netting covering an aircraft in one of the dispersal bays. Then I saw an '88 on what appeared to be the horizon and climbed slightly to attack. As I started to fire, an erk from the 'kite' ran like hell, off to the left. We attacked the *Freya* and stirred up a hornets' nest. We took a .303 in a feathering button, and Bud Badley had an engine shot up and diverted to Woodbridge on one fan and no rudder control. Both aircraft were damaged, one almost a write-off, so after that we stuck to straight intruding and night targets.

Stewart completed 50 trips on ops with 23 Sqdn at Little Snoring and returned to Canada as an instructor, all before reaching the age of 21. The Stewart-Beaudet crew went to 45 enemy aerodromes, 36 of them in Germany.

On 2 December 1944 W/C 'Sticky' Murphy, CO 23 Squadron, failed to return from a night operation, and S/L Philip Russell, who had

Mosquito F.II DZ238/YP-H of 23 Squadron, pictured on 22 May 1943. (BAe, via Philip Birtles)

returned to the squadron on 7 October complete-ly recovered from the after effects of untreated diphtheria he had contracted while the squadron was in the Mediterranean, was promoted to the rank of wing commander and given command of 23 Squadron. Returning to the squadron after a spell at the RAF rehabilitation unit at Loughborough College was a bit of a wrench, as he admits:

The unit was run by Dan Maskell, of subsequent ten-nis fame. I had to learn to walk again, helped with lots of massage from attractive nurses and swimming lessons with even more attractive ones. At the end of September I went for an RAF medical examination and, to my mild disappointment, was passed fit for flying duties. The European picture had changed con-siderably since we had left the UK and our targets were now principally in Germany and all rather heav-ily defended. In December we were fitted with radar and in January 23 Squadron became part of 100 Group.

Meanwhile, three more squadrons of Mosquito night-fighters had been released for bomber sup-port operations, but not in 100 Group. In December 1944 307 (Polish) Squadron's Mosquito NF.XXXs had been fitted with *Monica* tail warning radar and converted to the bomber support role, with a detachment at the famous Battle of Britain station at Coltishall. In January 1945 the Poles moved to Castle Camps in Cambridgeshire and continued their role until the end of the war. On 21 February 151 Squadron's

Mosquito FB.VIs and NF.XXXs began bomber support duties, having started installing *Monica* equipment in late 1944. On 1 March 1945 151 Squadron's Mosquito FB.VIs flew to Bradwell Bay from Hunsdon for anti-*Diver* operations against V1s, but soon returned to night bomber support operations. In mid-March the 456 (RAAF) Squadron, also at Bradwell Bay, equipped with the NF.XXX, and during April, Mosquito PR.XVIs replaced the PR.IVs in 192 Squadron, whose aircraft had been fitted with *Dina* and *Piperack* jamming equipment earlier that year.

On 13/14 April 515 Squadron flew its first Master Bomber sortie, dropping TIs, followed by the bombs and incendiaries of the Mosquito force. 100 Group Mosquitoes participated in *Spoof* raids on enemy airfields and cities. On the night of 14/15 April five Mosquitoes of 141 Squadron, each fitted with two 100-gal napalm gel drop tanks, carried out the first of 13 *Firebash* raids, on night fighter airfields at Neuruppin and Juteborg, near Potsdam and Berlin respectively. On 24/25 April 456 (RAAF) and 151 Squadrons both flew their last operations when four Mosquitoes of 456 and six of 151 flew *Night Rangers,* while 141 Squadron carried out another napalm attack on Munich-Neubiberg airfield.

The last operation by 100 Group was conduct-ed by 86 aircraft on the night of 2/3 May 1945, when Bomber Command flew the last operation of the Second World War. Some 126 Mosquitoes

Mosquito NF.XXX MM748 in flight. Fitted with AI.X radar in a thimble nose radome, the NF.XXX first entered service with 219 Squadron in June 1944. Six more squadrons were so equipped by the end of the year, including three which served in 100 Group on Intruder *operations. (ARP)*

Mosquito F.II 'Special' DZ238, Babs, of 23 Squadron, with AI radar removed and additional fuel tanks installed for long-range Intruder *operations over the continent. (via Jerry Scutts)*

W/C Philip Russell takes the salute from the WAAF 'Queen Bee' and her WAAFs at Little Snoring in 1945. (Philip Russell)

S/L Philip Russell receives the DFC from King George VI at Buckingham Palace. (Philip Russell)

I have to admit that when the end of the war came, I was extremely relieved. Courage is an expendable thing and mine was just about expended. With the exception of my time in hospital, I had been flying continuously from the outbreak of war and had completed 72 operational sorties (considerably more than the normal 30 sorties per tour applied in Bomber Command), and I had had enough – and then some.

In June-July 1945, Exercise *Post Mortem*, involving simulated attacks by aircraft from four RAF groups, proved the effectiveness of RAF 'jamming' and *Spoof* operations on the German early warning radar system. In September, 23 Squadron was disbanded and in May 1945 Philip Russell went to see King George VI to collect his DFC, and also to see the American Ambassador to the United Kingdom to collect the American DFC. Russell concludes: 'I was demobilized, given a demob suit and a felt hat, and sent on my way to Leicester; broke to the wide but all in one piece.'

* * * * *

from 8 (PFF) Group followed in the wake of another 16 PFF and 37 100 Group Mosquitoes, in attacks on the Kiel area. Honn and Flensburg airfields were bombed with napalm and incendiaries directed by Master Bomber, S/L Griffiths of 515 Squadron. 169 Squadron's Mosquitoes raided Schleswig and Westerland, while others dropped incendiaries on Jagel.

W/C Philip Russell concludes:

The part played by 100 Group, which was disbanded on 17 December 1945, cannot be overestimated. While it had developed electronic warfare to an almost state-of-the-art technology in just 18 months, its Mosquito force had accounted for many valuable German night fighters and airfields.

Chapter Thirteen

2nd TAF

Mosquito FB.VI squadrons in 2 Group, 2nd Tactical Air Force (2nd TAF) also intruded over the Reich, bombing and strafing German lines of communication and Luftwaffe airfields; but the aircraft is probably best remembered for daylight precision operations, particularly pinpoint raids on Gestapo buildings in occupied Europe which it made famous in 1943–45.

2 Group had been transferred to 2nd TAF on 1 June 1943. AVM Basil Embry replaced AVM d'Albiac at HQ, Bylaugh Hall with the task of preparing 2 Group for invasion support in the

A Mosquito FB.VI built by Standard Motors. (ARP)

Mosquito FB.VI LR366 of 613 Squadron being prepared at Lasham prior to an operation. (via Jerry Scutts)

run-up to Operation *Overlord:* the invasion of France. Embry was an excellent choice for the new-found role. On 27 May 1940 he had been shot down over France in a Blenheim and three times had been captured, but never made a PoW. On the second occasion, unarmed, he fought his way out; then, with a 'borrowed' German rifle, had killed three Germans, and escaped to England. Embry succesfully fought off an attempt to re-equip 2 Group with Vultee Vengeance dive-bombers and saw to it that his Lockheed Ventura-equipped squadrons were re-equipped with the Mosquito FB.VI fighter-bomber. Re-equipment with the FB.VI, which was armed with four cannon for night *Intruder* operations, began in August 1943 with 140 Wing at Sculthorpe, when 464 (RAAF) and 487 (RNZAF) Squadrons exchanged their obsolete Lockheed machines. They were closely followed, in September, by 21 Squadron, all three squadrons moving to Hunsdon in December 1943. On 15 October 138 Wing at Lasham began operating Mosquito FB.VIs when 613 (City of Manchester) Squadron joined 2 Group. In

December 305 (Polish) Squadron converted from the Mitchell, and in February 1944 107 Squadron converted from the Douglas Boston.

In 2nd TAF the Mosquito FB.VI carried out precision attacks, often on individual buildings, by day and night. Probably the most famous of these was Operation *Jericho,* which went ahead on 18 February 1944 after snowstorms and thick cloud had led to several postponements. A prison at Amiens, France, was known to be holding 700 French prisoners, among them Monsieur Vivant, a key Resistance leader in Abbeville. A dozen prisoners were due to be executed on 19 February. The prison was built in the shape of a cross and surrounded by a wall 20 ft high and three ft thick. The plan was to breach this wall by using 11-second bombs dropped by 12 Mosquito FB.VIs – six each from 464 (RAAF) and 487 (RNZAF) Squadrons – and hope that concussion from the explosions would open the cell doors, so that some prisoners at least might make their escape. There would be casualties, but better to die from RAF bombs than be shot by a German firing squad. If the first two waves of Mosquitoes

G/C Percy C. Pickard, CO 464 (RAAF) Squadron (pictured earlier (centre), during SOE operations, with his dog 'Ming', when he became legendary as 'Pick-up' Pickard, flying SOE agents into France), who commanded the Amiens operation. He and his navigator, F/L Pete Broodley were killed on the Amiens raid.

failed, four aircraft of 21 Squadron, led by W/C I. G. 'Daddy' Dale, had orders to flatten the prison complex.

Embry was forbidden to go so the raid was led by G/C Percy C. Pickard, CO 464 (RAAF) Squadron, with his navigator, F/L J. A. 'Peter' Broadley, in *F-Freddie*. Pickard was a brave and revered leader, and as a F/L he and Wellington *F-Freddie* had appeared in the British wartime film, *Target for Tonight*. Cpl Ralph Hunt, a wireless operator-mechanic at Hunsdon who carried out the Daily Inspection (DI) on the Mosquitoes, making sure his CO's GEC VHF set was in 'bloody good order', remembers: 'He was a biggish man with a big moustache. He was always smoking his pipe like a factory chimney, but in a hangar one day he'd ticked off an erk for smoking a cigarette!'

The formation of 19 Mosquitoes took off from Hunsdon with snow falling. Four aircraft imme-

A photographic still taken from W/C Bob Iredale's Mosquito, MM412/SB-F. The aircraft following is MM402/SB-A, flown by S/L W. R. C. Sugden and his navigator, F/O A. H. Bridger. (via John Rayner)

487 (RNZAF) Squadron crews, some of whom took part in the Amiens raid, are interviewed by the BBC. Top, L-R: P/O D. R. 'Bob' Fowler, pilot of HX974/EG-J; P/O M. Barriball; P/O M. L. S. Darrall, pilot of HX909/EG-C. Bottom, L-R: Robin Miller, NZ war correspondent; P/O Maxwell N. Sparks, pilot of HX982/EG-T; David Bernard (BBC); and P/O F. Stevenson, P/O Darrall's navigator on the operation. (via John Rayner)

P/O Maxwell N. Sparks (left) and his navigator, P/O Arthur C. Dunlop, of 487 (RNZAF) Squadron, who crewed HX982/EG-T on the Amiens raid. (Arthur Dunlop, via John Rayner)

In 1946, a French film celebrating the Amiens raid opened in Paris. L-R: Mrs I. S. Smith; W/C I. S. 'Black' Smith, CO 487 (RNZAF) Squadron, who led the New Zealanders in FB.VI LR333/EG-R; D. Ponchardier, leader of the local Resistance at the time of the raid and who sent a message of thanks to the Air Ministry in London in March 1944; Mrs and S/L Ian McRitchie. (via John Rayner)

Above left *P/O C. F. Redgrave, navigator (left) and F/L B. D. 'Titch' Hanafin, pilot, of 487 (RNZAF) Squadron, pictured earlier in their careers when the New Zealand squadron was equipped with the Lockheed Ventura. On the Amiens raid Hanafin led the second flight in HX855/EG-Q before his port engine caught fire en route to the target and he was forced to abort and return to Hunsdon on one engine. (via John Rayner)*

Above right *The southern wall, left of the main gate at Amiens. As none of the crews attacked from the south, it must be assumed that the breach was caused by a bomb that skidded through the prison after being dropped from the east or north. (via John Rayner)*

Below *The breached northern wall and the badly-damaged Amiens prison. Two pilots – P/O D. R. Fowler of 487 (RNZAF) Squadron, who flew HX974/EG-J, and Ian McRitchie, of 464 (RAAF) Squadron, claim the same hole! McRitchie states that the wall was unmarked when he made his approach. (BAe, via Philip Birtles)*

S/L Ian McRitchie DFC (left) and F/L R. W. 'Sammy' Sampson of 464 (RAAF) Squadron. Their Mosquito, MM404/SB-T, was hit by flak, but despite being wounded in 26 places, McRitchie managed to crash-land his shattered aircraft near Poix. Tragically, Sampson was killed. (via John Rayner)

diately became lost. Their Typhoon escorts also had problems with the weather and one of the squadrons failed to show. Two Mosquitoes, both from 21 Squadron, returned early when about 10 miles from the target. F/L 'Titch' Hanafin of 487 (RNZAF) Squadron was forced to abort because of an engine fire. The remaining Mosquitoes descended to 100 ft, their propellers swirling wispy snowclouds in their wake. At 12:01 hrs precisely, with the guards eating lunch, bombs from five of 487's aircraft, five of 464 and a sixth 487 aircraft, piloted by Pickard, hurtled into the snow-covered prison. The first bomb blew in almost all of the doors and the wall was breached. F/L Tony Wickham, in a specially-equipped Film Photographic Unit Mosquito, made three passes over the ruined jail which was now disgorging smoke and flame and fleeing men, and his cameraman, P/O Lee Howard, filmed the flight of some 255 prisoners. Some of the 37 prisoners who died during the raid were machine gunned to death by the sentries; another 182 were recaptured and 50 Germans were killed. Pickard cir-

cled the area at 500 ft and, satisfied that the leading elements had done their work, radioed 21 Squadron, circling 10 miles to the north, to return home. Almost immediately, *F-Freddie* was attacked by an Fw 190 of II/JG26, and Pickard and Broadley crashed in flames. A Typhoon flown by F/O Paul Renaud was shot down and the pilot taken prisoner. A Mosquito flown by S/L Ian McRitchie of 464 (RAAF) Squadron was hit by flak, but despite being wounded in 26 places, the Australian managed to crash-land his shattered aircraft near Poix. F/L R. W. 'Sammy' Sampson, his navigator, was killed.

Cpl Hunt remembers the 'general air of sadness' back at Hunsdon:

Everyone was miserable. We went into mourning. It was a sad night, but at a meeting we were told that we must carry on. When you are 20 years old, like I was, it was 'tough luck'; but when someone didn't come back the attitude was always, 'it's him and not me'.

More low-level daylight raids, for which 140 Wing would become legendary, followed the

Amiens strike. On 11 April 1944 six Mosquito FB.VIs of 613 Squadron, led by W/C R. N. Bateson, succeeded in destroying the Gestapo's records of the Dutch Resistance in the Kunstzaal Kleizkamp (Kleizkamp Art Galleries), a five-storey, 90-ft-high building situated close to the Peace Palace in The Hague. On 14 July 1944 the Gestapo barracks at Bonneuil Matours, in the north-east part of Foret de Mouliere, were attacked by Mosquitoes of 464 (RAAF) and 487 (RNZAF) Squadrons. G/C Peter Wykeham-Barnes DSO & Bar DFC and F/O Chaplin led 487's aircraft, and W/C R. H. Reynolds DSO DFC led 464's quartet. Their targets were six buildings inside a rectangle just 170 x 100 ft, close to the village which had to be avoided. The Mosquitoes dropped nine tons of bombs in shallow dives on the target.

On 1 August 24 Mosquitoes of 21 and 487 (RNZAF) Squadrons carried out a low-level attack on the Poitiers barracks, escorted by RAF Mustangs. The next day, 23 Mosquitoes of 107 and 305 (Polish) Squadrons hit the Sabotage School at Chateau Maulny. On 18 August 14 Mosquitoes of 613 Squadron, led by AVM Embry, attacked a school building being used as an SS barracks at Egletons, 50 miles south-east of Limoges, and delivered at least 20 direct hits to destroy the target. On 31 August, millions of gallons of petrol in a huge petrol dump at Nomency, near Nancy, were destroyed, thus depriving the German Panzer divisions in the Battle of Normandy of much-needed fuel.

On 31 October 25 Mosquitoes of 21, 464 and 487 Squadrons, each carrying 11-sec delayed-action bombs and led by G/C Peter Wykeham-Barnes, were sent to Denmark to destroy the Gestapo HQ at Aarhus University in Jutland. Included in the Mosquito formation was AVM Basil Embry and his navigator, Peter Clapham. Embry wore no medal ribbons and was known as 'W/C Smith'. The Mosquitoes escort was provided by eight Mustang IIIs of 315 (Polish) Squadron, 12 Group, which flew to Swanton Morley from their base at Andrews Field in Essex, led by the CO, S/L Tadeusz Andersz. One of the Mustang pilots was F/L Konrad 'Wiewiorka' (Squirrel) Stembrowicz, who recalls:

We landed at Swanton Morley early on the morning of 31 October. One or two of our Mustangs damaged their tailwheels on the grass field and were not ready in time for the escort. Eight of us refuelled and took off again to rendezvous with the Mosquitoes over the North Sea. When we saw them they were at 100 ft above the waves. Our two Finger Fours formated 50 ft below to starboard and slightly south of them. We crossed Denmark and dropped our auxiliary 90-gal petrol tanks, which by necessity were only half-filled. Mine fell near a Danish cottage surrounded by a mass of brown, yellow and orange chrysanthemums. People ran out of the house and waved their arms and large white tablecloths as we all roared past. Approaching Aarhus the Mosquitoes lifted slightly. They were to attack down a street west to east. The leading section of four Mustangs went left and we followed.

On 31 October 1944 25 Mosquitoes of 21, 464 (RAAF) and 487 (RNZAF) Squadrons, each carrying 11-second delayed action bombs, and led by G/C Peter Wykeham-Barnes, destroyed the Gestapo HQ at Aarhus University in Jutland. This remarkable still shows bombs leaving one of the Mosquitoes and explosions bottom right caused by bombs dropped from the right-hand aircraft. (via Philip Birtles)

The attack was carried out at such a low altitude that one Mosquito hit the roof of the building, losing its tailwheel and the port half of the tailplane, but it limped back across the North Sea and managed to land safely. The university and its incriminating records were destroyed. Among the dead was SS Obersturn Fuehrer Lonechun, Head of the Security Services. (via Philip Birtles)

F/L Stembrowicz concludes:

We saw explosions and very light ack-ack coming up in the Mosquitoes wake. All of us went to the right and put ourselves between the Mosquitoes and the German airfields. This time we were higher. We saw no fighters and the flight home was uneventful.

The attack was carried out at such a low altitude that one Mosquito hit the roof of the building, losing its tailwheel and the port half of the tailplane, but it limped back across the North Sea and managed to land safely. The university and its incriminating records were destroyed. Among the dead was SS Obersturn Fuehrer Lonechun, Head of the Security Services.

Altogether, nine Mosquito squadrons equipped 2nd TAF. In September 1944, following the outbreak from the Normandy beachhead, plans were in progress to move them to airfields in France. In November 1944 107, 305 (Polish) and 613 Squadrons, all of 138 Wing, were based at Epinoy, near Cambrai. Mosquitoes of 21, 464 (RAAF) and 487 (RNZAF) Squadrons remained behind at Thorney Island, but in December 1944 the RAAF and RNZAF squadrons both sent advance detachments to Rosieres-en-Santerre, France. In February 1945 the two squadrons, along with 21 Squadron, all of 140 Wing, left southern England and landed at Amiens-Rosieres-en-Santerre. Their arrival coincided with the first anniversary of the Amiens raid by 140 Wing Mosquitoes in February 1944, when the 'walls of Jericho' had come tumbling down.

In March 1945, Special Operations Executive (SOE) in London received intelligence that various Resistance and political prisoners held captive in the Gestapo HQ Shellhaus building in Copenhagen were to be shot on 21 March. The Free Danish Resistance movement had made repeated requests that the RAF should attack the building, even though most of the prisoners were held in the attic to thwart any attempt to bomb the

HQ. Basil Embry considered the implications and decided to send the low-level experts in 140 Wing, some of whom had flown on the Amiens prison raid and the attack on the Gestapo HQ in The Hague, to make a daring pinpoint raid on the Shellhaus.

To minimize the risks of flying over enemy territory, 18 Mosquitoes of 140 Wing flew to Fersfield, Suffolk, 350 miles from the target, on 20 March. Crews studied a model of the Shellhaus and were thoroughly briefed by G/C R. N. 'Bob' Bateson and Svend Truelsen, the Danish Resistance leader, who confirmed the absolute necessity for the raid, emphasizing that the Resistance members held in the attic would prefer to die by RAF bombs rather than be shot by the Gestapo. Finally, the 18 Mosquitoes, each loaded with 11-second delayed-action bombs, took off and headed out over the North Sea where they rendezvoused with Mustang IIIs of 64 and 126 Squadrons from Fersfield.

Bateson and Sismore led the first wave, which included Embry and Peter Clapham and four Mosquitoes of 21 Squadron, including one flown by the new CO, W/C Peter Kleboe DSO DFC AFC. The second wave of six Mosquitoes was led by W/C Bob Iredale DFC, who had flown the Amiens prison raid, and the third wave comprised six Mosquitoes of 487 (RNZAF) squadron, led by W/C F. H. Denton, who had flown the Aarhus raid. Still cameras were carried on aircraft in all three waves and Film Photographic Unit Mosquitoes bombed with the first and third waves.

At 11:14 hrs, amid light anti-aircraft fire, Bateson's bombs hit the first and second floors. Embry and Clapham, and then S/L A. Carlisle, the deputy leader, got their bombs away. Kleboe hit a 130-ft-high lamp standard 800 yd from the target and crashed. The Mosquito erupted in flames and scattered debris after three bombs fell from the bomb bay and exploded, killing eight Danish civilians. The last two Mosquitoes, flown by S/L Henderson and F/L Hetherington, put their bombs through the roof of the Shellhaus before they scattered and exited the city at roof-top height. Henderson was so low that Embry, below him, was forced down into the streets, and they missed collision by only a few feet.

The second wave followed. Iredale and F/O Standish had problems picking out the target because of smoke but got their bombs away on the correct target on their second run. F/L W. Shrimpton and F/O Lake also skirted the city twice, but had to abandon their second run to avoid collision over the target. They took their bombs home. Two 464 (RAAF) Squadron Mosquitoes following mistook Kleboe's burning Mosquito as the target. The Jeanne d'Arc school, only a few yards away, was destroyed by their bombs and 86 of the 482 children died in the conflagration. At least four Mosquitoes in the third wave hit the wrong area, but the two remaining aircraft realized the error and did not drop their bombs. Altogether, the four-minute raid cost four Mosquitoes and two of the Mustang escorts. F/L Pattison and F/Sgt Pygram's badly damaged Mosquito crashed, killing both crew, as they tried to run for Sweden.

That night the Danish Freedom Council radioed SOE headquarters in Baker Street that the Shellhaus had been completely destroyed and that 30 Danish hostages had escaped, including two Resistance leaders. Of four men who had leapt 50 ft to the street below during the bombing, only one survived.

140 Wing had one more low-level pinpoint raid to fly. On 17 April six Mosquitoes, led by Bateson and Sismore, taxied out for a daylight strike on a school building on the outskirts of Odense which was being used by the Gestapo as an HQ. Basil Embry went along, as usual, under the alias of 'W/C Smith'. Cpl Ralph Ramm and his two AC2s in 21 Squadron at Melsbroek filled Embry's petrol tanks with the requisite 50 gal and checked that both engine tanks were topped off with 29 gal of oil:

He came to the aircraft and I produced the 700A Travelling Aircraft Servicing Form for him to sign (this always went with the aircraft). Basil Embry took it, signed it, and handed it back. He looked me straight in the eye, as if to say, 'You don't expect me to keep it', knowing that if he was shot down the paper could be found and reveal his real name. I took it, saluted and said, 'Thank you Sir!' 'Chiefy' Lucas didn't want the 700A either so I kept it as a souvenir.

The six Mosquitoes destroyed the Gestapo HQ and 18 days later Denmark was free.

Chapter Fourteen

The Milk Run that Turned Sour

VE-Day was celebrated on 8 May 1945. Although the European war was over, Coastal Command Mosquitoes continued to mount operations after VE-Day for fear that the German crews aboard U-Boats had not received word of the surrender. Mosquitoes continued to escort convoys and carried out sea searches for crashed aircraft until 21 May, when four aircraft of 143 and 248 Squadrons flew the final patrol of the European war, between Svinoy and Terningen.

But this is not the end of our story about

Mosquitoes in the Second World War. In addition to those in service with Coastal Command, Mosquito ferry flights across the Atlantic, from May 1945 onwards, were still in full swing. Since early 1942 Canadian-built Mosquitoes had been flown to Britain, or directly to the theatres of war. By December 1944, when 17 Canadian-built machines were flown to Britain, some 230 Mosquitoes had crossed the Atlantic Ocean by means of the Northern Ferry Route, via Gander–Greenland–Iceland–Prestwick, and the Southern Ferry Route, via South America, Ascension Island and North West Africa. In January 1945 four Mosquitoes went missing over the Atlantic; two were thought to have been brought down in tropical storms. In February, KB562 also failed to arrive at its destination after leaving Canada and being flown across the Southern Ferry Route. The pilot was F/L David Backhouse, from Maxstoke Castle in Warwickshire, who recalled an earlier ferry flight:

In May 1943 I had flown one of the early Hudsons across the South Atlantic as a co-pilot to F/L Burzynsky, a short, dumpy Polish pilot, very pleasantly mannered. He was incredibly old; almost 30. He was known as the millionaire pilot because he had flown in Europe long before the war and had covered more than a million miles. He was killed about a year later, when a Liberator he was flying crashed into a high-rise building just outside Montreal. [Andrew Lavery, who had been the only other pilot in the same

F/L Denis Hudson and F/L David Backhouse (right), pictured in Nassau in 1945 during a ferry flight across the Atlantic. (Denis Hudson)

course as Backhouse to qualify for the elite role in Transport Command, was killed on his first trip as co-pilot in a Hudson. Training was rigorous. Potential ferry pilots had to qualify as a pilot, navigator and radio operator.]

After the Atlantic flight with Burzynsky I qualified at North Bay, Canada as captain, flying over 70 trips on Hudsons and 30 in Oxfords for instrument [blind] flying and radio range. By April 1945 I had made 36 Atlantic crossings, 18 as captain and 18 as passenger/co-pilot, delivering Baltimores, Dakotas and Marauders, and the Mosquito, on both the southern and northern routes. We called the much easier southern crossing, Bahamas–Puerto Rico–Trinidad–Brazil–Gold Coast, the 'Cream Run', while the recently navigated northern route was the 'Milk Run'.

On 17 April 1945 18 aircrew were *en route* to London, Ontario, to collect nine Mosquito aircraft which they would fly over the North Atlantic to Scotland. They were a set of Damon Runyan characters: a couple of expatriate Poles, a Czech and a Norwegian; a civilian pilot (who was a conscientious objector) with a South African radio/navigator; some RCAF and two RAF crews, 'Bingo' Clarke and Vladimir 'Laddie' Sopuk, a Czech-Canadian; myself and my observer-radio navigator F/L Denis Hudson, a Yorkshireman from Keighley. 'Bingo' had a jet black walrus moustache and was a most extrovert man and good company. 'Laddie' was squat, thickset, looking more like a wrestler than what would have been his future profession: a concert violinist. He had trained in Vienna just before the war.

At London we checked in to simple but decent bedrooms, breakfasted well on waffles and maple syrup, fried eggs and strong coffee, and went to the main hangar to identify our aircraft. I don't know how much KA146 cost to build, but I had signed for it in Montreal and it was now my responsibility! On a F/Lt's pay, even when seconded to the RCAF, I doubt if I could afford one of the large propellers.

Next day we took off for the 2 hr 40 min flight to Mont Joli in Quebec State. It was a pleasant flight in clear sky and bright sunlight. With a slight diversion south shortly after leaving London, you had an excellent view of Niagara Falls, and for this purpose I had kept the aircraft at 2,000 ft. Flying across the rest of Lake Ontario I climbed to 9,000 ft for the remainder of the flight to make best use of favourable winds, and yet not requiring oxygen which became necessary above 10,000 ft. A pleasant and easy job for me, and presumably also for Denis to navigate, for you met the St Lawrence River by Montreal and then followed its course north-east to Three Rivers and Mont Joli.

My allotted task was to deliver KA146 to the UK. The route was up to me. I could fly via Goose Bay in Labrador or Gander in Newfoundland, and thence to Scotland via Greenland and/or Iceland. With favourable tailwinds you could sometimes miss out Greenland, and with really favourable conditions and with extra drop tanks fitted under the wings, it was possible to fly from Goose or Gander to Prestwick direct. We had already made a direct crossing some months earlier in 6 hr 20 min, having the benefit of a 100-kt tailwind – which of course added well over 100 mph to our ground speed. However, in bad weather – and it usually was – it was prudent to fly what we called 'Round the Parish' – from Goose or Gander to Greenland (if necessary) to Iceland to Scotland. Earlier, Hudsons had to fly from Labrador or Newfoundland to Iceland on the first leg of the Atlantic crossing, until September 1941, when a quite remarkable landing strip was established in Greenland.

At Mont Joli we found that the weather in both Newfoundland and Labrador was so foul as to prohibit flying there, so we spent one full and pleasant week in and around Mont Joli. Huge T-bone steaks were served on wooden platters in local restaurants and there was plenty to drink. By comparison, we were immeasurably better off than civilians in London, Birmingham or Coventry [which he had seen burn from the castle battlements at Maxstoke Castle where his father was a tenant]. Once over the North Atlantic, however, the balance might be somewhat redressed.

In consultation with Denis I selected Goose Bay as the preferable taking-off point for the Atlantic crossing. The flight from Mont Joli to Goose was going to take less than three hrs in the fast Mosquito, and it was almost entirely over a vast and bleak expanse of whiteness. Frozen snow covered everything. The landscape had no depth, few undulations, no shadows, no roads, no trees, no habitation; nothing but a permanent whiteness without seasons. And the land seemed only to vaguely merge with the sky. The sky in daytime seemed darker than the snow-covered ground, locked in a freezing cold in which nothing could survive. And so, on the 25 April, we took off. Well out over the Davis Strait it seemed that one of the generators was giving problems, but we considered conditions reasonable to fly on to Greenland. Greenland is a misnomer, for there is nothing green about it, and this huge island, the size of a continent, seems to be a large block of ice.

The survey flight in 1941 by D. C. T. Bennett had suggested the possibility of a landing strip on the south-west coast of Greenland. It was achieved and so became the most remarkable and most hazardous airstrip in the world. Thought of originally as an emergency base, it had the wartime code of 'BW1', pronounced in radio terms as Bluie West One.

The generator seemed to be functioning again and we homed in to the radio range on Semitak Island. Ahead was the south-west coast of Greenland which, as we approached, became evident as a considerable number of rugged fjords along the coastline. Before leaving Goose there had been a thorough weather briefing and a movie showing which fjord to select if you had to land at Bluie, and how to navigate once in the long, narrow fjord. We must select the right one. There would be no flying back out if you got the wrong one, because low overcast meant you were, in effect, flying down a long tunnel. To attempt a climb you would almost certainly hit a mountain. Denis and I compared notes and agreed what we considered to be the right fjord. The length of the fjord was about 60 miles, so our journey down it at 200 mph would last 20 min. A very long 20 min. Where the fjord divided we took the right fork and saw a rusty old cargo ship half on its side. We had chosen correctly.

The fjord curved round to the left again and, quite suddenly, we arrived in a little bay where the fjord ended in a lake. The bay was filled with floating ice and on it's north edge – the very end of the glacier – the sheer rock gave way to a fan-shaped area of near flattish ground on which a metal link mat, or runway, provided a single uphill landing strip. A cluster of Nissen huts provided accommodation, Mess halls and the necessary administration buildings. Not far from the higher end of the landing strip the rock face rose for several thousand ft – which meant that you could only land uphill and take off downhill, regardless of the direction of the wind. We made a reasonably smooth landing although the metal links clanked a bit as we rolled along them. We then taxied to a dispersal point where we were met by a Jeep. Scattered around the base were a couple of Hudsons in RAF markings and some Liberators with the USAAF insignia. There were no other Mosquitoes. Presumably some had remained at Goose or Gander and others may have flown direct to Iceland with favourable winds.

After a good night's rest in comfortable enough, if primitive, accommodation, we rose for an early breakfast and went to briefing and the Met Office. Bluie West One and Meeks Field, Reykjavik were both

KB471, a Canadian-built B.25, fitted with Merlin 25 engines. (via Jerry Scutts)

'open', although the weather between was not good and liable to get worse in the next few days. The flight from Goose Bay to Bluie West One had taken three hrs. It would take about the same to fly from Bluie to Meeks Field, and as it was not thought the weather would deteriorate much for the next few hrs, it seemed reasonable to depart forthwith.

The Mosquito had already been refuelled and the reported fault repaired. Denis filed a flight plan and we boarded. I started both engines and carried out the usual pre-flight checks to see if everything seemed in order. It seemed so. I called the control tower and taxied to the top end of the runway, facing downhill to the water with its floating lumps of ice. The tall face of the glacier was only a few ft behind the aircraft. We rose into the air well before the end of the metal link strip, banked left and threaded our way back through the fjord to its mouth. Here we climbed steadily, flew around Cape Farewell and set course for Iceland.

Once out of the fjord and climbing, we continued up through the overcast, flying 'blind' or on instruments – for in cloud you can see nothing beyond your wing-tips. You climb steadily through the dark and gloomy cloud until, for a matter of a split-second, there is an almost imperceptible brightening in the cockpit – and then you burst into bright sunlight and clear blue skies. We climbed to 9,000 ft where I levelled out and put her 'on the step'. This was a method used by long-distance pilots of climbing a few hundred ft above the decided operational height and edging back down to keep the aircraft in a slightly nose-down attitude, so getting the best possible airspeed in relation to fuel consumption. You did not have the advantage of 'George', the automatic pilot, in this aircraft; but in clear atmosphere I could trim the Mosquito to cruise smoothly, requiring only a light touch of my fingers and feet to control it. Everywhere around was clear and bright. Two thousand ft below, the cloud-top bathed in sunlight looked like cotton wool. Now the cloud cover was complete and we could no longer see the cold, grey Atlantic. But you knew it was there! I had already been down 'in the drink' in another Mosquito in the South Atlantic. In the bleak North Atlantic, life expectancy was measured in seconds. But with the optimism of youth, neither Denis nor I gave it much thought and were little concerned. Time enough to be concerned if something went wrong.

After 2$\frac{1}{2}$ hrs of flight, Denis handed me a note. We had just passed our point of no return, meaning that with strong headwinds on the way back we would not have enough fuel to return to Bluie, and were therefore committed to landing at Meeks Field. There was no alternative airfield available. Reykjavik should still remain open, but the weather there was deteriorating. The second point was that the generator had packed up! We were without radio, which was the main asset to navigation in these latitudes. Having no direction-finding equipment, you can rely only on dead reckoning – a somewhat bizarre term for visual navigation. With 10/10ths cloud cover over the water below, this posed something of a problem. Iceland is a big island and we knew we were flying towards it. But with the cloud cover, would we see it? The alternative was to descend through the cloud, hoping that its base would be sufficiently above the sea for us to identify our position so that we could fly north or south until we spotted Reykjavik.

Given a reasonable cloud base this was the best option. At least the one to try first, I reasoned. So I started a gentle descent by throttling back a little and we left our bright sunny world for the dark murk of the cloud which, without the sun, was a dense blackish-grey. I throttled back a little more and pulled back on the centre column and trimmed the ship to lose sufficient airspeed to put down a quarter flap. This enabled me to lower more slowly through the overcast at a reduced airspeed. I wasn't unduly keen to be doing anything up to 300 mph in such conditions. Down we went, 8,000ft and into the cloud. The measurement of your height above the ground (or water), while being fairly accurate in those days, was not an exact science. At 2,000 ft I added a touch of throttle to decrease my rate of descent still further. At 1,000 ft, still in cloud, I crept downwards, hoping second-by-second for a glimpse of the sea. At 200 ft indicated, still no contact. Seldom do the cloud and sky meet. There was still hope. I must watch for any sign of contact while still flying only by instruments. 150 ft reached and still no visual contact. I held at this indicated height for perhaps half a minute and 'risked' perhaps another 15 ft. No contact. Held height. Then I saw it – the sea raging below us! Everything was water; the cloud was water and it fed hard, driving rain into the sea below. Worse still, the sea was so rough that it threw up waves 30 or 40 ft high. I was conscious of the fact that spray from wave tops was hitting the underside of our fuselage.

Suddenly, incomprehensively, there in front of us was a ship! It seemed almost below us. Denis saw it first and shouted. He told me later that as I pushed both throttles fully forward we passed over its top deck between its two masts. I now climbed back into the cloud, remembering to go up at least a 100 ft before raising the quarter flap. If you raise too quickly at the wrong speed the aircraft sinks a little, and this

Canadian-built B.XX. KB326, named ACTON ONTARIO, CANADA, was the first of two such aircraft to arrive at Hatfield on 12 August 1943. The B.XX was basically a Canadian-built B.IV. (via Jerry Scutts)

was clearly undesirable! With flaps up and full power, I climbed, feeling temporarily relieved but realizing we did not know what our second option would find back at 8,000 or 9,000 ft.

To say that during these few minutes down below, between life and death – and death surely must have been less than a split-second away – I was frightened, would not be true. The fact that I was not and acted instinctively is due to the excellent training undergone in the British armed forces. 'Square-bashing' – being shouted at by corporals and sergeants – followed by the knowledge imparted by instructors in flying, navigation, radio and mechanics, fits you for the job to be

done so that you react without question and do what has to be done. It is not too far-fetched to say that my survival on this fateful trip could be due to that little bastard of a corporal who seemed to pick on me when I first joined the RAF!

I broke out of the cloud cover again at 8,000 ft. Now we were back in the world of bright sunshine, blue sky and cotton wool clouds – but where was Iceland? Denis gave me a course to fly for Reykjavik. Down below my mind was fully occupied with survival. Now I fully comprehended what a close shave we had had. Most men will live their whole lives without being really tested. I think we were tested then.

We must fly on in the hope that the cloud might begin to break up over land and that we should see Iceland, and then by dead reckoning to find Meeks Field. Even if we could not make it, our chances of survival were not too bad. Going into the sea meant certain death, but on land, even though freezing, you could get some insulation by digging a hole for yourself in the snow and using the large nylon panels of the parachute to wrap yourself and to provide top cover. The single seat of a Mosquito was like an empty, elongated shallow bucket. Your parachute fitted into this bucket and you thus flew with the parachute already strapped on, using the folded 'chute part as a seat. In the base of the seat itself would be 'K' rations, a flare, and possibly even five cigarettes.

Our departure from Bluie West One was notified to Meeks Field, of course, and an estimated time of arrival given. We were now getting near that time, and because we had no radio contact, Meeks Field would already know that something was wrong and emergency procedures would be put into action. They could give us a good chance of survival, so I hoped I could look forward to my 22nd birthday the following month. Denis seemed to be working hard on some navigational feat. He said we must now be very near the coastline. Reykjavik is on the coast, although we could be well north or south of it. If north, we would already be over land. If south, probably still over sea.

Still in bright sunlight above the clouds, to my right, about two miles distant and 1,000 ft below, I saw an almost exactly circular break in the clouds, about half a mile in diameter. Then I saw other, smaller, breaks. Having no radio as a navigational aid, we could not know over what part of the Icelandic coastline we would arrive. And there below me it was not only the ground but, in clear view, the multi-coloured roofs of Reykjavik! Reds, yellows, blues and other colours. Why they painted their roofs, I did not know. Maybe it was to relieve the monotony of the bleak white countryside. They could be seen from higher ground, or maybe they were painted to be more easily seen by people like me. At that time I was not concerned but just thankful they were there.

I did a tight turn, banking around the inner edge of the cloud, and descended in this manner for about 1,000 ft. Now the cloud was breaking up and we came out in the clear under the clouds, about 5,000 ft above Reykjavik. Meeks Field was immediately evident. I could not call up the control tower for permission to land so I decided to do a conventional approach and landing. I flew over the centre of the airfield at 1,500 ft, keeping a watchful eye for other aircraft. Although it was daylight I put on my downward navigation

lights and 'waggled' my wings as I flew past the control tower. Now they would have the binoculars on me and had probably already identified me as the 'missing' Mosquito. They would know that something was wrong and would warn any other aircraft in the vicinity to keep clear. In the white square adjacent to the control tower was an arrow marking the direction of landing and figures showing the height of the runway above sea level. I checked the landing direction with the windsock and noted there would be a fair crosswind from left to right; where there is only a single runway you cannot always land directly into the wind, as you would wish to. I banked and turned 180° back across the field, and then turned again and flew towards the runway in the correct direction for landing. I had now reduced height to 1,000 ft. The runway at Meeks Field was short in length and although four-engined planes could use it, it meant building up extra revs with brakes on for a quick take-off. For landing you wanted to touch down as soon as you could near the beginning of the runway. Near one end of the runway – the one we were now approaching – the land fell sharply away towards the sea, so that the runway began almost on top of a huge boulder. A hundred yds or so in front of this runway we could see a broken Mosquito where it had in fact evidently throttled back too early and had flown straight into the hill. There it lay, just before the end of the runway. Its occupants would be dead.

I flew over it at 1,000 ft and flew exactly over the length of the runway, turned left and flew downwind, parallel to the runway, losing height and speed. With the speed low enough I lowered the wheels and put down half flap. Past the end of the runway I turned crosswind still losing height and then turned into wind on final approach. I put down full flap. As we passed some 20 ft over the crashed Mosquito I cut the throttles, and we settled down comfortably some 30 yds down the runway. I taxied in and parked in a dispersal point. A Jeep was out to meet us and I could see a fire engine and an ambulance at the end of the runway.

I reported the failed generator and went to the Operations Room, where they would want to hear our story. But first, who was in the crashed Mosquito? The pilot was 'Bingo' Clark. His radio-navigator was Vladimir 'Laddie' Sopuk. They must both have been killed instantly. We buried them both a few days later in Montreal with full military honours.

That evening, Dennis and I had a reasonably good meal; probably better than you could get in England. I would sometimes buy food, even fresh steaks, in Mont Joli. There was no problem in finding a cold place to store them and normally you could reach Prestwick in

Mosquito B.IX LR503/F of 105 Squadron which completed a Bomber Command record of 213 opera-
tional sorties in the Pathfinder Force. F/L Maurice Briggs (right) and navigator John Baker flew the
Mosquito on a goodwill tour of Canada, but were killed when the aircraft crashed at Calgary on 10
May 1945. (via Jerry Scutts)

two or three days according to route. After dinner a
few drinks in the bar, to which we felt entitled.

We left the next day after an early lunch so we
would arrive at Prestwick in daylight. Night flying
was not permitted because of German intruders. The
flight was uneventful, which meant it was also pleasant. First the long haul across the water, flying for a
while at 20,000 ft to be over the cloud top. Then the
descending to my more customary height of 9,000 ft
as the skies were clear about 400 miles out of Iceland.
The weather forecast for Prestwick was fair; but even
if Prestwick itself had not been clear, there were many

alternative landing places, this part of the world being
rather more populated than Labrador or Greenland or
Iceland.

Our first landfall was Stornaway; soon the Isle of
Skye. Now gradually descending at more than 300
mph across the beautiful lochs and firths of the
Scottish Highlands until, passing to the west of
Glasgow at 1,500 ft, we approached and landed at
Prestwick, where we handed over the aircraft. I gave a
little pat on the fuselage. Someone else would fly it to
its selected home. (We had just flown it for over 4,000
miles.)

Chapter Fifteen

Far East Ops

One of the myriad of problems facing South-East Asia Command (SEAC) in India in 1943 was the aerial reconnaissance of Burma and Malaya from its far-flung bases in Ceylon and India. Only the camera-fitted Mitchells of 681 Squadron based at Dum Dum, Calcutta, possessed the range and speed for long range photo-reconnaissance (PR) over the Bay of Bengal and the Rangoon area. At the beginning of April 1943 three Mosquito FB.IIs and three FB.VIs were allotted to 27 Squadron at Agartala: three for performance tests and familiarization, three to be used for weathering trials during the coming rainy season, under the supervision of Mr F. G. Myers, de Havilland's technical representative in India. Late in the month, however, it was decided that the Mosquitoes should supplement the squadron's Beaufighters for *Intruder* operations.

The first Mosquito operation over Burma was a reconnaissance on 14 May 1943. It is reported that Maj Hereward de Havilland, visiting 27 Squadron, was horrified to find that the FB.IIs were being put to operational use, and attempted to have them grounded because he considered that the casein glue with which they were bonded was unlikely to withstand insect attack and the tropical weather. The FB.VIs, yet to arrive, were supposedly bonded with 'waterproof' formaldehyde adhesive. 27 Squadron used the FB.IIs again on only one occasion: one crashed and another was damaged by ground fire on 5 June.

The aircraft situation in 681 (PR) Squadron at Dum Dum was causing great concern. Two serviceable Mitchells had been in use for over 12 months and there were no aircraft in the command, other than the Mosquitoes, with equivalent operational range and high speed. After some delay, while Air Ministry approval was sought for their conversion to PR aircraft at No 1 CMU, Kanchrapara, two Mosquitoes and their flight crews were transferred in August to the twin-engined Flight of 681 Squadron, followed by the three newly-arrived FB.VIs.

On 23 August F/O Dupee DFM reconnoitered the Mandalay–Shewbo-yeu–Monywa–Wuntho area. The following day a second Mosquito sortie was flown when F/L Picknett made a reconnaissance of Akyab Island. During September 681 Squadron flew eight PR sorties over vast areas of Burma, and on occasion a Mosquito FB.VI was employed. One of the Mosquitoes became a victim of enemy action, but after a forced landing, it was repaired and returned to Calcutta after three weeks. The feared deterioration of adhesive did not happen despite the aircraft being continually exposed to high temperatures and humidity, so approval was given for the delivery of more Mosquitoes to India.

In September five Mosquito PR.IXs arrived in-theatre. In October 47 Squadron, which was equipped with Beaufighter Xs at Yelahanka, India, began receiving a few Mosquito FB.VIs. On 21 October 681 Squadron flew the first of 33 PR sorties over Burma as far as Rangoon and the Akyab Trail, before their Mosquitoes were transferred to 684 Squadron, which had been formed from the twin-engined Flight of 681 Squadron on 29 September with two Mosquito FB.IIs,

684 Squadron used several different marks of PR Mosquito in the war in the Far East, including the PR.IX (pictured here), the PR.XVI and PR.34. (MoD)

three Mosquito FB.VIs and four Mitchells. The first Mosquito PR.IX was added to its strength on 18 October and the second followed five days later.

On 24 October F/L McCulloch with Sgt Vigors flew a reconnaissance of Rangoon and Magwe. On 24 October McCulloch and F/L Reeves made a reconnaissance of the Andaman Islands to bring back photos of Japanese shipping and flying boat activity. Three Ki-43 Oscar fighters tried to intercept the high-altitude Mosquito, but could not match the British aircraft for height. That same day, F/S Johnson with Sgt Willis in a Mosquito FB.II, returned safely with photos of Rangoon despite another attempted interception, this time by two Japanese fighters, and anti-aircraft fire at 27,000 ft.

The first Mosquito loss while on operations from India occurred on 2 November 1943, when F/O Fielding and F/O Turton failed to return from a PR of the Rangoon area. On 9 December the six remaining Mosquitoes and four Mitchells

of 684 Squadron moved to Comilla in East Bengal, where it formed part of 171 Wing. Their stay was short, just one month, and their debut was marred by the loss of two crews. On 10 December a Mosquito FB.II flown by Sgt Boot with Sgt Wilkins, was shot down over Rangoon, and an FB.VI piloted by F/O Orr with Sgt Johnson, suffered a fatal crash after structural failure. Operations now involved distances of over 1,000 miles from base and an 8-hr mission duration was not uncommon. On 15 December S/L B. S. Jones, the CO, with F/O Dawson, reconnoitered Bangkok for the first time; a feat which earned both men the DFC.

On Christmas Day 1943 27 Squadron, equipped with a mixed inventory of Beaufighters and Mosquito FB.VIs, despatched its first Mosquito sorties proper. The 'Flying Elephants' were commanded by W/C E. J. B. Nicolson, famous as the only Battle of Britain pilot to have been awarded the Victoria Cross, which he had gained for his actions on 17 August 1940.

A Mosquito PR.XVI taxis out at an airfield in Bengal. (via Philip Birtles)

Despite terrible burns sustained in the action, Nicolson recovered, and in 1942 he had been posted as station commander to Alipore, Calcutta. On 25 December he and F/O Thompson made strafing attacks on Japanese railway targets. Nicolson flew 27 Squadron's final Mosquito operation on 9 March 1944: a reconnaissance of Japanese airfields. Later, as commander of training at SEAC, he spent some time with Liberator crews, studying the results of aircrew training operationally. On 1 May 1945 Nicolson was lost aboard a Liberator involved in a night raid on Rangoon.

Meanwhile, in January 1944, the Air Ministry decided to equip 22 bomber and strike squadrons with Mosquito FB.VI aircraft to replace the Vultee Vengeance and some Beaufighters. De Havilland were to produce replacement airframe components at Karachi. In February 684 Squadron, now back at Dum Dum, received nine pressurized PR.XVIs, and sorties at higher altitudes were subsequently flown. The remaining

FB.VIs were retired but were a valuable source of spares, because parts were in very short supply. At the beginning of the month 684 Squadron had begun a photographic survey of Burma, while reconnaissance flights to islands in the Indian Ocean continued. On 7 February W/C W. B. Murray, who had taken over command in December 1943, with F/O Hawson, tussled with an A6M3 Hamp over Port Blair. Later that same day another Mosquito was intercepted over Bangkok and had to abort.

In March 684 Squadron made regular flights to the Andaman Islands and reconnoitered the Japanese railway system in Burma. On 22 March F/L Robin Sinclair with F/O R. Stocks of 684 Squadron, made the first sortie by an RAF aircraft over Malaya since the fall of Singapore when they reconnoitered the Bangkok–Singapore railway line. On 27 March F/L Newman with F/Sgt Smith flew a 1,860-mile trip to photograph a stretch of the Burma railway and airfields at Bangkok and Hua Hin. Four days later F/O

and F/O Gerald Stevens flew to Tenasserim and Kra via the advanced landing ground at Kyaukpyu and took high-level verticals, before dropping to just 50 ft for oblique photos of St Luke, St Matthew and Domel Islands. On 28 May F/O C. G. Andrews and W/O H. S. Painter reconnoitered targets in the Siam Valley. They observed shipping at Sattahib which led, two days later, to Liberators making attacks on two merchant ships and, on 1 June, on port installations.

With their operations restricted by monsoon storms, on 16 June F/L G. Edwards and F/L J. Irvine flew north to the peak of Makalu in Nepal, then to Mt Everest, 10 miles further west. Edwards circled the mountain for 20 min, taking photographs with cameras mounted in wing-tanks. W/C Pearson of 681 Squadron, in a Spitfire, had flown over Everest on 26 May – the first pilot to do so since the Houston Expedition of 1933 – and had taken photos of the mountain and the Rongbuk Glacier. Nepal was a neutral country and the Everest flights caused a minor diplomatic upset when details were released to the Press. It was explained that the aircraft were lost, due to the extensive cloud cover, and were only able to fix their positions by recognizing the mountain.

On 4 July 1944 82 (United Provinces) Squadron at Kolar, and 84 Squadron at Quetta, India, were to begin conversion to the Mosquito FB.VI from the Vultee Vengeance dive-bomber. (45 Squadron at 1672 MCU at Yelahanka, near Bangalore, had been the first to convert from the Vengeance to the Mosquito, in February 1944.) 82 Squadron began conversion at Kolar, 35 miles to the east, in July. Heavy monsoons prevented any operations at all until mid-September, but 45 and 82 Squadrons moved, in turn, to Ranchi, 45 flying their first Mosquito sortie on 1 October. 47 Squadron moved to Yelahanka on 7 October, followed by 110 Squadron three weeks later.

In October 684 Squadron Mosquitoes at Alipore were using Cox's Bazar at the Mouths of the Ganges to make long-range flights into Burma. Terence Boughton and his navigator, Bill Rhodes, who had joined 684 Squadron in July, had flown their first op on 6 September: a survey of the Japanese-held Mandalay area. Boughton recalls:

A Mosquito navigator, W/O Davison of 684 Sqn, about to board PR Mk. IX MM295:C on the brick-paved dispersal area at Alipore during a lull in the monsoon rains of 1944.

Dupee DFM and F/O McDonnell brought back the first photos of Car Nicobar Island.

In April 684 Squadron continued flying long-range missions, with sorties to places as far afield as Khun Khaen in central Siam and Vientiane in Laos. On 4 April Sgt Cocks with F/Sgt Smith brought back photos of the Sittang bridge on the Burma railway. The photos revealed that repairs to earlier bomb damage had been carried out and that the rail line was free between Martaban and Rangoon. A few days later the bridge was bombed, and subsequent PR sorties by the Mosquitoes showed that it was again out of commission. In May a 684 Squadron detachment began operations from Alipore, a suburb of Calcutta. On 24 May W/C W. E. M. Lowry DFC, the CO,

Mosquito HR551 of 82 (United Provinces) Squadron. On 4 July 1944 the squadron, then based at Kolar, began conversion from the Vultee Vengeance dive-bomber to the Mosquito FB.VI. (ARP)

Mosquito TE594 of 82 (United Provinces) Squadron. (ARP)

Flying up and down parallel lines at a mere 10,000 ft or so was a bit anxious, but no one seemed interested in us and we did a second trip over the Chindwin River a few days later. By October we were venturing further afield, moving forward to Cox's Bazar to fill up with fuel and usually spending the night in grass-roofed huts, before taking off early in the morning. From here we could cover Rangoon, Moulmein, Akyab, Chiengmai, and as far south as Bangkok. This was very high-altitude work using long-focus cameras to photograph ports, railways, roads, airfields; though on one occasion we had to cover the road from Chiengmai to Hluang in northern Thailand from only 5,000 ft. Our extreme range took us down to Victoria Point and Phuket. We flew photographic sorties as far as Bangkok and north Thailand. About this time the wooden glued-together Mosquitoes were giving trouble and there were cases of wings collapsing, so I was sent to Colombo on a ship recognition course.

All Mosquito operations came to an abrupt halt on 12 November 1944, when a signal to all units required Mosquito aircraft to be grounded pending inspection. The cause of the accidents was, supposedly, destruction by 'termites' and deterioration of glue. In May W/C A. C. Stumm, CO 45 Squadron, and F/L McKerracher, both RAAF, were killed at Amarda Road when their Mosquito broke up during a practice attack. On 13 September F/O W. C. Tuproll and F/Sgt V. A. Boll of 82 Squadron died when their FB.VI crashed while making dummy attacks on another aircraft. W/C L. V. Hudson, the CO, thought that a glueing fault had caused failure of the wing or tail. Then, on 4 October, the wing leading-edge of a 45 Squadron FB.VI buckled in flight, but the pilot, S/L Bourke RAAF, was able to land safely. On 10 October F/L Campbell RCAF and F/L Rimmel, 143 RSU's Chief Technical Officer, were killed in a crash near Bishnupur. S/L C. J. Cabot arrived from HQ Base Air Forces the following day to investigate the accidents.

On 20 October two more Mosquitoes crashed. An 82 Squadron aircraft flown by F/O A. E. Parker with his navigator, F/O M. D. Randall, shed half its starboard wing during a practice bombing attack on Random Range, and a 45 Squadron aircraft flown by S/L Edwards broke up when about to land at Kumbhirgram, Assam. Glue failure was suspected as the cause of both accidents. It was supposed that, as the aircraft

were left standing in the open, 'extreme heat has caused the glue to crack and the upper surfaces to lift from the spar'; but it soon became clear that the adhesive was not the cause of the trouble.

In March 1944, production of the first batch of Mosquitoes in Australia had been disrupted when it was discovered that components in the wing failed to 'mate'. Consequently, gaps occurred in the glued joints between the main spar and the plywood stressed-skin of the wings (under load the plywood upper wing surface could become detached and the box-section spar assembly could collapse). The wings for the first 20 Australian-built aircraft were scrapped. In the UK a series of fatal flying accidents among Mosquitoes of various marks (at the rate of two to four per month from January to June 1944) was attributed to failure of the wing structure. HQ 8 Group reported alarm over nine accidents in the 10 weeks from 27 June to 16 September, some caused by wing failure.

The effects of the accidents in India were far-reaching. The intended manufacture of components at Karachi was abandoned and the re-equipping of squadrons delayed. Structural failures and added troubles with the engines meant the wooden aircraft was never a favourite with the crews of 27 Squadron, who preferred the Beaufighter for their low-level strafing sorties. All 14 Mosquito FB.VIs in 110 (Hyderabad) Squadron, which a few days earlier had retired its

Damage in India was not always caused by glue and wood problems. This Mosquito (RF650) of 1672 MCU is in for repairs at Yelahanka following a bird strike. (ARP)

Vultee Vengeance aircraft, were grounded by 6 November.

De Havilland still maintained that the failures in India resulted from climatic conditions and ordered the destruction of all parts made with casein glue. At first it seemed that the defects were restricted to the Mosquito FB.VIs built at Canley by Standard Motors Ltd. Of 24 such aircraft inspected by 8 November, 23 had defects adjacent to Rib 12, located six ft from the wingtips. But within four days, similar faults had been found in 16 Mosquitoes produced by de Havilland at Hatfield. An investigating team led by Maj Hereward de Havilland arrived in India on 26 November and a week later reported that the accidents were not caused by deterioration of glue, but by extensive shrinkage of airframes during the monsoon season. However, an investigation by Chabot and Myers attributed the accidents definitively to faulty manufacture. Myers signalled: 'Defects not due to climatic conditions. The standard of glueing...leaves much to be desired.' Meanwhile, an inspection team at the Ministry of Aircraft Production at Defford found that six different marks of Mosquito, all built by de Havilland at Hatfield and Leavesden, showed signs of similar defects. Yet none of the aircraft had been exposed to monsoon conditions, nor had they been attacked by termites!

In 684 Squadron there was no uncertainty about the cause of the grounding of the Mosquitoes. The 12 November 1944 entry in the Operations Record Book says: 'Section of wingtip splicing on some aircraft found to be defective due to inferior workmanship at the factories building these components.'

A meeting at the Air Ministry on 1 January 1945 heard an explanation of the Mosquito defects from Maj de Havilland on his return from India. He again attributed the faults to the entry of water, differential shrinkage and unsatisfactory gluing, admitting that there was scope for improving manufacturing techniques, particularly the method of assembling glued joints. Although records show that accidents classified as caused by 'loss of control' were three times more frequent on Mosquitoes than on any other type of aircraft, the Air Ministry forestalled pos-

S/L Newman arrives in the first PR.34, painted aluminium and blue, after a flight from RAF Benson to Karachi in a record-breaking 12 hr 45 min, on 1 June 1945. (IWM)

Australians of a Far East Mosquito squadron pose for the camera in front of a Mosquito FB.VI resplendent with 'door art' and bomb log showing an impressive operations score. (via Jerry Scutts)

sible loss of confidence in its Mosquito squadrons at home and abroad by holding to Maj de Havilland's assertion that the accidents in India were caused by 'faults largely due to climate'.

To cure the problem, a plywood strip was inserted along the span of the wing to seal the whole length of the skin joint along the main spar. Despite this remedy altering the aerofoil section of the wing, it seems that Mod 638, as it was called, had no effect on performance. The modification was applied to all Mosquitoes in production in Australia, but few, if any, sets were sent to India, where Mosquitoes found to have skin defects were simply struck off charge. The number of aircraft available to 684 Squadron, for instance, dropped from 21 in October to just four

airworthy PR.IXs by 20 November, and 84 Squadron did not complete conversion to the FB.VI until March 1945. (84 Squadron Mosquitoes saw no action against Japan but they were used, along with 47, 82 and 110 Squadrons, in late 1945 against Indonesian separatists until more faulty wing-structures were discovered in some FB.VIs. The aircraft were again briefly grounded for inspection.)

Meanwhile, starting in December 1944, 47, 82 and 110 Squadrons had commenced day and night *Intruder* sorties on the Japanese road, rail and river network system. On the night of 1 February 1945 F/L G. F. Mahony and W/O Roy Trew, of 82 Squadron, were hit by flak during the bombing of Heho aerodrome in Burma. Mahony recalls:

The weather had become very bad and we diverted to Kalemyo, but Kalemyo had been caught before by intruders and declined to put on a flarepath. We had now been airborne for $6\frac{1}{4}$ hrs and could not wait for first light. With about 10 min fuel remaining we headed a little way toward the Chindwin, feathered the starboard prop' and abandoned. I may have discovered a new experience by hitting the back of my neck on the tailplane as I left through the side exit!

Eventually, I joined up with habitation and I sought to know where my navigator was. Some difficulty, but a lot of beating of drums seemed to be going on and eventually the penny dropped that this was broadcast signalling, and distant replies could be heard. I believed I understood that Roy was safe some 20 miles down the Chindwin. We took a dugout and paddles, and lo and behold, there he was – beside the Chindwin, expecting us! His parachute sustained a tear and kept twisting and untwisting on the way down. We were at Mawleik, on the Upper Chindwin, a remote supply-drop strip. They had radio and it took days to get through to Kalemyo (drums did it much quicker). The supply drop strip was made good enough to tempt a Stinson Sentinel to arrive and we were lifted out, one by one.

During February 1945 89 Squadron at Baigachi began converting from the Beaufighter to the Mosquito FB.VI, but they were never used. In March 82 Squadron flew some 269 sorties, while 47 and 84 Squadrons were used on bomber support operations for the Army.

Meanwhile, in January 1945, the Mosquitoes of 684 Squadron flew over 70 sorties, including survey flights to Phuket Island. A detachment at China Bay, near Trincomalee in Ceylon, made sorties to the Andaman and Nicobar Islands and the tip of Sumatra – almost 1,000 statute miles across the Bay of Bengal, so each sortie was the equivalent of a transatlantic flight and lasted some eight hrs. Terence Boughton, who was posted to China Bay on 13 February, recalls:

Our aircraft were fitted with drop tanks from Hurricanes under the fuselage; rather bluff and draggy things which got us on 100 or 200 miles and were then dropped into the ocean. We were then back on internal fuel plus the well streamlined underwing drop tanks, which we didn't drop as there weren't any more available. For these trips we were kitted out with jungle survival suits, revolvers, booklets and cards in various Far Eastern languages, and bags of Maria Theresa silver dollars which were apparently acceptable every-

where. If we had had trouble 1,000 miles from home, we should probably have done well to land on a beach and survive as best we could, for the Bay of Bengal was utterly empty of shipping, although there was a slim chance of being picked up by one of the Catalina flying boats of a Dutch squadron which was also based at China Bay. These were slow but had an immense endurance and flew regularly across to Sumatra, which before the Japanese invasion was part of the Dutch overseas empire.

The detachment commander, F/L Henry Lowcock, with F/Sgt Lewin, had, on 10 February, photographed five Sumatran airfields. Four days later the Mosquito PR.IXs made low-level PR flights over the notorious Burma–Siam railway. By March 1945, record-breaking flights of around nine hrs were made to Phuket Island, to reconnoitre possible landing beaches. Terence Boughton adds:

These trips across the water continued through the spring of 1945. On several we met the intertropical front, a fearsome barrier of cloud which reached from

During March–April 1945, 684 Squadron regularly reconnoitred the Japanese railway system in Burma, to provide intelligence for B-24 Liberator bombing strikes. On 4 April Sgt Cocks with F/Sgt Smith brought back photos of the Sittang bridge on the Burma railway. They revealed that repairs to earlier bomb damage had been carried out and the rail line was free between Martaban and Rangoon. A few days later the bridge was bombed, and subsequent photo-reconnaissance by the Mosquitoes showed that it was once again out of commission.

Above *Mosquito NF.II DZ695, the first Mosquito delivered to India and used by 27 Squadron. (IWM)*

Left *Mosquito PR.34 of 81 Squadron. (Bruce Robertson via Geoff Thomas)*

Below left *Mosquito PR.XVI NS645 of 684 Squadron at Alipore in March 1945. (IWM)*

the sea up to above our cruising level and gave heavy airframe and carburettor icing, forcing us to turn back. On 4 April we had an unusual task, a very low-level sortie with an oblique camera, flying along the coast of Camorta Island at a mere 1,000 ft. I have no idea what we were looking for as the island appeared to be utterly deserted. In all this work Bill Rhodes handled the navigation, the radio (except for short-range VHF) and the photography. Flying the aeroplane was comparatively relaxed, although we had no autopilot and there were long hrs of holding a steady course and height and occasionally watching the fuel gauge.

Operation *Dracula,* the seaborne invasion to capture Rangoon, took place on 1/2 May with support from 82 and 110 Squadrons, but the Mosquito PR.IXs of 684 Squadron were grounded by bad weather. By the end of May 1945 Mosquitoes using Ramree Island as an advanced landing strip were flying regularly over Siam. Terence Boughton and Bill Rhodes' last trip together was on 18 May. Boughton recalls:

We were bound for Sumatra but found that the port pesco pump had failed. This pump (there were two)

On 20 August 1945 eight Mosquito FB.VIs of 110 Squadron were used to dislodge Japanese troops at Tikedo, east of the Sittang river, who had refused to surrender. It was the final RAF operation of the Second World War. Thereafter, one of the duties involving Mosquitoes of 47, 82, 84 and 110 Squadrons, was their use late in 1945 against Indonesian insurgents in the Dutch East Indies. Here, crews explain how things went on a raid on an Indonesian separatist radio station. (ARP)

pumped air to drive the pilot's instruments but also served to force fuel from the wing drop tanks into the outer wing tanks. So we had a drop tank full of fuel that couldn't be used. We therefore abandoned Sumatra and went off to 'do' the Nicobar Islands, which were nearer. After a long photographic session we were on our way home and had sighted the high clouds which covered a still-invisible Ceylon. At this point it was my habit to start a slow descent, to maximize range. At 19,000 ft I switched the superchargers into 'Low' and there was the usual 'chug', but the port engine quietly died and stayed in idle. Sod's Law had ensured that this was the engine on the same side as the failed pump, and this meant we had lost still more fuel as the outer tanks could not be cross-fed. I feathered the dead propeller and we lost height steadily and were anxiously looking out for land – and watching the fuel gauge heading for the zero mark. I put out a Mayday call on the VHF and hoped that China Bay

would send out help if we had to ditch and climb into our dinghies. At last the coast appeared, well south of China Bay, and we flew northward, keeping the beach in range for a power-off landing. When the airfield came in sight we put the landing gear and flaps down and went straight in, to find after landing that we had just five gal of fuel left. The cause of the failure was very simple: a split pin in the throttle linkage had not been opened out during maintenance and the jerk of the supercharger gear change had pushed it out. The engine was quite serviceable but had become disconnected from the pilot's throttle lever.

I had a short spell with the Photographic Reconnaissance Development Flight, taking pictures of beaches in Ceylon by the so-called transparency method which enabled beach gradients to be deduced from wave patterns. This was in preparation for the invasion of Malaya, called Operation *Zipper,* which never happened.

Mosquito PR.34 RG203 of 684 Squadron is towed into position at the Cocos Islands Detachment in July 1945.

In June the PR.34, a very long-range version of the Mosquito PR.XVI entered service, and, based on the recently completed airfield at Cocos Island, carried out reconnaissance missions to Kuala Lumpur and Port Swettenham. On 3 July a Mosquito PR.34 of 684 Squadron crewed by W/C W. E. M. Lowry DFC with F/Sgt Pateman, made that model's first reconnaissance sortie, to Point Pinto via Morib and Port Swettenham area via Gedong and, finally, Sumatra. Next day seven runs were made over Kuala Lumpur. By the end of July some 25 sorties had been carried out by PR.34s from Cocos Island, and a further 13 more by VJ-Day.

On 12 August 47 Squadron flew its last sortie of the war before its Mosquitoes were taken out of service to have rocket projectiles fitted. (These were used late in 1945 against Indonesian insurgents in the Dutch East Indies.) With the unconditional Japanese surrender on 14 August 1945, the Mosquitoes were sent to reconnoitre the oilfields at Palembang in Sumatra and Japanese dispositions and PoW camps in Malaya. Some of the flights, which included reconnaissance of Penang and Taiping in northern Malaya, lasted over nine hrs.

On 20 August eight Mosquito FB.VIs of 110 Squadron were used to dislodge Japanese troops at Tikedo, east of the Sittang river, who had refused to surrender. It was the final RAF operation of the Second World War. Ironically, 110 Squadron had also flown the first operation of the war, when equipped with Blenheims in France. A more contrite band of Japanese soldiers welcomed the crew of a 684 Squadron Mosquito which put down at Kalland on Singapore Island with engine trouble on 31 August following a reconnaissance of the Palembang oil refineries, rather than risk the long overwater flight back to Cocos Island. They were the first Britons to arrive in Singapore since the Japanese surrender. On 3 September Gen Itazaki, the Japanese Southern Area Commander, formally surrendered to VA Lord Louis Mountbatten in Singapore, thus bringing the war against Japan to an end.

Chapter Sixteen

'Jane'

By 15 August 1945, VJ-Day, 1,032 Mosquitoes had been built in Canada. One of the Mosquito men who had double cause to celebrate the night in some style was Philip Back, who, on 25 May 1945, with his navigator, Sandy Galbraith, had been posted from 139 Squadron to Woodhall Spa to join 627 Squadron: part of the 'Tiger

F/O Philip Back (right) and F/O Derek Smith DFC (left), of 692 Squadron at Graveley, in front of T-Tommy. After completing his tour, Philip Back was posted to 162 Squadron where, as a pilot in the fast ADLS, he was provided with many more opportunities for adventure.

Force' earmarked for the invasion of Japan. On 28 July 1945 Philip had married his fiancée, June Debenham, a nurse at King's College Hospital, London, whom he had met in September 1944 when she attended the University Air Squadron Passing Out Parade, accompanied by her father, Prof Frank Debenham. In 1910–12, the professor had been the geologist on the ill-fated Scott Expedition to the Antarctic. More recently, he had been one of the lecturers who had taught Philip during his RAF Short Course at Corpus Christi College, Cambridge.

June and Philip motored home from their honeymoon in Dorset in their 1937 black Ford, stopping off at Blackbushe to find that his old 139 Squadron friend, W/C Mike K. Sewell, was in command of 162 Squadron and that the *crème-de-la-crème* of PFF and 8 Group Mosquito crews had been posted to the Surrey airfield. When RAF Transport Command required a fast Air Delivery Letter Service (ADLS) for Europe, the Mosquito was considered most suited for the task. It was also considered essential that the most experienced aircrews available should be employed. 162 Squadron had therefore exchanged its Pathfinder eagle for the greyhound of King's Messenger and moved from 8 Group, Bomber Command to 46 Group, Transport Command, and had begun flying diplomatic mail all over Europe and the Middle East.

Philip Back asked for a 'job'. Sewell granted his wish. Elated, the Backs set off again, but they only got as far as Stevenage. It was VJ-night, so they turned around and drove to London to join in the wild celebrations. It was Philip Back's second appointment with destiny. On 23 September 1944, on his first leave from 692 Squadron, he had talked his way aboard a USAAF C-47 Skytrain flying from Northolt to Paris shortly after liberation. Col Shultz had driven his Jeep into the transport plane and the two men had flown straight to Versailles, where Back got a gendarme to flag down a car to drive him into the teeming French capital. There was still shooting in the streets, and for the British, Paris was off-limits. Back went to US HQ, told them he was an RAF liaison officer, and that he needed a taxi! One was duly provided. After an exciting 48 hrs he wondered how to get home. The taxi took him to the Ritz! The hotel was bursting with American staff officers and war correspondents, including Ernest Hemingway. At Reception, Back even brushed shoulders with Fred Astaire. When the girl behind the desk announced that the transport to take Hemingway's party to Orly Airport had arrived, the RAF 'liaison officer' promptly followed and got a lift back to Orly and, eventually, a flight to Heston in another C-47. He hitched a ride into London armed with scent, songs of the Resistance, secret newspapers and a wealth of stories to tell his envious squadron!

Philip and his bride headed for London, but their black Ford got only as far as Oxford Street, which was blocked by thousands of delirious, flag-waving and cheering crowds. Their car was picked up bodily by an enthusiastic throng and carried through Oxford Street, until they were lowered gently onto the road. They made their way, with the rest of the milling crowds, to Buckingham Palace, where Philip and June climbed onto the Queen Victoria memorial amid the gathered news cameramen to witness the grand sight of HRH King George VI, Queen Elizabeth, the princesses, and Winston Churchill, wave to the massed crowds.

Philip Back motored back to Woodhall Spa and a few days later drove down to Blackbushe again to take up flying duties with 162 Squadron. He was crewed with Tim Baron. As well as delivering documents and diplomatic mail to many European capitals, 162 Squadron was also tasked with making regular deliveries of daily newspapers to these capitals and to certain RAF bases in Germany and Holland. Peter Richard, a pilot in the ADLS, recalls:

This latter operation was officially known as 'Jane', after the lady of that name who appeared in the *Daily Mirror* strip cartoon. It consisted of dropping newspapers in specially designed canisters on marked-out 'target areas' at these airfields. It was a kind of bomb run.

The fast ADLS was officially known as 'Jane', after the Daily Mirror *strip cartoon heroine.*

A Mosquito NF.XXX night fighter of 125 Squadron. The squadron first received the type in March 1945 and used it until the unit was disbanded at Church Fenton on 20 November 1945 and renumbered as 262 Squadron. (via Philip Birtles)

Only some of 162 Squadron had continued with their unit – the bulk were brought in from tour-expired aircrews selected from the other 8 (PFF) Group Mosquito squadrons. Sadly, some, like Pat Duncan, who had been Charles Parker's pilot on 50 operations in 8 (PFF) Group, died while flying in peacetime: Pat was killed just after the war in a training accident. To the victors the spoils. On 25 May Charles Parker had been awarded the DFM. Although he was now a P/O, the award was for his ops as a sergeant, which was fortuitous because a gratuity of £50 came with the award. Had he received it as an officer the award would have been for the DFC, with no gratuity. Derek Smith got a Bar to his DFC and Philip Back got his DFC (both for the 50 ops in 692 Squadron). Ed Boulter too received the DFC.

After their fortieth op, John Clark and Bill Henley, who had flown 51 ops together in 571 and 162 Squadrons up until 25 April 1945, had gone on leave, only to return to Bourn to discover that the airfield was deserted. Crews had either been pensioned off or posted to a holding unit.

Ground crews had been offered 'Cooks Tours' over bombed-out German cities, although some had refused to go, claiming the trips were too dangerous! For Clark and Henley there would be no more flak, no more fighters, no more searchlights and no more night fighters. There would be no more passing the cemetery the Americans were making at Madingley, either. Their war might have been over but their days flying the Mosquito had not ended, for they, too, joined the 'elite' at Blackbushe. Henley could have returned to his native New Zealand if he had wanted, but he said to Clark:

I've been thinking about it, and I've decided it would be stupid not to see Europe and elsewhere at the Air Force's expense, before heading back home. I might even find my brother's grave in Crete. From what the Adj said, we'll be swanning around all the capital cities and seeing a bit of the world we've never seen before.

John Clark was delighted. They had been a team, the two of them, and he would have felt 'pretty lost' without him. But Bill Henley had made the wrong decision when he decided to see Europe and the Middle East. John Clark explains:

A month or so after our arrival in Blackbushe, I was detailed by the CO to navigate a W/C from Air Ministry to Cairo. We spent a week there. Meanwhile, Bill had been crewed up with another navigator and detailed to ferry a Mosquito to Malta. He and the navigator were returning in a Dakota transport. The pilot was flying serenely through a layer of cloud embedded in the stratus layer; a death's head if ever there was one! The aircraft was torn to pieces. The passengers and crew were flung out and scattered over the countryside. I learned about it on my return from Cairo.

I felt almost guilty when I heard the news. It was the only time Bill and I had not flown together. Better that he had returned to New Zealand and had tried to teach the Kiwi birds there how to fly.

Philip Back and Tim Baron also had a close shave. The flight on 23 December 1945 to Kastrop in Denmark with a consignment of diplomatic mail went well enough and they returned late on Christmas Eve with a radiogram, Christmas turkey, cutlery and Copenhagen china secreted in the bomb bay. As Philip approached Blackbushe in the dark, halfway down the runway the chap in the tower turned off the perimeter lights. Philip had yet to cross the A30 road which bisected the end of the landing strip!

All I could do was run-up my engines and flash my landing lights on to warn the cars on the road to stop while I crossed in front of them! Fortunately, they did, and I crossed to my dispersal without further incident. I arrived at my in-laws' home at Camberley laden with presents from Denmark like Santa Claus.

* * * * *

In all, 55,573 Bomber Command crew did not return during the war. Virginia 'Peggy' Dow had waved her husband, S/L Roy Dow DFC, off from their house close to RAF Upwood on a sunny morning, 2 April 1945. The popular Canadian's red hair was groomed neatly under his RAF cap,

and his gilt PFF wings, awarded to the 139 (Jamaica) Squadron pilot on 23 October 1944, shone proudly beneath his RAF wings on his best blue uniform. The one with the faded wings which he wore on ops hung, unwanted, in his wardrobe because he was not scheduled to fly that night. Before mounting his bicycle for the short ride to the base, he said: 'I'll be in for dinner, Peggy. Be a good girl!'

Later that day, Peggy heard four Mosquitoes take off and thunder over the house on their nightly operation. They were Berlin-bound. Peggy had heard the sound of the Merlins hundreds of times before. On 89 occasions, Roy had come back safely, and anyway, hadn't he said he wasn't on ops that night? She only began to worry much later. Lying in bed, she heard three Mosquitoes return. One was missing. She had a premonition that something was wrong. A key turned in the front door and she heard footsteps on the stairs. The bedroom door handle turned. She called out, 'Roy!' He didn't come in. She knew then that her Canadian pilot was dead.

Peggy was distraught. Next morning she ran outside into the back garden, a 4-lb hammer and a chisel in her hand, and destroyed the Anderson shelter Roy and her father had built while on leave. Roy and his 28-year-old navigator, F/L J. S. Endersby, were laid to rest in the Olympische Strasse British Cemetery in the Russian Zone in Berlin, after the Russians had given permission for their bodies to be interred there. Endersby left a young, pregnant widow, Margaret. Years later, Peggy found these words, penned by Roy, tucked away in her household recipe book:

'I'll gird tighter my armour and advance
in the fight with a brave heart.
And bravely I'll battle for right.
I'll blanch at no danger and guard at
no might – If you will pray for me.'

Index